SIMULATION IN MANAGEMENT & BUSINESS EDUCATION

Acknowledgements

The editors wish to thank Sally Pratten, Brenda Highbee and Christine Fernando for their invaluable assistance in shaping the materials here into book form

PERSPECTIVES ON ACADEMIC
GAMING & SIMULATION 7

Simulation in Management & Business Education

The proceedings of the 1981 conference of SAGSET,
The Society for Academic Gaming and Simulation
in Education and Training

Edited by Lynton Gray and Ian Waitt

Kogan Page

sagset
SOCIETY FOR ACADEMIC
GAMING AND SIMULATION
IN EDUCATION AND TRAINING

NELPCO

Perspectives on Academic Gaming and Simulation is the series title
of the proceedings of SAGSET's annual conferences.

General Editor, SAGSET: Jacquetta Megarry

Uniform with this volume:
Perspectives on Academic Gaming & Simulation 1 & 2:
Communication, Computer Basis and Education edited by
Jacquetta Megarry (1978)

Perspectives on Academic Gaming & Simulation 3:
Training and Professional Education edited by
Ray McAleese (1978)

Perspectives on Academic Gaming & Simulation 4:
Human Factors in Games and Simulations edited by
Jacquetta Megarry (1979)

Perspectives on Academic Gaming & Simulation 5:
Simulation and Gaming for the 1980s edited by
Philip Race and David Brook

Perspectives on Academic Gaming and Simulation 6:
Simulation and Games: The Real and the Ideal edited by
Betty Hollinshead and Mantz Yorke

First published 1982 by
Kogan Page Limited
120 Pentonville Road
London N1 9JN

In association with
NELPCO Limited
Danbury Park
Chelmsford
Essex

British Library Cataloguing in Publication Data
Simulation in management and business education.
— (Perspectives on academic gaming 7)
1. Management games — Congresses
I. Gray, Lynton II. Waitt, Ian
III. Series
658.4'0353 HD20.7

ISBN 0 85038 583 0

Distributed in the United States of America by
Nichols Publishing Company, Post Office Box 96, New York,
NY 10024

Copyright © SAGSET and contributors 1982

SAGSET is the Society for Academic Gaming and Simulation
in Education and Training. Its address is:
The Secretary, SAGSET, Centre for Extension Studies, Loughborough
University of Technology, Leicestershire LE11 3TU, England

Printed in Great Britain by The Anchor Press Ltd, Tiptree, Essex

Contents

Alphabetical list of authors

Introduction
The Twelfth Annual Conference of SAGSET
at Anglian Regional Management Centre, Danbury Park, Essex

The twelfth annual SAGSET conference was held at Danbury Park on 17-19 September 1981. As befitted the location, the central emphasis was on simulation and gaming in management and business, but this was not exclusively so. The conference's nine main sessions offered up to four parallel presentations, demonstrations and participative activities, of the high calibre which has by now become a hallmark of the SAGSET conferences.

Participation in conference activities was stressed from the outset, with an enjoyable goal-setting exercise (COUNTERPOINT), which not only shaped social interaction throughout the conference, but led to some informal simulation sessions in the conference's *drop-in* session, where new ideas could be explored with sympathetically critical colleagues, and problems in designing or using simulations could be shared and discussed.

The atmosphere of involvement through formal and informal activities was enhanced by the availability of a variety of micro-computer-based simulations and a relaxed and informal conference dinner. As in the most successful conferences, the boundaries between formal sessions and informal and social activities soon blurred and became indistinct.

My thanks for a successful and enjoyable venture go out to the Conference Secretary, Mrs Diana Wignall, and to the catering and domestic staff at Danbury Park, whose unobtrusive yet tireless endeavours ensured high levels of satisfaction by all participants.

Lynton Gray
Conference Organizer
September 1981

9

Editorial and Introduction to the Papers

While this is the first volume in the *Perspectives on Academic Gaming and Simulation* series to focus specifically upon management and business education, examination of previous volumes indicates clearly that this is one of the least neglected areas, and, as Hollinshead and Yorke stated in their editorial to *Perspectives on Academic Gaming and Simulation 6*, it is one of the few areas where simulation and gaming have already long been accorded academic respectability.

However, this volume does more than present a summary of the level of development reached to date in a well established area of academic activity. Rather, it presents a series of ideas and initiatives which, while small-scale and specific when looked at individually, when taken together suggest a radical new paradigm in management and business education.

To the disinterested observer this area has all the confusing characteristics of the terrain of the broad world of education. The dichotomy between education and training is clearly visible in the UK, despite EEC policies of integration. Governmental, local authority, training board and company policies and provision jostle and conflict, while still leaving vast areas of unexplored territory. Research activities are limited, and those which exist tend to be poorly focused and heavily criticized. The literature inclines to the prescriptive, attracting little credibility amongst practitioners, yet with a firm belief in the quest for some philosopher's stone which will reveal and transmute all. As properly conceived — to introduce now the note of advocacy which will characterize this editorial — education is about the human experience in life and about reflection upon that experience. This is as unsurprising as the reader may find it obvious. Yet, throughout management and business education, as throughout education as a whole, theory is separated from practice, with consequent problems, to the illumination of which this book is addressed.

To recognize the radical nature of the perspectives here, it is necessary to consider the impact of the burgeoning output of research, theory and prescription about management and business, an output which seems to have grown exponentially in proportion to the growth of disenchantment both with the performance of managements and businesses and with the absence of apparently effective panaceas from the groves of academe. It is our view that such dissatisfaction is both understandable and justifiable. It is a commonplace that, wherever the relationship between theory and practice is debated, the Hegelian solution of praxis is proposed. How effective, appropriate or even meaningful a particular praxis might be then becomes the topic of further debate. However, we discern in such debates that the articulation of theory takes precedence over practice. Practice in business and management is dismissed as so pragmatic as to lack justifiable theoretical underpinnings, based upon recognizable models of the real world: this is confirmed by a growing catalogue of failures, while successes are discounted as fortunate and temporary accidents. In turn, practitioners consider management thinking and theorising either as impractically idealistic, or as based upon perceptions of reality which bear little accord with day to day experience. Imported notions such as systems theorising tend to fit into each of these categories.

The subject of this book is the deployment of simulation and gaming in management and business education. As this is an approach which makes legitimate claims to span the fields of education and training and to bridge the gulf between theory and practice, the dichotomies therein become central dilemmas. Conventionally, training programmes in this field fall fairly neatly into a theoretically-oriented, classroom-based component, supplemented by practical on-the-job experiences, and the conjunction between the two, if it occurs at all, is wished rather than planned. However, theory tends to be the preserve of the literate and the articulate: it can thus easily be equated with status, with the consequent risks of snobbery, special pleading and isolation from reality. Theory may be derived from practice or from observation of practitioners and their clients, and this process is well established in management education. However, while the theorist has always to cope with the impulse to find a defence for his or her activity — academic status, breadth of research or the conceptual *tour de force* — the practitioner, mindful of the absence of relative status, can find easy refuge in the simple language of common sense and immediate perceptions of reality, succinctly expressed.

This is where this volume suggests a modest revolution. Educators who use simulation and gaming are, usually, attempting deliberately to resolve the dichotomy considered above by incorporating approximations of the real world into the theoretical components of training programmes. There is little that is new in this attempt at praxis. However, a significant focus of the papers here is the conscious recognition of the difficulties in attempting this form of reconciliation. Again, there is nothing new in this. What is novel, we believe, is that several of the papers here address themselves *directly* to achieving the resolution of deeply entrenched problems; while other papers suggest, albeit more obliquely, directions whereby praxis might be attained.

This is not to suggest that the volume is peddling panaceas. Solutions proffered might involve batteries of micro-computers, but other papers are included which, for example, modestly draw attention to a simple teaching device, the sandbox, which few would claim to answer global questions, and to the uses of simple games in the teaching of languages. The commitment of educators using games and simulations to active, experiential forms of learning is well-established. In the following pages we offer a guide through the papers collected here, which attempts to draw links between the practical experiences described by some and the conscious reflections on the use, design and evaluation of simulations by others; between the *cris de coeur* of some and the bold solutions proposed by others.

We believe that papers here, taken together, represent a significant step forward for management and business education and for SAGSET. It is no accident that it comes at a time when the Society's Council is recommending the abandonment of the word 'academic' in its title and its replacement by 'advancement'. The contributions here advance the techniques and concepts of simulation and management education. Some of them can be used immediately, with little or no adaptation and development: others carry further the questioning of simulation philosophy and process. The range of activities covered is deliberately wide. The advancement of simulation and games demands a process of experience, linked to reflection, leading to further experience and reflection—with the emphasis upon relevance, practice and reality.

The papers

This volume differs from previous ones in the *Perspectives on Academic Gaming and Simulation* series in that it includes articles which did not first appear as conference papers. There are two reasons for this. The first is the very practical one that, in an experientially-oriented conference, an increasing proportion of the activities do not take the form of formal papers, and therefore are not readily available for inclusion in a volume such as this, for the central experience is participative and affective. The second reason is that a conscious attempt has been made to provide here a distinctive approach to management and business education, which, while not excluding contributions from peripheral areas of interest, nonetheless tries to offer a coherence of intent which, *in toto*, may have some impact upon the practice of management and business education.

The philosophy underlying the arrangement of these papers has already been outlined. In accord with this, the contributions are arranged in two broad groups. *Experiences* form the first group of 10 papers: *reflections* characterize the second 10. This might appear strange, given the preceding remarks on reconciling the distinctions between theory and practice. However, we believe it to be both sensible and justifiable, and to emphasize first the practical dimension.

The first part of the book comprises those papers which present and describe, in complete or abbreviated forms, specific simulations or games. With only one exception these are centrally related to aspects of management and business education, albeit ranging broadly from managing national economies to managing schools and land administration.

The second part comprises papers which, while referring perhaps to specific games and simulations, are primarily concerned with reflections upon their design, uses, evaluation or their underlying philosophies. It is our hope that the ideas of this section will be used in conjunction with the practical suggestions of the first, to stimulate in turn ideas for the more effective design, uses and evaluation of simulations and games, both in and beyond the territories of management and business education.

PART 1: EXPERIENCES

The papers in this section all contain substantial descriptions of games and simulations which, with due acknowledgements, can be used or adapted by teachers and trainers within and outside management and business education. Jaques (1) provides one answer to the question of how to utilize further the experience of people gathering at conferences. He suggests that, in his simulation COUNTERPOINT, conference participants can be led into closer contact, and also gain more from the gathering, by setting themselves objectives which involve risk-taking. The exercise is operated through groups, controlled by brokers and contains a reward element.

Schofield (2) describes innovations in video-based simulations in management training. The simulation CALL YOURSELF A MANAGER? employs two novel techniques: the devising of material which is not sequential, allowing the trainer to select that which is most appropriate at any juncture, while also achieving economy through multi-purpose design, and the placing of the viewer into a position demanding a response. This is a powerful use of the television medium, requiring a positive input from the trainer, and has implications for training activity design. Schofield gives directions for use, identifies potential difficulties and produces an interesting vehicle for the examination of interpersonal behaviour, as well as indicating miniature case study possibilities.

Beckwith (3) sets out in PIGS or SNAKES' EYES a game of chance in which results are influenced by players' strategic decisions. Thus he seeks to provide a medium for the exploration of risk-taking, holding that the exercise can lead to consideration of successful entrepreneurship, as well as distinguishing a risk from a gamble — hinging upon the degree of personal influence on outcome.

Bassey (4) has developed a highly sophisticated computer-based simulation which possesses the attractive virtue of simplicity in expression. While the central theme is that of political education in world development, the simulation provides opportunities for a wide range of approaches, involving negotiation, interpersonal skills and the ability to master a brief. At heart the simulation examines the interdependence between developed and developing countries, with different possible social and economic priorities and political philosophies.

The next two papers deal specifically with the sphere of education management. Waitt (5) observes that the teaching of elements of law to managers requires approaches which will encompass what managers need to know and to experience, and through which they can view human behaviour in its potential conflict with legal, quasi-legal, and administrative procedures. He uses two simulation exercises to illustrate his arguments. One refers to a simulation which led directly to change in a local authority's procedures. The other demonstrates the inter-related complexities of law, managerial behaviour, subordinate reactions, and how vehicles for exploitation may be both legitimately and illegitimately used. In both instances he has approached his simulation construction from the perspective of the dramatist but, having developed his characters and set out the boundaries for their action, he welcomes the pedagogical risk of allowing the characters to take over.

Taylor-Byrne (6) presents a case study which considers the devising, implementation and evaluation of his SORTHAM OUT simulation. His goals in the simulation are experiential in that he seeks in the debriefing for each participant to have been exposed to the experiences of role play, and to have identified issues and lines of argument. The simulation itself is based on the competing values and arguments which are deployed to decide which temporary, part-time teachers in a comprehensive school lose their posts. Thus, decision-making processes are reviewed.

Antia (7) advances the proposition that power, defined as the ability to get action, is a key to behaviour patterns within organizations. He seeks by the means of drama and therapy to exorcise a variety of power-related problems. Central to his argument is that the use of drama and therapy, expressed ultimately in the making of a rigorously enforced contract with the subject, can

13

and should be extended to the repertoire of the trainer. He recognizes that the trainers themselves should have acquaintance with professional training and be secure in their personalities—and the editors would emphasize this. Whatever the virtues of this adventurous approach, the practice by the untrained upon subjects who may well be, or become, distressed is profoundly dangerous, and we underline Antia's warning of these dangers.

Wynn *et al* (8) consider a comprehensive simulation devised for the teaching of land administration in higher education. The authors argue that, as an essentially multi-disciplinary subject, land administration teaching is well suited to simulation techniques. Their example, THE COFFERIDGE CLOSE GAME, is concerned with the purchase and development of land by a New Town Development Corporation, and the reactions of local administration, landowners, and a pressure group. This sophisticated game is well developed, and includes the effects of the intervention of economic forces.

Naetscher (9) is also concerned with simulating the built environment—a theme which occurs yet again in Gibson's paper (14). Like Gibson, Naetscher looks to the potential of simple readily available materials, and argues for the use of the sandbox as an educational medium whose value as a basis for simulation is demonstrated with reference to locational economics and geography teaching.

The final contribution in this section also demonstrates the educational potential of simple, readily available materials. Wright (10) argues for the use of games such as MONOPOLY when teaching English as a foreign language to business students. He shows how such games stimulate the acquisition of useful vocabulary, and encourage active participation.

PART 2: REFLECTIONS

The second section of the book develops from the first. The first two papers consider the problems involved in simulating real life in management training. Woolliams and Moul (11) identify a number of deficiencies in conventional approaches to management training, and present some striking alternatives. Using banks of linked micro-computers and visual display units they indicate, with technical detail, how simulation exercises for managers might resemble more closely real life experiences, by separating the managerial decision-making processes from the continuing development of business activities. Hence, using their simulation DYNAMO, managers on training programmes are required to make decisions while information changes and time is limited.

Brand and Walker (12) address similar problems. They comment upon the problems of designing games which are realistic simulations of real-life organizations. They offer guidance to game designers for undertaking research, preparatory study and design, so that the simulation is recognized by participants as having the essential flavour of reality.

Gray (13) draws attention to the variability of user skills in games and simulations. He suggests that it should not be assumed that simulations are 'teacher proof', or that didactic teaching skills are sufficient for simulation users: and goes on to outline the characteristics of successful simulation users, in both single trainer and group-managed simulations.

The following papers similarly address the problem of simulation use. Gibson (14) evaluates the uses made of a series of 'neighbourhood packs', which, like the work of Wynn *et al* (8) and Naetscher (9), are concerned with the management of the built environment. His materials are flexible, readily manipulated, and have been used to bring together professionals and lay people in situations where they can address common problems practically and without the barrier of professional jargon.

Rolfe and Waag (15) concern themselves with the management of military training, and evaluate the use of simulators in the training of pilots. Their findings not only provide some clear guidelines for assessing simulated as against real-life experiences, but point out some distinct advantages in the use of simulated models of reality, rather than experiencing the reality itself — a lesson which is directly relevant to the earlier papers (11 and 12) on real-life simulation.

Holding still to the theme of simulation uses, Ellington, Addinall and Langton (16) examine the possibilities of adapting technologically-based simulations for uses in management training. They indicate how four simulations, originally designed for aspects of technological education, have been and can be adapted so that they not only focus upon managerial activities, but do so in a context which creates for managers a realistic — yet possibly unfamiliar — technical and scientific setting.

Diehl (17) reports on the first products of a major research study which examines the impact of a number of management simulations. Her evaluation of the PLANET MANAGEMENT GAME identifies, by statistical analysis, a number of the game's strengths and weaknesses. These can be of great assistance to potential game users. The analysis points to the game's qualities in developing group cohesion and decision-making skills, and it also highlights some interesting differences in the perceptions of specified groups of participants.

Brand and Walker (18) develop the theme of their earlier paper (12), in commenting upon the selection, design, organization and operation of management games. They stress the value of feedback in ensuring that greater reality is achieved, so that learning objectives might be met.

Linda di Desidero (19) offers a very different perspective, but one which is of equal relevance to business and management education. Her concern is research into the processes of creativity. She indicates how simulation and gaming has a distinctive contribution to make in this sphere; she goes on to suggest how specific simulations might stimulate creative thinking; and she concludes by pointing out how such activities can facilitate the activation of leadership potential. Her conclusions, on the importance of simulation and gaming in developing human potential, are echoed by Rockler (20), who takes the notion of 'fallibilism' (that, since absolute truth is unobtainable, the ultimate task is not certainty but improvement), and suggests how the problems of curriculum management might be approached through the uses of gaming and simulation. His diagnosis of curriculum reform would, like di Desidero's, require the use of simulation and games as integral parts of its expression.

The papers in this second section thus traverse the spectrum from analysis of very specific problems of simulation design and use through to contemplative reflections on the nature of education, and the place of simulation and gaming in a more effective educative process. Taken together, in spite of significant differences of perspective and attitude, they provide a striking new focus for management and business education, in which emphasis is placed upon the provision of experiences which encapsulate real life, and which reflect upon the nature of the simulation/game activities in ensuring that participants are offered

15

an education designed around the twin objectives of surrogate reality and purposeful experience.

The editors would wish to conclude by emphasizing that, throughout these contributions, the traditional distinctions between education and training and theory and practice have been purposefully ignored. We would express a personal view that simulation and gaming provide some of the most powerful tools for the demolition of some unnecessary and harmful dichotomies: and this book demonstrates ways in which such tools might be used.

Lynton Gray
Ian Waitt

Part 1: Experiences: Simulations and games for use in business and management education

1. COUNTERPOINT – opening a conference

David Jaques

Abstract: Conferences often do not live up to participants' expectations of them. Their potential is rarely fully exploited. COUNTERPOINT is designed, specially for the SAGSET '81 Conference, as a participative exercise designed both to build small social groups at the conference and to provide a means for evaluating the conference. The exercise, involving negotiation and decisions about real-life risk taking, is described, and its impact upon the conference evaluated.

Introduction

'Experience is not what happened to you. It's what you do with what happens to you.'

I confess to being an inveterate conference-goer. Making new acquaintances, renewing old ones, and swapping ideas and gossip, free from the vortex of institutional life: these are all the stuff of the conference culture. The very temporariness of conference allows me to do things in the knowledge that there are boundaries beyond which news will not travel. Yet I frequently feel let down at conferences. They are not what I expected; I am bored by such and such a session; I am not getting what I wanted from the presentations; the best bits are the coffee breaks—after all that's what the conferences are really about isn't it? But is it? Is it the best use of our time and someone else's money? Perhaps we could make greater capital of the rich potential of conferences (so many fine people gathered together) if we were to make use of links between our inner and outer world, between the cognitive and the social. Put into less theoretical terms this would mean:

(a) having some idea of what we want to get out of the conference;
(b) recognizing and making available to others what we bring to it;
(c) finding a way of integrating disparate experiences;
(d) getting to know new and even unlikely people;
(e) putting newly acquired ideas into action when we return home.

COUNTERPOINT is intended to go some way to meet these needs. Its guiding principles embody two more, perhaps complementary aims:

(f) to belong to a 'family' group—one in which our membership is accepted without question;

(g) to monitor consciously what we are getting from the conference, and to change tack as we need to.

The exercise starts with individuals writing down their goals and strategies, following which they coalesce into small 'family' groups where they introduce themselves and share their written comments. The achievement of their goals may mean taking risks. Each group is invited to declare to two risk brokers the risks its members intend to take. A prize is awarded at the end of the conference to the group taking the most and the greatest risks. The groups are also encouraged to meet at odd breaks and discuss progress and risk taking, and their strategies. Before the conference ends they can meet to review what happened and discuss what they intend to do with what they have gleaned.

COUNTERPOINT—Participants' Instructions

Welcome to SAGSET '81!

The opening exercise is a new and, therefore, somewhat experimental one. It involves clarifying intentions for the conference with a small group, and devising strategies for fulfilling them. A reward system has been built in to add a competitive spark to the proceedings.

STATEMENT OF INTENT (10 MINS)

Could you please fill in the following matrix and boxes with as nice a compromise between the abundance of your ideas and the boundaries of the boxes as you are able.

	Requiring *LOW risk initiatives*	*Requiring* *HIGH risk initiatives*
What I want from the conference		
What I bring to the conference		

(Answer these questions according to what *you* consider to be a low or high risk for *yourself*, ie by your own standards, not those of others.)

How I can maximize my interests at the conference.

How I can sabotage my interests at the conference.

GROUP TASK (30 MINS)

Now find *three* fellow participants whom you do not know very well, or at all, and

(a) introduce yourself;
(b) share with each other what you have written overleaf;
(c) work out, as a group, a way of
   (i) monitoring what you are contributing to/getting from the conference and the risks you are taking in the process;
   (ii) checking, as the conference proceeds, whether the monitoring is working and how you might change it if necessary;
(d) briefly check out how you feel about the idea of monitoring your experience of the conference.

There are two rules which must apply in COUNTERPOINT.

1. All discussion about risks and initiatives are confidential to each group and the brokers (see next section).
2. Sex and physical aggression are not permissible topics.

NEGOTIATION (40 MINS)

At this point in the proceedings two *risk brokers* will manifest themselves: one marked 'LOW' and the other 'HIGH'. Their job is to give out counters to each group according to how many risks or initiatives it is intending to take.

Yellow counters are given for LOW risks.
Red counters are given for HIGH risks.

You may claim up to *one* red and *three* yellow counters for each member of the group. These counters refer to individual risks. A further red counter may be taken if the *group as a whole* decides to take a high risk.

Each group must send a *representative* to the brokers to ask for the counters appropriate to the number, and kind, of risks the group has assembled. The brokers will need convincing that a risk is what it is claimed to be. As they are busy people they will probably have time only for spot checks. If they suspect any fraud over a claim they may refuse to issue counters.

While your representative is bargaining with the broker you could discuss how you are going to monitor the risk/initiative taking. For instance you will probably find it useful to schedule one group meeting about half-way through the conference, and one at the end.

CONTINUATION AND FINALE (UP TO TWO DAYS)

The long-term goal in COUNTERPOINT is for representatives of each group to present a set of claims, to one or other of the brokers, that the initiatives and risks proposed in the first session have been carried out. To do this they must convince the brokers of the validity of their evidence and that the claims have the groups' backing.

The rewards for successful claims are:

HIGH risk initiative: three prize tokens for one red counter.
LOW risk initiative: one prize token for one yellow counter.

The worth of a claim is at the discretion of the broker who, on the one hand, may give tokens for brave but unsuccessful attempts, or, on the other, impose a penalty for fraudulent claims.

At the end of the conference, or at some other agreed time, the group with the highest number of prize tokens will be awarded a special prize. Additional prizes will be given for the group coming up with the best (in the brokers' view) ideas for: (a) improving COUNTERPOINT; (b) improving the conference.

COUNTERPOINT—Brokers' Instructions

Two of you will take the part of brokers and must sit close enough to each other to be able to make occasional cross checks (back-to-back may be a suitable arrangement). One of you will be responsible for HIGH risk—red counter claims, and the other for LOW risk—yellow counter claims.

Please read the instruction sheet for the general body of participants.

You will be visited by representatives from each group after about 40 minutes from the start of COUNTERPOINT. Your task will be to judge the validity of claims made on behalf of each group: whether a high risk is what it purports to be, or whether a proposed initiative represents any risk at all.

If you consider any claim to be inflated you may reject it and give a lower rate of counters in return. If you reckon a claim is frivolous or fraudulent you may impose a penalty, the choice of which rests with you.

While the groups are sharing their thoughts (Stage 2) you will probably find it useful to check with each other what criteria and standards you will operate and how you will ensure they are related to the sort of initiatives the group is discussing. You may also wish to eavesdrop on one or two of the groups.

You will need to devise a means of recording and scoring the transactions.

Your reward will be in heaven/hell depending on which constitutes the bigger risk for you!

Evaluation

Perhaps because they were all pre-conditioned to strange events, everyone at the conference seemed to fall in with the instructions, even if they were a little puzzled about the way things would go. Some, I think, did not see conference problems the same way as I did and others saw no risks on their horizons. While some groups gelled, therefore, a few carried on perhaps out of a sense of duty rather than of involvement.

When the risk brokers opened business, however, the interest and action soared to a higher plane. In retrospect I realize how crucial is their role and how important it is that they be people of wit and imagination.

The first three stages ended in a flurry of activity and hilarity around the brokers' stalls as groups tried to trade last-minute risks for more counters. On the more serious side, the whole exercise produced some fascinating statements of intent. One participant, for example, admitting to a deep-rooted shyness which prevented her meeting new people at conferences, undertook to introduce herself to strangers — within the conference! One group agreed to stage a workshop of its own invention during one of the free 'slots' in the conference timetable. In the end it was this group that received the apt prize of a bottle of sparkling wine. Another group that came up with a suggestion for improving COUNTERPOINT was given a bag of peanuts, on the grounds that the game was designed for peanuts!

The overall view, if that is what one should call a few hasty remarks collected during the disorder of people leaving and clearing up as the conference finished, seemed to be that COUNTERPOINT had worked well:

(a) in getting people to move out of their cliques of old buddies;
(b) in stimulating everyone to be a bit more purposeful about their time at the conference;
(c) as a warm-up exercise which both brought people together and mixed them up (in the positive sense).

One colleague remarked:

> I'd never realized before how prone I am to just teaming up with my old mates and ignoring newcomers. First of all I resented the way the exercise pushed me to meet up with strange people but then I saw the sense and it was just what I needed to stir me out of my lethargy.

Several others commented that the exercise as a whole could have held together better if a short meeting of the groups had been scheduled into the timetable, both in the middle and at the end of the conference.

For my part, the anticipated risk of devising and running a game to help gamesters work on games proved minimal in reality. That is the way with so many risks!

Biographical note

David Jaques, who first qualified as an engineer and taught engineering for several years, now teaches communication skills at Hatfield Polytechnic. His interest in gaming and simulation derived initially from his recognition of the limits that traditional teaching methods impose upon the outlook of engineering students. He currently uses experiential learning in training higher education staff and is particularly interested in the more imaginative side of learning when looking at the very personal qualities involved in communication skills. He has designed games for staff development (THE ACADEMIC GAME) and also games for use by the World Health Organization.

David Jaques
Centre for Educational Development
The Hatfield Polytechnic
PO Box 109
College Lane
Hatfield
Herts AL10 9AB
England

2. CALL YOURSELF A MANAGER? – a new approach to using simulation in management training

Allan Schofield

Abstract: The paper describes the development and use of a new method of using video-based simulations in management training. Two programmes have currently been produced, one on Meetings and the other on Managing Staff. Five more are in preparation.

Introduction

In a society such as SAGSET the advantages of using simulation and gaming as forms of experiential learning need no advocacy, and they have been widely discussed in the previous volumes in this series. Their uses in management training have also been widely considered both inside the society and outside (see Elgood, 1976) and a large number of materials have been developed.

However, despite their widespread use, a number of warnings have been sounded about the effectiveness of many simulations in management training. Stewart and Stewart (1977) have discussed the difficulties of role playing in developing, reviewing and appraising skills; Twelker (1977) has written of the need for full evaluation of simulations to determine their effectiveness; while Hart (1978) has gone one stage further and concluded that no known link exists between ability in management games and coping with real-life management problems. He concludes: 'Enjoy your gaming. It may do you no good but it is unlikely to do you any harm.' Such sentiments are unlikely to satisfy the trainer, nor indeed the organization supporting training, since the whole point of such activities is to bridge the gap between current and potential performance.

CALL YOURSELF A MANAGER?

It was against this background, and with a desire to overcome some of the potential difficulties in using simulations in management training, that CALL YOURSELF A MANAGER? was developed. This was coupled with a secondary wish to try and develop a more creative use of video in training than had previously been produced and published in the UK. (See Turner, 1982, for criticism of the unsuitability of most existing management training films and videos.)

The approach used in CALL YOURSELF A MANAGER? introduces two important innovations to the use of video in management training (Boud and Pearson, 1979). Firstly, unlike most of the existing material described above, it neither presents factual information nor relies on a single 'story line'. Instead the programme consists of a large number of very short scenes, each depicting a different type of management problem. This means that trainers can select appropriate episodes to meet their particular training needs. The programme has a very wide range of possible uses with the same group, and is therefore very economical, whereas conventional films are usually only used once for each group and purpose.

The second innovation is that by the use of subjectivity the viewer is placed on the spot: immediately dropped into a problem to which he or she has to respond. In most episodes what is being said is directed at the viewer who, imagining himself or herself as the person being addressed, has to respond to the issues presented. Thus the viewer is placed in a situation much like the one he or she faces at work: face-to-face with the boss or a subordinate, at a selection interview, dealing with a trade union official, and so on.

In developing the programme, considerable attention has been given to the question of immediacy. This brings a reality to the issues and dispenses with the need for a lengthy build-up to a training exercise. This technique is regarded as important in the training of managers, since the most difficult problems are often those which occur suddenly, with no prior warning: the member of staff who walks into your office, the trade union official who has asked to see you, and so on—any one of these may suddenly lead to difficulties. The response to that situation could be crucial to the future relations with the staff concerned. Many episodes take place from behind a desk so that the viewer is placed in the position of the employee being spoken to by a superior. Some episodes involve the viewer responding as a trade union official or as a candidate for a job. Thus with relative ease the trainer can summon up a whole range of staff management situations. In this way the programme is economic, flexible and convenient.

Two programmes have so far been produced, one on Meetings and one on Managing Staff, and each contains approximately 50 very short scenes showing different types of problems, some including episodes which have two or more versions with variations in the sex, age, tone of voice, etc of the person making the statement. In all the scenes professional actors were used to play the various simulated roles. The episodes are anything between 10 and 40 seconds long.

Trainer skills

Unlike many existing films and video tapes, CALL YOURSELF A MANAGER? requires a positive input from a trainer, but its flexibility means that it can be used by trainers of varying experience, ranging from those who have relatively little practice in conducting small group training sessions to those with extensive expertise. It is, of course, important that trainers are reasonably aware of small group training techniques (Berger, M L and P J, 1972, and Ayres, 1977)— particularly the role of the facilitator—but, providing they are careful in their selection and use of episodes and limit their objectives to those that they feel they can meet, the relatively inexperienced trainer should be able to cope adequately.

It is, however, important to stress that any training activity where these programmes are being used should be appropriately designed: this will include the identification of training needs (both personal and organizational), the setting of agreed objectives, the selection of appropriate teaching methods, and the construction of evaluative mechanisms. This can only be done through an understanding of the job(s) of those participating and the context in which they are undertaken. There are, in addition, within each of these categories many differences in such factors as the organizational context and the experience of individuals (Boydell, 1976).

Using the programme

The programme can be used in two main ways:

(a) as a means of looking at interpersonal behaviour and relationships in certain aspects of management;
(b) as miniature case studies.

The episodes are very short. This is to increase their impact on the viewer, but it does mean that they contain only the essential information about the particular incident portrayed. This method does not require a build-up of additional information, but trainers may find that for some groups it will be necessary to set the episodes in a specific context to make it easier for viewers to assimilate the situation in the time available. This depends greatly on the nature of the group and of the training activity itself: in the area of interpersonal behaviour, background information will usually be less relevant.

Trainers will obviously decide for themselves how to organize the group to view the episodes depending on the circumstances; however, there is no doubt that this type of training demands a small group approach. Where plenary sessions are used (to compare responses or to pool information, etc) then there should be a strict limit on numbers (say no more than 24 people), and where interpersonal relations are being discussed 10 or 12 may be appropriate. Groups can be arranged in a variety of ways depending on the nature of the exercise and the experience of the group, but two main arrangements are recommended.

1. WORKING IN PAIRS

The group is divided into pairs to watch the episodes. After each episode, one of the pair responds to what he or she has seen on the screen. The partner then helps the respondent to articulate and examine that response. Their roles are reversed for the next episode and so on, giving each of them experience of responding and of facilitating the other's response.

2. WORKING IN THREES

The group is divided into threes to watch the episodes. After each episode, one of the trio responds, another helps the respondent examine the response and the third observes the whole process. The facilitator role is the same as in the first method, but the way it is undertaken, the support given, the questions asked and so on are later considered by the triad with the help of the observer. In a sense, a secondary purpose — that of examining the facilitator functions and the interview process — emerges. For subsequent episodes the roles are varied, giving each member of the trio experience of each role. Thus this technique provides interviewing skills practice within the main staff management skills exercise.

The process of clarifying and reviewing a response provides the basis for the second level of activity—the development of skills of observation (both aural and visual) and of questioning. Most staff managers spend a lot of their time either in listening to other people, in observing their activities, or in asking questions. Therefore the facilitator and observer roles are, in themselves, an integral part of the development function of the episodes. The facilitator will be given a list of questions set by the trainer—or set by the participants if it has been decided to make building lists of suitable questions part of the exercise—and can use these to structure the discussion. The method of questioning and discussion that the facilitator chooses (including the way the various questions are introduced, and the extent to which they are pursued or followed up and so on) can then be commented upon by the observer where that role is part of the exercise.

The selected episodes should, of course, be played singly to the group so that an immediate response can be made to each one. It is probable that, initially, some type of review session will be needed to compare the responses of individuals in the groups and to discuss the learning points that arise from individual episodes; this may then become less necessary as the participants grow more used to responding to what they see. Indeed, where personal feelings are being considered in a small group, any subsequent plenary session would probably be inappropriate. The nature of any plenary review will vary according to the particular circumstances concerned and may be dealt with by the trainer in various ways. Obviously, care needs to be taken on the timing of such a review session, and it is recommended that not too long should elapse between seeing and responding to an episode and discussing it.

The trainer's role can then be summarized as ensuring that each episode is considered as part of a continuous cycle of activity: first the use of the programme must be explained and related to previous activities; second, the individual episodes must be shown and the issues arising explored in the manner already described; third, the trainer must ensure that such issues are clarified, summarized, and their implications pursued (either in a plenary session or by working with the small groups as appropriate); and fourth, the overall outcome must be related to further parts of the training programme or to some positive developmental strategy (for example, action planning).

An example

An example may help to clarify the way the programme can be used in looking at aspects of interpersonal behaviour. During a course on 'Effectiveness in Meetings' one group was shown an episode in which someone is saying directly to the viewer:

> Look, I know you people are very good at shuffling the papers around and all that but when are you actually going to do some real work around here?

One particular respondent's reaction to being asked what he felt about the episode was to say that he felt angry that someone should talk to him 'like that', and that the other person had 'no right to do so'. As the discussion continued with his partner in the small group it slowly emerged that his reaction was due not only to the manner in which the remark was made, but also to some of the implications that he read into it.

His job was largely concerned with relatively routine administration and arranging some fairly straightforward meetings, and he felt that his contribution

25

was being devalued by such comments. As he responded to other questions it emerged that he sometimes felt just like that in his real job, and this coloured his relationships with some of his colleagues and led him to refuse to take responsibility for assisting with new ideas or innovations. A plan was made to raise the issue with a sympathetic head of department in order to take some remedial measures, and this was linked to other learning on the course.

Some potential difficulties

In using this training method, the authors have found that, although most people involved find the programme both enjoyable and valuable as a learning experience, there are a few who will react against this technique and claim to be unable to respond to the episodes. Clearly, different individuals will respond in different ways to the same situation—this, after all, is the reason for examining interpersonal behaviour. However, there will be cases where participants may be deluding themselves in their claims to be unaffected, and the trainer should pursue and clarify such comments. Work carried out in the United States (Kagan, 1975) using a similar training method for counsellors and doctors measured the physiological responses (sweating, pulse rates, etc) of participants shown various confrontational episodes. This demonstrated that in many instances, although individuals had claimed to be unaffected by what they had seen, their physiological responses had shown that the reverse was true.

A study in Australia (Boud and Pearson, 1978), where this technique was also used for training in medical education, has suggested that three main problems may exist which can in some cases inhibit the uses of particular episodes with certain participants:

(a) There are different levels of readiness amongst participants to appreciate the issues which are illustrated in the programme, and this is largely related to the experience of those involved.

(b) There are the general social norms which inhibit acknowledgement of feeling and emotion to be overcome.

(c) Some participants may not be able to cope easily with the expression of emotion shown in certain episodes, and this barrier may have to be overcome before genuine discussion can take place.

Examining interpersonal behaviour and relationships

Many existing training methods do not bring out the importance of interpersonal behaviour and relationships at work. Conversely, some methods which attempt to do just that may be unpopular with managers, who will sometimes strongly resist taking part. Many people do not like to discuss openly their feelings about other people or difficult situations. The episodes in this programme can trigger a response in the viewer which can be taken and discussed in relatively supportive surroundings, but, even so, the trainer should be aware that there will still be problems in getting people to identify their real feelings. Different episodes will affect different emotional levels. In most cases the initial feelings will be exposed and discussed without too much difficulty: however, the process becomes more difficult the further one tries to dig down into people's emotions. For that reason, it is important that feelings should be discussed only at a level which is legitimate for the particular training purposes, and which the trainer can manage. The use of the episodes in this context should provide a basis on which individuals can identify and understand feelings which are relevant to their managerial role.

Trainers will discover that one short episode can provoke a wide range of responses. For example, when asked 'How did you feel?' about some of the episodes which place the viewer in front of an authoritarian manager, the individual may express feelings of anger, inadequacy, resentment, defensiveness, etc. When asked 'What would you probably do?' about an episode in which the viewer is placed in front of an apparently unco-operative employee, people may find themselves rapidly asking questions like: 'How can I get round him? How can I force him to do the work?'.

By use of these episodes and with appropriate interventions from the trainer, individuals can come to appreciate the important distinctions between how they feel and what they think, between what action they would take and what they would really want to do, and so on. For example, a particular incident may make them feel very angry, but expression of that anger may be dysfunctional and an important learning point is the need to identify those personal feelings, to understand the reasons for them, and their effects on the other people involved.

The trainer working in this way must ensure that there is a suitable working climate, and that appropriate support is provided in the small groups. Adequate time should be allowed for personal feelings to be identified and explored, and due attention paid to the effectiveness of the facilitator and observer roles (Cooper, 1976).

Using the episodes as miniature case studies

Used as miniature case studies the episodes involve techniques similar to those described above. However, the emphasis is different: individuals are not asked for their feelings about what they saw, but about more cognitive issues in the situation concerned. Thus the group might be asked to describe the main points arising in an episode and to identify the organizational issues, to analyse the communications between manager and employee or to determine and examine the behaviours identified. The subject groupings on the tape may often form the basis of the use of the episodes as miniature case studies. For example, in running a session on interviewing, the trainer might make use of several of the appropriate episodes either to introduce the topic or to supplement learning points made by other methods during the session. In this context the use of CALL YOURSELF A MANAGER? is similar to an ordinary written case study, but adapted to take account of the visual content.

Using the programme with other training methods

The trainer should regard CALL YOURSELF A MANAGER? as a multi-purpose training aid which can be used either on its own in short sessions, or in conjunction with other material on longer courses or workshops. For example, if the trainer is running a course on working relations, CALL YOURSELF A MANAGER? might be integrated into a range of training methods including simulations and role-plays. The extent to which any method dominates will depend entirely on the trainer's perception of need and the specific objectives of the activity. In a similar way, the episodes can complement written exercises — case studies, critical incidents, and the like — by bringing to life staff management situations that cannot be satisfactorily reviewed without observing behaviour. This could be carried further by writing case studies based on selected episodes, and comparing the way participants respond to the two methods.

The programme can be particularly valuable in assisting in the identification of different styles of management behaviour, leading to the completion of some of the written exercises which can be used in this area (Margerison, 1979, and Francis and Woodcock, 1975). The identification of management styles leads directly to consideration of the effectiveness of performance, and on to organizational issues. Behavioural analysis (Rackham and Morgan, 1977) can also be used in identifying issues occurring in the episodes. Whatever training methods are used with CALL YOURSELF A MANAGER? it will usually be important to ensure that participants make some type of personal commitment to build on the issues raised in responding to the episodes, for example, by means of action plans or follow-up meetings.

Evaluation

This article has been written some three months after CALL YOURSELF A MANAGER? became publicly available, and so far evaluation has solely been on the 'reaction level' (Hamblin, 1972). This has been extremely positive, both from other trainers who have used the programmes, and also from participants on workshops led by the author where, almost without exception, the programmes have been the most popular item according to questionnaires completed at the end of the event. In a way, the programmes seem for participants to combine the value of good experiential learning with the appeal that is sometimes found of using television as a learning medium.

As a result of the interest shown in the programmes, five more are being produced on: supervision, leadership, working relations, industrial relations, and interviewing. Additional applications in the social work area and in teaching and learning are being considered. The authors are currently trying to develop a more systematic strategy for evaluation, both as a way of comparing effectiveness against other training methods, and also in its own right.

References

Ayres R (1977) *A Trainer's Guide to Group Instruction.* BACIE: London
Berger M L and P J (eds) (1972) *Group Training Techniques.* Gower Press: Farnborough
Boud D and Pearson M (1978) *Bringing Reality into the Classroom: The Use of Trigger Films in Introducing Socio-Emotional Aspects of Learning in the Health Sciences.* Tertiary Education Research Centre, University of New South Wales, Australia
Boud D and Pearson M (1979) The Trigger Film: A Stimulus for Affective Learning, *Programmed Learning and Educational Technology* 1, 16
Boydell T (1976) *The Identification of Training Needs.* BACIE: London
Cooper C L (1976) *Developing Social Skills in Managers: Advances in Group Training.* Macmillan: London
Elgood C (1976) *Handbook of Management Games.* Gower Press: Farnborough
Francis D and Woodcock M (1975) *People at Work: a Practical Guide to Organizational Change.* University Associates: Mansfield

Hart R T (1978) Simulation and Gaming in Management Education and Training. In
    McAleese R (ed) *Perspectives on Academic Gaming and Simulation 3.* Kogan Page:
    London
Kagan N (1975) Influencing Human Interaction—Eleven Years with IPR, *The Canadian
    Counsellor,* 9
Margerison C (1979) *How to Assess Your Managerial Style.* MCB Publications: Bradford
Rackham N and Morgan T (1977) *Behaviour Analysis in Training.* McGraw Hill: Maidenhead
Stewart V and Stewart A (1977) *Practical Performance Appraisal.* Gower Press:
    Farnborough
Turner P (1982) Is Anybody Out There?, *Audio Visual,* 121, January
Twelker D (1977) Some Reflections on the Innovation of Simulation and Gaming. In
    Megarry J (ed) *Aspects of Simulation and Gaming.* Kogan Page: London

Biographical note

Allan Schofield has been Administrator in the Centre for Staff Development in Higher
Education at the Institute of Education, University of London, since 1974. A sociology
graduate of the Polytechnic of Central London, in recent years he has worked on
administrative staff development. He has organized and participated in numerous courses for
administrators, and is co-author (together with Roger Mayhew) of the CALL YOURSELF A
MANAGER? video-based programmes, available from the University Teaching Methods
Unit.

Allan Schofield
University of London Institute of Education
University Teaching Methods Unit
55 Gordon Square
London WC1H 0NU
England

3. PIGS, or SNAKES' EYES – a simulation for entrepreneurs

Stuart Beckwith

Abstract: PIGS or SNAKES' EYES is a simple game of chance and strategy whose rules are
described here. The strategic decisions made by players before and during the game make it
an interesting medium for exploring the differences between a risk and a gamble, and the
characteristics of successful entrepreneurship.

Introduction

PIGS or SNAKES' EYES is an amusing game of chance and strategy that may be
played by any number of people. The playing time for each set is from five to 15
minutes, dependent upon the number of players, and each set may be repeated
as many times as is required or until an element of boredom creeps in. A limited
range of equipment is required, viz two dice and a throwing cup, plus a set of
score cards (which may be on a stencil—see Appendix 1).

The Game

The object of the game is to acquire 100 points and some form of monetary penalty or reward may be used in the parlour (as opposed to the classroom), although readers are not issued with any further advice on this aspect.

THE PLAY

The order of play is determined by each player throwing both dice, and the first player is the one with the highest score (which is not counted as a score for the game). The first player now rolls two dice. If he throws an ace with either die he does not count a score on that throw and must pass the dice to the next player (clockwise direction). If he throws any other numbers he scores that number of points and may continue to roll until such time as he decides to finish that innings, or until he throws a single ace in which case he loses the score *for that innings*. If he throws two aces—the snakes' eyes of the title—he loses not only the score of the current innings but also any previous score he has accumulated.

POINTS

Points are accumulated by adding together the face values of all dice thrown in a player's turn. A player may make as many throws as he wishes in each turn (subject to throwing either one or two aces, in which case he must cease that turn, as indicated above). Therefore, a player may elect to stop his turn at any time, scoring his total for that turn and adding it to his previous total, and passing the dice to the next player. However, there is another exception to this rule, in that a player may *not* end his turn on a double. If he throws a double two, three, four, five or six he must add the face value (four, six, eight, etc) to his previous score and throw again *even if he wishes not to do so for whatever reason*. (Clearly if a double ace is thrown the earlier rule applies and the player's cumulative score is wiped out and he must re-start from zero at his next turn.)

THE WINNER

The first player to reach 100 points *may* be the winner, but the complete innings must be played out before this is determined. So, if Player A scores 105 points and quits (but not on a double), Player B gets his turn. If Player B subsequently scores 107 he beats Player A, but he, in turn, may be beaten by Players C, D, etc. The game is not over until each player has completed his throw for the round in which one of the players declares, having passed 100 points, that he wishes to end the game. Play must continue even if all players have reached 100 points, until one of the players declares that he wishes the game to end; which he must do on completion of his throw (having exceeded 100 points) *before* handing the dice to the next player. It must be stated that the throwing order is important, as no new rounds are undertaken once any one of the players has indicated in the appropriate manner that he wishes the game to end.

STRATEGY

The last player knows how his opponents have fared and may adjust his strategy accordingly. He also knows that they have no chance of another throw if he declares the game to be over. Does this mean that there is an advantage in being the last to throw?

There are advantages and disadvantages in all positions. Luck on its own will not enable a player to win. He needs to evolve a strategy to cope with the luck of others. Of course, we all know what can happen to the best laid plans of mice and men, and the success of an earlier player may force a later one to press his luck too far and wipe out a promising turn — but he could still come back and win next turn!

Purpose of the game

This is a game which can be played at all levels of sophistication. In management education the aim is to simulate risk in conditions where strategy may be changed swiftly, and effects of other factors are immediately apparent and measurable.

The objectives in such cases would be twofold:

(a) to determine whether a strategy is apparent to others;
(b) to determine the effects of other factors and events on a chosen strategy.

Method of play

It helps to get players to treat the game as a strategic exercise if they are asked to write down their strategy before play starts (after a brief explanation of the game has been given), and to ask them to note down any changes (and reasons) as play develops.

As it is impossible to eliminate all risks, it is necessary to devise a strategy for dealing with them; rather, a range of strategies. It is hoped that this game will allow players the opportunity of devising strategies in a situation where most of the variables are measurable (eg, probability of numbers being thrown — see below) and there is limited damage (except to one's ego) if the chosen strategy is 'wrong'.

Another dimension of the game is to attempt to predict what effect a 'scientific' approach makes to final results. At the discretion of the tutor, discussion on probability may take place before or after a game — see Appendix 2.

Risk or gamble?

The author believes that the differences between risk and gamble hinge upon the degree of personal influence on outcome. The greater the degree of personal and individual involvement, the greater the shift from gamble to risk on this spectrum.

Risk ⟵───────────────────────────────────⟶ *Gamble*

| High degree of personal involvement, eg, betting on running a marathon race that one is entering. | Others decide, eg, betting on which fly will take off first from a wall. |

This may be illustrated as follows.

On which of the following gambles would you prefer to bet £100, and why?

31

(a) Liverpool to beat a non-league team in the cup, at 10 to one on.
(b) Your favourite sport against a player who is normally twice as good, at odds of two to one against.
(c) A 50 to one chance of striking oil, with a return of around 200 to one if you do.

The chances are that the entrepreneur, who enjoys risk but wishes a high degree of personal involvement will opt for the second choice; the others, although offering a higher possible reward, are further away from the sphere of his influence. Certainly, my own experience of using this with entrepreneurs and others has been that the choice of the second gamble marks out the entrepreneur.

Other learning applications

A further development is for observers to be appointed who watch the ways players act and speak. Records may be kept (in note form or on tape) and comparisons made after the game between previously determined and actual strategies employed. Therefore, the game may be used as a behavioural exercise as well as in the ways that the author has identified. And it is certainly a question of considerable interest to those, like myself, engaged in the training of entrepreneurial managers and businessmen (and businesswomen), to ask whether the ability to hold to a previously determined strategy, in spite of the pressures incurred by the actions of others, is a necessary behavioural skill for the successful entrepreneur.

Appendix 1: Scoresheet

◄─────────────── PLAYERS ───────────────►

	A	B	C	D	E	F	G	H	I
1st Innings									
2nd Innings									
Total 1 + 2									
3rd Innings									
Running Total									
4th Innings									
Running Total									
5th Innings									
Running Total									
6th Innings									
Running Total									
7th Innings									
Running Total									
8th Innings									
Running Total									
9th Innings									
Running Total									
10th Innings									
GRAND TOTAL									

Appendix 2: Calculating odds

ODDS

There are 36 possible combinations of two dice. (For each of the six ways one die may turn up, there are six ways the second die may turn up: 6 x 6 = 36.) The results range from 2 (1-1) to 12 (6-6). These two throws are known as 'snakes' eyes' and 'boxcars', respectively.

Here are the various ways a number can come up from a roll of two dice:

2 can be made one way: 1-1
3 can be made two ways: 1-2 or 2-1
4 can be made three ways: 1-3, 3-1, or 2-2
5 can be made four ways: 1-4, 4-1, 2-3, or 3-2
6 can be made five ways: 1-5, 5-1, 2-4, 4-2, or 3-3
7 can be made six ways: 1-6, 6-1, 2-5, 5-2, 3-4, or 4-3
8 can be made five ways: 2-6, 6-2, 3-5, 5-3, or 4-4
9 can be made four ways: 3-6, 6-3, 4-5, or 5-4
10 can be made three ways: 4-6, 6-4, or 5-5
11 can be made two ways: 5-6 or 6-5
12 can be made one way: 6-6

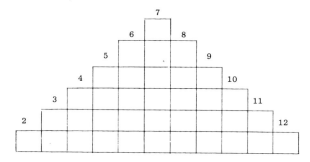

Biographical note

Stuart Beckwith is a senior lecturer in the Small Business and Innovation Studies Division of the Anglian Regional Management Centre. Having spent 14 years running his own small businesses he is used to risk and uncertainty. Although a relative newcomer to education and training, he has achieved some successes in simulating real events within the classroom.

Stuart J Beckwith
Anglian Regional Management Centre
North East London Polytechnic
Danbury Park
Danbury, Essex
England

4. The COCOYOC simulation – political education in world development

Michael Bassey

Abstract: The COCOYOC SIMULATION is a 'committee' activity in which participants role play cabinet ministers of five countries engaged in development planning. Avia and Bevia are industrial countries similar to Britain; Xavia, Yakia and Zebria are third world countries. Avia and Bevia are faced with problems of rising unemployment and potehtial shortages of fuel, raw materials and possibly food. They are partly dependent upon imports of these from Xavia, Yakia and Zebria. These latter countries are concerned to feed a rapidly expanding population and to meet aspirations for a better life; in particular they are concerned with the extent and form of industrialization. In all five countries these major problems are set in a matrix of domestic issues, including military policy, education, health provision, communications, etc.

Participants are provided with cabinet papers and briefs for individual ministers. Print-outs from a micro-computer aid the flow of information and contribute to the impression of reality. A full run can involve 50 participants for one or two days. It is also possible to carry out a 'one country' run with between five and 15 participants and lasting about three hours. The inclusion of 'wealthist' and 'convivialist' political factions is sometimes appropriate.

The author's aims are political awareness of national and international issues and the development of political attitudes in the context of the United Nations 'Cocoyoc Declaration'.

Introduction

The COCOYOC SIMULATION is a 'committee' activity in which participants role play cabinet ministers of five countries engaged in development planning.

Participants are provided with cabinet papers and briefs for individual ministers. Print-outs from a micro-computer can aid the flow of information and contribute to the impression of reality.

A full run can involve 50 participants for one or two days. It is also possible to carry out a 'one country' run with between five and 15 participants and lasting about three hours. The inclusion of 'wealthist' and 'convivialist' political factions is sometimes appropriate.

The author's aims are concerned with political awareness of national and international issues and with the development of political attitudes, in the context of the United Nations 'Cocoyoc Declaration'.

Figure 1: *The 'world' of the COCOYOC SIMULATION*

Description of the simulation

The 'world' consists of five countries: Avia, Bevia, Xakia, Yakia and Zebria. Avia and Bevia are industrial countries similar to Britain; Xavia, Yakia and Zebria are third world countries. Avia and Bevia are faced with problems of rising unemployment and potential shortages of fuel, raw materials and possibly food. They are partly dependent upon imports of these from Xavia, Yakia and Zebria. These latter countries are concerned to feed a rapidly expanding population and to meet aspirations for a better life; in particular they are concerned with the extent and form of industrialization. In all five countries these major problems are set in a matrix of domestic issues, including military policy, education, health provision, communications, etc.

Avia and Bevia import half of their food, half of their fuel and nearly all of their raw materials from Xavia, Yakia and Zebria. In exchange they export consumer goods, heavy goods and armaments. There is an international currency unit called the 'buk'. One million buks, or one megabuk, is represented as 'Mbuk'. This currency is free of inflation. (This represents a major simplification from the real world; another is that capital investment is omitted from financial planning.)

Participants take on the role of cabinet ministers and engage in preparing five-year plans. (As a simplification these plans are made in relation to the last year of the five-year period, ie 1990.)

Cabinet papers of about 25 A4 sheets of typescript set out the matters which require decision. For each minister there is also a special brief, which enables him to monitor the effects of decisions in his field of responsibility.

There are 11 named cabinet posts in each country:

Prime Minister
Minister for Finance
Minister for Overseas Trade
Minister for Employment
Minister for Energy
Minister for Raw Materials
Minister for Food & Agriculture or Internal Affairs
Minister for Defence
Minister for Education
Minister for Health, Housing, Transport and Communications
Minister without Portfolio

If necessary ministers may be responsible for more than one ministry. If there are more than 11 participants, under-secretaries may be appointed. Prime ministers can be chosen beforehand by the simulation director, or elected by the participants. It gives the prime minister a firmer power base if he, rather than the simulation director, invites ministers to take particular briefs. The simulation materials are:

Notes for participants
Cabinet papers for Avia
Cabinet papers for Bevia
Cabinet papers for Xavia
Cabinet papers for Yakia
Cabinet papers for Zebria
Ministerial briefs for senior ministers for Avia
Ministerial briefs for senior ministers for Bevia
Ministerial briefs for senior ministers for Xavia
Ministerial briefs for senior ministers for Yakia
Ministerial briefs for senior ministers for Zebria
PET cassette for 1990 predictions for Avia and Bevia
PET cassettes for 1990 predictions for Xavia and Zebria
PET cassette for 1990 predictions for Yakia
PET cassette for World Bank report
PET cassette for *Times of the World* issues
Notes for simulation director

There are two modes of play and a 'political' variation.

ONE COUNTRY MODE (FIVE TO 15 PARTICIPANTS)

Participants from the government of one country only. This is either Avia (an industrial country) or Xavia (a third world country). No information is available about the decisions of other countries and the cabinet has to make reasonable guesses about international trade and aid. In this mode there is no inter-government negotiation.

Although it is possible to complete the cabinet agenda in two hours (particularly if all participants have thoroughly read through the papers and made their own, preliminary, decisions), it is preferable in this mode to spend longer.

WORLD MODE (25 TO 75 PARTICIPANTS)

Participants from the governments of the five countries. The activity requires at least a day and entails three sessions. The first session is devoted to cabinets meeting in isolation from each other for two hours or longer. The second session is spent on inter-government negotiations, for one or two hours, or longer. The third session entails cabinets again meeting in isolation and balancing their budgets in terms of the trade and aid matters which have been negotiated.

In this mode meetings of the United Nations General Assembly can be called. At a first meeting the Cocoyoc Declaration can be presented and member states invited to endorse it. Subsequent meetings may be called by the simulation director (role-playing as UN Secretary-General) when requested by members and as a finale for statements on future planning by prime ministers.

POLITICAL CREDOS

A variation which can be introduced to either mode of play entails two political credos, namely the wealthist credo and the convivialist credo. These are described in Figure 2. They can be used in a number of ways. One way is for participants to divide themselves into wealthists and convivialists and for, say, Avia to be wealthist and Bevia convivialist, etc. Alternatively, as in the 'one country' mode, a coalition government can be formed with equal numbers of wealthists and convivialists who, from time to time during the cabinet meetings, call for party meetings.

COMPUTER PRINT-OUTS

In the cabinet papers participants receive a statistical report for 1985 (last year) on government income and expenditure, trade imports and exports, energy consumption and supply, raw materials consumption and supply and food consumption and supply. A series of PET programmes (each of about 10,000 bytes) enables each cabinet to receive a statistical report of predictions for 1990 based on their decisions, coupled with a prediction of the likely popularity of the government. Ministers have been able to monitor changes in these balances throughout the cabinet meetings but the computer print-out serves to bring these reports together—and to check on the arithmetic of participants! It also adds to the impression of reality. An example of a print-out is given in Figure 3. (see p 40).

The economic models on which these calculations are based are unsophisticated: their purpose is to stimulate the thinking of participants rather than give accurate mirrors to reality. Another programme provides a *World Bank Report* which in the world mode facilitates inter-country negotiations. There is also a programme which produces issues of *The Times of the World*. The simulation director can use this to add to realism, for example by provoking antagonisms between nations.

Both parties believe in democratic government which is representative of and accountable to the people. Both see the functions of government to be to safeguard the lives and interests of the people and to promote their welfare and happiness. But they differ fundamentally as to how welfare and happiness should be promoted.

	WEALTHIST	CONVIVIALIST
Mainspring of society	The creation of wealth. Greater wealth implies that people become more affluent, so that they gain satisfactions from greater access to goods and services.	The creation of conviviality. Greater conviviality implies that people are more in harmony with themselves and their social and physical environment, so that they gain satisfactions from their own activities and from interaction with one another and with their surroundings.
Attitude to work	A man works in order to create wealth (through manufacturing goods or providing services); he works for maximum profit.	A man works in order to create conviviality (through developing his talents and through relating to his fellows and his environment); he also works in order to provide for his needs.
	Work is undesirable, but necessary.	Work is enjoyable and necessary.
Attitude to the use of natural resources	Resources are a source of wealth. They should be exploited to produce maximum profits.	Resources should be used in relation to need and not greed. Renewable resources (eg wood) should be consumed no faster than they are renewed; non-renewable resources (eg coal) should be conserved as far as possible.
Attitude to trade	Trade is essential for creating wealth and for acquiring resources which can be turned into wealth.	Trade makes people less self-reliant and so tends to reduce conviviality.
Attitude to leisure, music, art, literature	These are an extrinsic product of wealth.	These are an intrinsic part of conviviality.
Attitude to education	Education is initiation into the creation of wealth.	Education is initiation into conviviality.
Attitude to the future	Progress is essential.	Stewardship is essential.

Figure 2. *Political philosophies of the wealthists and the convivialists*

```
####################################################
GOVERNMENT OF AVIA
COMPUTER PREDICTIONS FOR 1990
. . . . . . . . . . . . . . . . . . . . . . . . . . . . . . . . . . . . . . .
GOVERNMENT EXPENDITURE AND INCOME:MBUK

EXPENDITURE. . . . . . . . . .          INCOME. . . . . . . . . . . . . . .

EDUCATION          020.0               INCOME TAX          040.0
HEALTH             015.0               PURCHASE TAX        025.0
COMM & TRANS       005.0               HEALTH TAX          019.0
HOUSING            010.0               HOUSEHOLD TAX       011.0
AGRICULTURE        004.0               COMPANY TAX         005.0
SOCIAL SECURITY    021.0               OTHER TAX           000.0
OVERSEAS AID       006.0
DEFENCE            020.0
OTHER              000.0
TOTAL              101.0               TOTAL               100.0
. . . . . . . . . . . . . . . . . . . . . . . . . . . . . . . . . . . . . . .
NATIONAL TRADE IMPORTS AND EXPORTS:MBUK

IMPORTS. . . . . . . . . . . . . .      EXPORTS. . . . . . . . . . . . . .

FROM BEVIA         025.0               TO BEVIA            025.0
FROM XAVIA         025.0               TO XAVIA            020.0
FROM YAKIA         025.0               TO YAKIA            030.0
FROM ZEBRIA        025.0               TO ZEBRIA           025.0
TOTAL              100.0               TOTAL               100.0
. . . . . . . . . . . . . . . . . . . . . . . . . . . . . . . . . . . . . . .
ENERGY CONSUMPTION AND SUPPLY:MBUK

CONSUMPTION. . . . . . . . . .          SUPPLY. . . . . . . . . . . . . . .

INDST C GDS        016.0               YAKIAN IMPORTS      025.0
INDST A/H GDS      007.0               NUCLEAR ENERGY      000.0
INDST GOV S        002.0               SOFT ENERGY         000.0
DOMESTIC H/L       010.0               HOME MINES          025.0
TRANSPORT          010.0
AGRICULTURE        005.0
TOTAL              050.0               TOTAL               050.0
. . . . . . . . . . . . . . . . . . . . . . . . . . . . . . . . . . . . . . .
FOOD CONSUMPTION AND SUPPLY:MBUK

CONSUMPTION. . . . . . . . . .          SUPPLY. . . . . . . . . . . . . . .

HOME CONSUMPTN     050.0               HOME GROWN          025.0
                   000.0               XAVIAN IMPORTS      015.0
                   000.0               ZEBRIAN IMPORTS     010.0
TOTAL              050.0               TOTAL               050.0
. . . . . . . . . . . . . . . . . . . . . . . . . . . . . . . . . . . . . . .
RAW MATERIALS CONSUMPTN & SUPPLY:MBUK

CONSUMPTION. . . . . . . . . .          SUPPLY. . . . . . . . . . . . . . .

INDST PRIV SEC     027.0               XAVIAN IMPORTS      010.0
INDST GOV S        003.0               ZEBRIAN IMPORTS     015.0
                   000.0               HOME RECYCLED       000.0
TOTAL              030.0               TOTAL               025.0
. . . . . . . . . . . . . . . . . . . . . . . . . . . . . . . . . . . . . . .
PREDICTED LEVEL OF UNEMPLOYMENT IN 1990  =    9 %
PREDICTED LEVEL OF POPULARITY IN 1990    =   41 POINTS
PREDICTED RESERVES OF FUELS IN 1990      =   36 YEARS
####################################################
```

Figure 3. *An example of computer prediction for Avia*

Aims of the simulation

The intentions of the simulation are to develop awareness of:

(a) some of the problems of industrial countries, and in particular the resource and employment difficulties which are currently predicted;

(b) some of the problems of third world countries and in particular the issues of industrialization and agricultural development in the context of rapidly expanding populations;

(c) the strong dependence of the industrial countries on other countries as sources of fuel, food and raw materials, and as markets for manufactured goods;

(d) the relatively weaker dependence of the third world countries on the industrial countries;

(e) the possibilities of self-reliance in national planning with an emphasis on stewardship rather than on economic progress.

The simulation also provides opportunities for participants to develop their political attitudes towards these issues. The political dimension is not the conventional 'left-right' one but the wealthist-convivialist dimension, as set out in Figure 2. Careful attempts have been made to ensure that the simulation materials do not force a particular perspective, but can support a variety of political attitudes. The Cocoyoc Declaration can be used to stimulate thinking on this wealthist-convivialist dimension. It was drawn up in October 1974 at Cocoyoc in Mexico and expresses three concerns:

(a) that development should be of man, not things;

(b) that for nations there are many different roads of development towards the goal of a satisfactory quality of life for all, which is achieved in ways compatible with the needs of future generations;

(c) that nations should strive for self-reliance, with trade providing mutual benefits and not involving exploitation of one nation by another.

The research programme through which this simulation has been developed is now turning to evaluating it and trying to determine the extent to which these aims can be achieved. At present only case study material is available.

Case study one

This is a report of a two-day run of the simulation in 'world' mode with 80 sixth-formers in a comprehensive school.

XAVIA

Xavia decided to spend one-and-a-half Mbuk/year on population control; to feed the increasing population, an agricultural policy was developed based on increasing crop yields and on developing virgin lands.

A policy of steady increase in urban industrialization was adopted and a 50-year agreement signed with SILICOM for the manufacture of microchips in Xavia. In order to provide the power needed for industrial growth a massive investment (four Mbuk/year) in biogas was decided on. Also one Mbuk/year was spent on new forest planting. From the start a policy of increased military expenditure was chosen.

Technical education was seen as the first priority and religious education was rejected. Originally, expenditure on education, health, and the radio network was to increase, but later these plans were scrapped.

Xavia planned originally to maintain the previous levels of trade with the hope of increasing raw material exports to Bevia. Requests for increases in the aid from Avia and Bevia were made.

After the period of negotiation, Xavia broke all links with Avia; there was no trade and no aid. However, exports of food and raw materials to Bevia were stepped up and overall this led to an increase in tax income from exports.

YAKIA

Similar plans to those of Xavia were made in terms of population and agricultural policy. Steady development of industry in the urban areas was planned for.

Top priority in education was to be technical education, with literacy second and political education third; religious education was ruled out. An increase in educational spending was agreed.

Yakia decided early on to increase its military expenditure.

Originally it was proposed to continue the 1985 level of exports of fuel to Avia and Bevia; since it was realized that these countries depend heavily upon Yakian fuel, considerable increases in aid were sought.

After the period of negotiation all fuel exports to Avia were stopped and instead the exports to Bevia were nearly doubled. In return Bevia upped its aid from three Mbuk/year to 11 Mbuk/year. This enabled Yakia to finance its various development schemes. All aid and trade from Avia ceased.

AVIA

Avia decided originally on a steady increase in production of consumer goods for both home and export. This reduced unemployment as did the raising of the school-leaving age to 18.

Originally no action was taken to restrict the development of the micro-chip, but later a tax raising five Mbuk/year was introduced.

Investment in nuclear power was part of the answer to the energy crisis and was coupled with measures to reduce energy consumption by better domestic insulation and by reduction in private transport (through a doubling of the petrol tax). Imports of fuel from Yakia were planned to remain at the 1985 level.

More food was planned to be home grown and so a reduction of imports of food from Zebria and Xavia was envisaged. An increase in the level of recycling of raw materials was planned and this was coupled with the intention to import less from Xavia, but not from Zebria. Overseas aid to Yakia (two Mbuk/year) and Zebria (three Mbuk/year) was to remain as before, but the allocation to Xavia (one Mbuk/year) was to be doubled.

For reasons that are not clear, during the period of negotiations Avia became isolated among the nations and diplomatic relations with Bevia, Xavia and Yakia were severed. All trading stopped. The government of Avia was faced with a desperate situation; how could they obtain sufficient supplies of food, fuel and raw materials. They tried to plan for total self-sufficiency, but the consequent reduction in the standard of living was unacceptable. They decided to increase expenditure on armaments and planned an attack on Bevia with biological weapons. A secret meeting with the Secretary-General of the UN made little impression on their militant mood. However, the tide turned and, again for reasons which remain obscure, a strong relationship developed with Zebria. The seat of government of Avia moved to Zebria and the formation of the United States of Azebria was proclaimed. This union ensured that Avia had the raw materials and food required to maintain her standard of living; for Zebria it supplied the requisite industrial goods. The energy requirements of the union would come from Avia's own fossil fuel mines and her investment in nuclear energy.

BEVIA

Bevia decided to increase slightly its production of consumer goods for both home use and for export. This reduced unemployment.

Energy policy entailed heavy taxation on petrol (three-fold increase) thus reducing consumption, and also a request to Yakia nearly to double supplies. Thus home fuels were conserved and it was expected that these would now last for at least 200 years.

Home food production was to be increased and imports reduced. Defence expenditure remained as before.

After the period of negotiation all trade with Zebria ceased and imports of food and raw materials from Xavia were increased. Aid to Zebria was stopped and the amount of aid sent to Xavia increased from three Mbuk/year to 12 Mbuk/year and to Yakia from two Mbuk/year to 11 Mbuk/year.

In order to pay for these increases expenditure on education was cut (although the school-leaving age was raised to 18) and the housing budget was slashed from 10 Mbuk/year to four Mbuk/year. A tax on microprocessors was also introduced.

A plan for a four-day working week was implemented and this resulted in a very low level of unemployment.

ZEBRIA

Zebria adopted the same policy on population control as its two neighbours and spent one-and-a-half Mbuk/year. In order to provide sufficient food for the increasing population it decided to improve farming methods and develop virgin lands.

A policy of steady industrial development in the urban areas was chosen and the necessary energy was to be supplied by investment in biogas plants.

Initially educational spending was to remain at the 1985 level and priorities were determined as: first: technical, second: literacy, third: political, fourth: religious. Slight increases in expenditure on health, housing and communications were proposed. These depended upon increased levels of aid.

When the *World Bank Report* was received it became clear that both Avia and Bevia planned to take less food from Zebria than hitherto. This would lead to economic difficulties for Zebria.

At the end of the period of negotiations *The Times of the World* carried banner headlines about Zebrian plans to invade Xavia and Yakia. At once these two countries cut all diplomatic links. Zebria protested that these plans were not

43

theirs but had been drawn up by a previous government; they assured Xavia and Yakia that they had no intention of attacking them.

The details have not been revealed, but at this stage a secret meeting between the prime ministers of Zebria and Avia led to the decision to form a union. This safeguarded the economy of Avia, who in return gave massive aid to Zebria, which was spent on education, health, roads, and armaments.

Case study two

This is a transcript of five minutes of decision-making. It arises from a Xavian cabinet engaged in a two-hour run through the papers, as a preliminary to interacting with the other countries.

So far the cabinet has decided to spend two Mbuk/year on population limitation and has chosen an agricultural policy entailing more intensive farming methods (two Mbuk/year) and some development of virgin territories (two Mbuk/year). They have also decided upon a limited development of urban industry (referred to as Scenario 1). The prime minister now moves the discussion on to energy:

☐ Right, Energy Policy.
☐ It depends largely on how much we've got to spend and what we want to do with it. If we follow Scenario 1 we've got to increase oil imports anyway.
☐ To five.
☐ Does this reduce unemployment?
☐ What other fuel do we need?
☐ Seven units.
☐ That's the alternative to getting fuel from Yakia. What we're saying is if we can't get any fuel from Yakia we can spend some money on biogas plants. So, we ought to link that with the previous one and say if we find that fuel's not coming then we'll spend some money on biogas plants.
It'll reduce unemployment and we'll only be spending money on biogas plants instead of on oil. I think biogas plants is an either/or situation. If we get the oil we don't need them, if we don't get the oil, we do.
☐ So that's one that's got to wait.
☐ What about firewood?
☐ That's up to me, isn't it—to get oil from Yakia. It's my attitude as your Energy Minister.
☐ We'll send a combined delegation.
☐ What about fertilizers? They're going to use it all up aren't they?
☐ It needs to be going back into the soil. And again because of our previous decision to increase our agricultural policy, we can't keep draining the land of all its fertilizers.
☐ Mind you, it's going to be 15 years before anything happens.
☐ It's a long term thing, but if we don't do it, in 15 years' time we say 'Christ, we should have done that, we're in right trouble now'.
☐ Even if you go over to biogas, with people working on the land we've got to have some local fuel.
☐ We can't say 'Wait', until we've got a decision on how much oil we get.
☐ We've got to put an initial proposal forward, so we'll have to assume that we will get the five units we require from Yakia.

☐ This biogas policy looks good though really – to have some energy of your own.
☐ Do you want to say, 'All right, we'll try to get three from Yakia and produce two of our own from biogas?
☐ I think it's a good idea to start the biogas plants.
☐ Also, it reduces unemployment by one per cent so if we go in for the demilitarization that only leaves us with another one per cent to offset.
☐ That gives us a lot more money to spend.
☐ If we use money for biogas plants you're using up material that would otherwise go back into the land as fertilizers.
☐ So, we're after two units, are we?
☐ Biogas plants.
☐ Which make fertilizer.
☐ Does that mean we're going to spend the full amount of four million buk on biogas plants?
☐ No.
☐ You said two units – two units is four million buk.
☐ Possibly, but it saves us on oil, of course.
☐ We'll only need three from Yakia.
☐ This is the initial decision.
☐ But it's one unit or two units – that'll cost you two million or four million.
☐ The thing to do is to put down the most appropriate alternatives in terms of the advantages and then we've got to go back to the beginning. We've got to spend 25 million – now what are we going to have?
☐ Can we just decide on DX7? Provisionally.
☐ Put the maximum of four.

This gives an indication of the extent to which participants act out their respective roles.

Case study three

These are extracts from diaries kept during a Xavia 'one country' mode run with 16 senior managers from industry and commerce. The extracts show how participants at this level enter into the spirit of the activity and are particularly concerned with each others' performance.

PRIME MINISTER

There is a problem in cabinet trying to keep people to the subject of the agenda. Some do not listen well to points being made. There is too much talk and attitude striking.

MINISTER FOR ENERGY

A better understanding of ministerial briefs would enable a more efficient use of time. We need a stronger lead from the PM. Political aspects and realities of government are being underrated. This is especially true of the government's standing in the country and the fight against subversive elements in society.

UNDER-SECRETARY FOR INTERNAL AFFAIRS

I received a phone call this morning from the Head of Security who is seriously concerned that rumours in the country areas might spread to the urban areas. The rumours are telling of increased taxation, birth control, resettlement of peasants, and exploitation of the urban workforce. There are also hints of certain ministers with commercial interests.

(On the basis of the above he proposed a motion of 'no confidence' in the PM. It was not carried, nobody else voting for it.)

MINISTER FOR INTERNAL AFFAIRS

I feel that the prime minister is far too democratic. His personality (a nice person who wants to help others) is coming through. As a result he is more concerned with making sure everyone has a fair hearing rather than getting on with decision-making.

UNDER-SECRETARY FOR INTERNAL AFFAIRS

I feel that the cabinet is totally mesmerized by the PM.

MINISTER FOR OVERSEAS TRADE

I feel that the cabinet is interacting effectively but the financial implications of decisions are not being recognized.

UNDER-SECRETARY FOR OVERSEAS TRADE

I am somewhat concerned at a lack of real accord within the cabinet. The unity which we enjoyed in achieving power seems to be fragmenting.

MINISTER FOR OVERSEAS TRADE

My Under-Secretary is not competent at calculating the trade statistics and so the strategic fight to maintain the balance between exports and imports is totally at risk.

UNDER-SECRETARY FOR FINANCE

I have resigned my cabinet post because of an increasing sense of isolation on the fundamental issues needed to guide the country over the next 25 years. A lack of policy and objectives has led, it seems to me, to confusion between the long and short terms; between what is critical and non-critical.

Biographical note

Dr Michael Bassey is Reader in Education at Trent Polytechnic. He has devised a number of simulations concerned with social responsibility and environmental conservation, including EUROPEAN ENVIRONMENT 1975-2000 (1972) and CORPORATE HEMLOCK (1974). The COCOYOC SIMULATION is his most ambitious venture and has been under development for nearly six years, going through six versions and many trials. It has received grant support from the Anglo-German Foundation for the Study of the Industrial Society.

Michael Bassey
Centre for Educational Research
Trent Polytechnic
Clifton Hall
Nottingham NG11 8NJ
England

5. Uses of simulation in education management and the law

Ian Waitt

Abstract: This paper discusses the teaching of elements of law to education managers. It attempts to demonstrate that simulation is a highly appropriate technique in this endeavour in that the interplay of legal or quasi-legal requirements and human behaviour as illustrated in role-play requires such a vehicle for their appreciation. The paper discusses the necessity for managers to have some grasp of legal requirements and illustrates this through one simulation which was devised as a specific problem-solving exercise, and another designed to have a wider scope.

Introduction

This paper describes two uses of simulation in the author's work in the Education Management Division of the Anglian Regional Management Centre (ARMC). The first is concerned with a specific, problem-solving programme for a local education authority. Because of the confidential nature of this exercise, not all of the detail of the simulation can be given, for such disclosures might lead to identification of the authority. The second simulation is one devised for use in the Diploma in Management Studies (Education) (DMS (Ed)) course at ARMC on which the author is responsible for teaching the topic of education and the law.

The two simulations serve different purposes, one being concerned with problem resolution, and the other having more diverse and general aims. However, both show common characteristics in their attempt to teach elements of law to education managers. It is self-evident that law should form some part of an education manager's training. This need has become more acute since the onset of contraction in education. Put simply, when a system is squeezed, those who suffer and believe that they are suffering will look for redress—quite possibly through the law. Recent examples of this abound: the two students who, at the time of writing, are each suing a university for breach of contract because, in response to expenditure restraint, the university did not honour its offer of a place on a certain course; the decision of the High Court in the case

47

against Hereford and Worcester LEA in the matter of charging for music tuition; and the successful copyright action brought against Oakham School.

As well as the legal remedies which may be sought by sections of society against the providers of education, there are also the problems for education managers of the divisions of legal responsibility within the education service. These are two-fold. In times of contraction, the inherent tensions between education law and employment law become explicit. To give an example, in public sector further and higher education, education law under the Education (No 2) Act 1968 (associated regulations and DES advice) grants a degree of autonomy to institutions but that autonomy can conflict with the local education authority's policies, and indeed its duties under the Local Government Acts, and Employment Protection Acts. Thus, a governor's decision can be overruled by an LEA, and governors' decisions can place the authority in the position of having to authorize that which it would rather not. Staff redundancy, for instance, could result *de facto* from relatively independent decisions of governors or the authority, leaving the staff unions without a clear body with whom to negotiate. Yet employment law demands the right to consult with the actual employer in such circumstances. While the unions can have the right to redress in the courts, the education manager, caught in the crossfire, is attempting to hold a position which may be almost untenable. This difficulty is compounded within some authorities where a result of corporate management has been effectively to separate the legal and personnel departments from the education department, with the result that inappropriate employment regulations may be applied. Both of these circumstances point to a further severe problem.

The law has evolved over a very considerable period of time. Whether in common law, or under statute, it seeks to achieve the impossible in that it exists to bring order into human affairs. Its principles have undergone lengthy development. However, the application of those principles to the education service are not necessarily those which educators imbued with their own professional ethics might expect; and certain educational practices may come as something of a surprise to the legal mind. At a simple level, teachers and educational administrators, accustomed both to control and to the behaviour patterns of their professions, can find that the due process of law as expressed in court comes as a severe shock. In attending many industrial tribunals during the late 1970s, the author noted how many educationalist witnesses, in what are fairly friendly and informal proceedings, were shaken, and often performed very badly. For those entertained by the macabre and by the distress of their seniors, the spectacle of a professional cross-examination of a senior educationalist ultimately unsure of his or her ground is certainly one to relish. However, the whole point of *schadenfreude* is that it happens to others. Authorities and individuals are better advised to avoid it.

In sum, then, the education manager has to understand legal principles, to be aware of possible legal problems even though she or he would need to seek specialist advice elsewhere, to implement legal requirements, and to avoid wasteful recourse to the courts. The latter issue is of prime importance, especially since in the education system it is often possible for an issue to reach the courts which should have been dealt with satisfactorily at institutional level. However, one is not training education managers to be lawyers. Rather, the training is concerned with appropriate managerial behaviour and the possession of a legal awareness. It is in this context that simulation becomes of prime importance. While the prior mastery of documentary evidence, and even brief summaries of legal provision, is necessary, the technique of simulation is particularly appropriate to learning for it involves human interaction. As the two following examples illustrate, however, the process can be pedagogically dangerous for the exercises are designed to provide natural development — and the trainer must therefore be equipped ultimately to deal with a multiplicity of consequences.

The Case of Stephen Jonas Olley

The essential problem for which the LEA (which shall remain nameless) had sought ARMC's assistance was its sorry record in cases at tribunal concerning its employees. The authority was consistently losing cases which it felt it should be winning, and did not understand why. Thus a simulation was devised using all the authority's relevant administrative procedures: instruments and articles of school government, standard contracts of teaching employment, conditions of service agreements and disciplinary and other procedural documents. All that was required was the devising of a fictional case, and everything which stemmed from it could then be taken through the authority's procedures — and perhaps to tribunal. The stated objects for the simulation were:

(a) to demonstrate how employee relations difficulties could result in recourse to law;
(b) to assist participants in the gaining of an understanding of legal processes;
(c) to explore through participation the ways in which employment problems might be encountered.

The group with whom the exercise was to be carried out was large, for it was composed of all the authority's senior educational administration staff and its senior advisory staff. The ARMC team was supplemented by a senior NATFHE official, who was to act in an adjudicatory capacity; and the authority's team was joined by representatives of its personnel department. The group was given the following brief:

ORGANIZATION OF THE EXERCISE

The group will divide into four teams. Each team is to be comprised thus:

☐ an applicant;
☐ a witness;
☐ a headteacher;
☐ a chairman of the governing body;
☐ two governors who are LEA members;
☐ two representatives of the LEA (chief adviser/assistant education officer);
☐ a chief education officer;
☐ two representatives of a teacher's association (lay officer, who happens to work at the school; full-time official).

Each team has to study the case; this is to be done individually in the first instance. Individuals may then consult with whom they wish, negotiate with other parties, and consider or decide upon their actions. The meeting of the governing body will then take place.

Actions are to be written down. This written evidence may be submitted to a tribunal, or may be required by a tribunal. The tribunal, should it meet, will require that a bundle of papers, agreed if possible, be presented to it. The bundle should consist of paginated documents.

Copies are available of: conditions of service agreements; individual grievance procedure; the instrument and articles of government; disciplinary rules applicable to the teacher in employment; disciplinary procedure applied to the teacher; and such procedural documents concerning the confirmation or rescinding of a dismissal effected by the school's governing body, and including the constitution of that confirming or rescinding body.

Teams and individuals will be able to request advice from those responsible for the exercise, but this advice will of necessity be restricted.

It is important that each team (or if it is their prerogative one of its sub-groups) submits its timetable of events. Each team or sub-group must also specify who attended any relevant meeting, and also who was entitled to attend. The following format may be used, for example:

> Extract from the minutes of the meeting of the Governing Body held on 24 September 1979: 'Apologies for absence were received from ... It was resolved that Mr Olley's contract be terminated...'

Should the case come before a tribunal, the tribunal may wish to know who submitted evidence to the governors, and which governor, if any, had an interest in the case.

Certain actions, such as the timing of certain events, may have to be 'agreed' by the team, but it is expected that each stage of events, within the brief laid down in the case below, will be determined either by negotiation or the actions of any of the participants. Names and designations not contained in the documents below are to be invented by the teams.

THE CASE

Stephen Jonas Olley was appointed to the Sandwick School with effect from 1 September 1975 to teach the subjects of French and German. He is a teacher of experience, and has achieved some eminence abroad by his publication concerning the composer Berwald. He is well qualified academically. In 1977, a new head of the languages department, Ms Kelly, was appointed to the school. Unlike her predecessor, who taught Spanish and French, Ms Kelly teaches French and German. Spanish was dropped from the timetable; there had been little demand for the subject. Until the end of the academic year 1978/79, Ms Kelly and Mr Olley shared the teaching of French and German, there also being another member of staff, Mr Rose, who taught languages part-time. Mr Rose left the school at the end of the academic year 1978/79. Ms Philips, a probationary teacher, was appointed to the school to teach English and languages, commencing on 1 September 1979. Mr Macleod, who taught music, retired at the end of the academic year 1978/79.

For a variety of reasons, the school roll had fallen from 1,200 in 1977/78 to 900 in 1979/80. The languages work of the school declined in a greater proportion. It was possible for all such work to be undertaken by Ms Kelly and Ms Philips. There was a vacancy in the teaching of music. Although technical and concert work was mainly undertaken by a peripatetic teacher, a substantial proportion of the teaching of music was offered to Mr Olley. The timetable he was offered in July 1979 for the year 1979/80 consisted of 18 periods of music, four periods of games, and the residue of languages work (examination classes). Mr Olley refused to teach this timetable. He held discussions which were acrimonious with the headteacher, Mr Wilshaw, and with representatives of the local authority. He also discussed the case with his professional association. Mr Olley stated to Mr Wilshaw: 'I love music too much ever to wish to teach it in any establishment of which you are the head.'

In February 1976 Mr Olley began a private music school. He is known to have encouraged certain pupils of the Sandwick School to attend. Mr Olley charges a fee for private tuition.

In May 1977 it came to Mr Wilshaw's attention that Mr Olley was using school and LEA musical equipment at his private classes. Mr Wilshaw informed Mr Olley that while the children were free to practice on instruments which they had on loan from the LEA where and how they wished, he required Mr Olley to return to the school the tape recorders which he had taken without permission; and also in the same way never to use the school harpsichord. This instrument, bequeathed to the school, is extremely delicate, requiring some hours of tuning after being moved. Mr Olley promised not to use such equipment at his private classes, although he pointed out that it had never been damaged, and that he tuned the harpsichord himself, and in his own time. Although he had made a note of the incident on Mr Olley's file, Mr Wilshaw did not report the matter formally to the LEA; the subject was discussed informally with an LEA adviser.

On 17 July 1979 it was discovered that Mr Olley had hired out school musical equipment. He had on three occasions made loudspeakers available to 'The Sniff', a group of ex-pupils of the school specializing in punk music. He had also hired out a set of drums to another musical ensemble. Mr Olley had access to the equipment since it was stored in a cellar beneath the school hall to which, because of his drama and concert work, he had a key. When challenged about the removal and hiring of the equipment, Mr Olley stated that he had intended to make recompense, but had forgotten to do so. He had not requested permission since the requests for equipment had been urgent, and he did not wish 'bureaucratic delay' to be the cause of the groups' not being able to perform. On 23 July 1979 it came to light that Mr Olley had hired out a set of Grecian costumes to a local dramatic society for their production of 'Lysistrata'. Again, payment had not been made to the school or LEA, and nor had permission been requested. Mr Olley, who admits that he does not adopt any clear accounting procedures in his financial affairs, had neglected to pass the payments to the school.

Acting on the advice of the LEA, Mr Wilshaw and the chairman of the governing body decided not to inform the police. On 25 July Mr Wilshaw suspended Mr Olley. Mr Wilshaw and the chairman of governors met to discuss the case on 26 July 1979. A meeting of the governing body was called to discuss Mr Olley's case on 14 August 1979. It was decided that . . .

No role details were given, but a biography of the leading character was provided (see Figure 1 p 52).

The four parallel exercises were then set in train. Each group behaved differently. Midway through the first part of the exercise the situations were:

Stephen Jonas Olley: Curriculum Vitae

Address:	22 Hastings Street . . .
Born:	Harrington, Cumberland, 12 November 1929
Education:	King George V Grammar School, Workington; University of Sheffield; BA (Hons) French and German, Class 1, 1965; PGCE, 1966.
Employment:	Royal Navy, 1944-1962; rank of lieutenant on leaving the service.

Assistant teacher (languages) Scale 1 and subsequently 2, the Grange School, Sheffield (a secondary school, comprehensive in 1967), 1966-69.

Assistant teacher (French and German) Scale 3 equivalent, Haslam School, Bradford (a direct grant preparatory and secondary school), 1969-72.

Teacher of languages, and subsequently assistant to the director, Ganoyanni Language School, Gondi, Athens, 1973-75.

Assistant teacher, French and German, Scale 2, Sandwick School, 1975-.

Activities:	Responsibility for a rugby and cricket team, The Grange School; responsible for a soccer and a cricket team, Haslam School; producer of several school plays and musical entertainments.
Publication:	*'In den Rachen': Leben und werk von Franz Berwald,* Neef, Mannheim, 1974. This is a work of scholarship, written in German, and represents a major biography of the nineteenth-century composer Berwald. Research was carried out in Sweden and Germany in 1972-73.
Interests:	Music, sport, travel. Expertise in the playing of keyboard and string instruments; knowledge of wind and percussion.

Figure 1. Curriculum vitae *for central role*

☐ Group one was disposed to make a deal, settling everything before the governors' meeting;

☐ Group two had endeavoured to make a deal, but without success, and confrontation was imminent, there being a significant movement towards dismissals;

☐ Group three were proceeding very slowly and displaying signs of considerable uncertainty;

☐ Group four governors were preparing to reprimand Mr Olley severely, their final decision being deferred until he had been fully heard.

Within the groups, it was noticeable that many governors and LEA officers were being both cautious and charitable—even over-generous. This reaction was understandable, but a hard interpretation would be that the employers were merely storing up trouble for themselves. On the other hand, the head's previous leniency did not allow the governors much room to manoeuvre. The union officials did not perform at all well: clearly, the role players had not grasped either the tactics or mental attitudes adopted by experienced union negotiators. This lack of appreciation was perhaps indicative of some of the reasons for the authority's poor industrial relations record. The various Mr Olleys all involved themselves in their role, and were plausible examples of altruistic financial incompetents.

At this stage, the ARMC team made an intervention. A telegram from Greece arrived for Mr Olley, offering him a teaching post in that country. One of the Mr Olleys left the governors' meeting in which he was being at least reprimanded, and after conferring with his union official, complained to the tribunal of constructive dismissal.

Thus far the exercise had revealed a positive wish to avoid action by many, and a wish for confrontation by some. The options open to the governors had ranged from the overruling of the head and chairman of governors by calling in the police, to reprimand, transfer, an action for breach of contract, and dismissal. Mr Olley's options were less open: to avoid reprimand or dismissal; to have a re-affirmation of support sufficient to ensure no further encroachment on his language teaching; to institute separate grievance proceedings; or to engineer a dismissal—or claim constructive dismissal—so that he might profit. The Greek telegram strengthened the latter option.

THE TRIBUNAL

When the tribunal members entered, the group were required to stand. This small piece of verisimilitude assisted greatly in creating a court atmosphere. After an hour of the proceedings, one of the group—a senior member—became restive, and whispered to a neighbour. Fixing him with a basilisk stare, the chairman remarked: 'You are interfering with the course of justice. Were you a younger man, I should have you imprisoned for contempt.' This remark, and the fascination engendered by examination and cross-examination, sufficed to command complete attention to the proceedings.

The case before the tribunal was that of constructive dismissal. The burden of proof lay on Mr Olley to show that his employers and their agent had acted so unreasonably that their behaviour was tantamount to the repudiation of his contract. He contended that the erosion of his languages teaching was unreasonable, and that the offer of music teaching was no recompense: as the school roll fell, he would lose his job, and he was being manoeuvred into this position. This was compounded by unfair allegations of peculation: the failure to process monies was due to carelessness, and in any event what he had done was a service to the community. The authority contended that Mr Olley was contracted as a teacher, and could be expected to teach subjects in which he was competent. He did not have the right to insist on language teaching only. As Mr Olley had resigned claiming constructive dismissal before the financial issues had been resolved, he could not claim that he had been subjected to harassment. It was revealed in cross-examination that Mr Olley had been offered, and accepted, a teaching post in Greece, and that his resignation and tribunal application coincided with this acceptance. Mr Olley claimed that, knowing that he was being constructively dismissed, he needed quickly to find alternative employment. The authority's witnesses stuck to procedural arguments which the chairman described in one interjection as being 'inadequate'.

The chairman in his summing up gave a rehearsal of the points of law at issue. He indicated that there were conflicting precedents concerning how far a teacher could be required to depart in his or her work from the specialist subjects he or she was appointed to teach, but that it was clear that there could be considerable flexibility. The financial and unauthorized uses of LEA property allegations against Mr Olley could have amounted to breach of contract, but since the authority had declined to press charges, Mr Olley had only to bear the burden of his own revealed carelessness: the authority, by its own actions, could have no complaint. However, both in the manner of the erosion of Mr Olley's languages teaching and in the inappropriateness of both its written procedures (specifically, instruments and articles, and suspension/dismissal) and their implementation, he felt that the authority deserved castigation.

He did not find the case proven. To be proven, a complaint of constructive dismissal must go to the root of the contract. The chairman felt that progression towards that root was clear, but that it had not been achieved. It was unfortunate that Mr Olley had 'jumped the gun', and in this regard he had to take note of the teaching appointment in Greece. He wished Mr Olley well in Greece. On the one hand he regretted Mr Olley's impatience, which had probably prevented him from winning a just cause; but on the other, if Mr Olley had merely been seeking to use the law for his own ends to achieve a profit, then he was getting no more than his proper reward: nothing. The authority, he stressed, had nothing to be proud of.

The tribunal being concluded, Mr Olley read a letter to the group. This letter made it clear that Mr Olley, for part of the period 1972-73, had been in prison, having been convicted of a sexual offence with a minor. One reason for his return to Greece was the renewal of a homosexual relationship. The authority's application form for a teaching post made no mention of the requirements of the Rehabilitation of Offenders Act 1974. The provisions of this Act would have required a statement from Mr Olley which, if truthfully submitted, would have prevented his appointment and, if untrue, would have justified subsequent dismissal.

THE RESULTS

In its formal written evaluation of the simulation, the authority stated that it 'was considered very valuable, with significant lessons learned by participants'. The trade union official who had played the role of chairman 'was regarded as extremely successful and effective'. Informally, the participants stated that his performance had convinced them even more of the value of negotiation rather than confrontation with his union, and that such a display of expertise demonstrated how careful the authority would have to be in instituting any proceedings. One subsequent direct result was that the authority changed its disciplinary procedures. The personnel department representatives present (whose participation was important to the success of the exercise) were sufficiently impressed by what they had witnessed to recognize the need for greater cognizance of the nature of the education service within the authority's procedures. All the participants had been impressed by the formality of the legal process when it was brought to bear on the record of internal quasi-judicial proceedings, and how improper or carelessly derived motives could be harshly exposed. They perhaps knew but little more of the law itself, but they had been made sharply aware of the possible consequences of unreasonable behaviour, whether in commission or omission.

It will be noted that the progress of the exercise was not predictable. This does require the trainer to have a very wide knowledge of the possibilities, and the relevant legal machinery, principles, cases and statute for each. Pedagogically as stimulating as it is dangerous, this open-endedness is illustrated further by the second simulation to be considered. Here, the purposes are different in that DMS(Ed) students are being asked to master a brief legal digest, and then to use their various skills in acting out a situation. The results of such actions may bring about a hearing in a simulated governors' or LEA committee meeting, or in court, or be resolved formally or informally within the educational institution.

In the following simulation concerning the Grimethorpe Institute of Higher Education roles and events are fully documented. The purpose here is partially stimulation – to capture the students' interest – and partially to determine via set roles the parameters of the consequential individual and collective behaviour.

Incidents at the Grimethorpe Institute of Higher Education

> 'Convey a libel in a frown, And wink a reputation down'
> *Jonathan Swift*

The Grimethorpe Institute is a former college of education which survived the 1970s by diversifying its courses. It now operates DipHE, BEd, BA(Combined Studies) and BA(Humanities) courses as well as a variety of short courses. There are about 800 full-time students and 110 staff. Part-time student numbers have fluctuated. Recruitment is variable: only five students are currently following rural studies courses; recruitment for arts and social science courses is steady and adequate. There are those who maintain that the Institute is over-staffed; the Academic Board is showing a reluctance to sanction the discontinuation of the rural studies courses because it anticipates that the staff will then be made redundant. There is a strong staff lobby seeking to establish masters' degrees and further award-bearing courses. While the impact of FECL 1/80 has not been felt directly, there is great discontent among staff concerning the way in which course development has been handled. This has been made more acute because many staff feel that course development failures (in particular the production of allegedly incomprehensible documents and a critical response from a CNAA visit) represent threats to their livelihood. Hostility has centred around Ms Mary Strickland, one of two vice-principals of the Institute, and the former principal of the Grimeville College of Education. When this college was closed in 1977, she obtained redeployment at the Institute.

Ms Strickland in turn feels somewhat beleaguered. Her relations with the principal, Dr Henry Block, are not good. She finds it difficult to communicate with him and views as a considerable threat his tendency to release information only when it suits him. She considers that the CNAA disaster (the masters' degrees having to be resubmitted) resulted from his not informing her fully of what the Council wanted: she had not been shown the whole CNAA correspondence, particularly that referring to the terms of the visit; she had produced documents for two new largely free-standing courses, but the Council wished to review existing courses, and particularly to examine links between existing and projected courses before giving attention to the masters' courses; it did not want free-standing masters' courses. Similarly, Ms Strickland feels that the male heads of the humanities and combined studies departments do not give her full support and are, in fact, obstructive. There has been a history of quibbling over the style of documents, for example.

In November 1980, Dr James Bluthal, head of humanities, wrote to Ms Strickland concerning resources. Ms Strickland's reply (Document A) angered him to such an extent that he responded in intemperate terms (Document B), and also circulated copies of the correspondence to the senior and principal lecturers in his department. On 11 November 1980 a letter appeared in the *Grimethorpe Evening Gazette* (Document C) which excited local comment and caused the principal to investigate its authorship. When questioned, Mr Arthur Vicary, senior lecturer in the humanities department, freely admitted authorship and added: 'OK, you're bound to be annoyed—but how else do we get any progress in this place? And I'm being straight in telling you. The public doesn't know who wrote the thing.' The principal, who interviewed Mr Vicary in the latter's office, asked him if he recalled the instructions concerning press relations (Document D), to which Mr Vicary responded: 'Yes—but I was writing anonymously, wasn't I?' The principal then thanked Mr Vicary for his candour but warned him that he was now going to consider the matter further.

The principal left Vicary's office. Vicary followed him, and then entered the room of his colleague, Mrs Tomkins, leaving the door open. The principal heard —and believed he was intended to overhear—Vicary's remark to Mrs Tomkins: 'Hey! There's just been a reversal of the natural order of things: would you believe that worms now go hunting moles? That man is to the office of principal what Nicholas II was to the throne of Russia. I think that man is despicable, don't you?' Mrs Tomkins replied: 'Come off it, Arthur, you're exaggerating again.'

On the following day the incident was being discussed among staff in the senior common room. Conversation ceased when Mary Strickland entered the room. She asked if her presence was inhibiting her colleagues. Mrs Tomkins replied: 'We were discussing Arthur and the principal. Join in if you want.' Ms Strickland replied: 'I can make no comment on the matter, but you scarcely need me to give any information on Arthur.'

Mrs Tomkins asked what Ms Strickland meant by her reference to Arthur

Vicary. Ms Strickland replied: 'Merely that you clearly enjoy a close relationship. And that Arthur is not noted for his continence in most matters. At one stage it seemed as if he was becoming a professional co-respondent.'

The next day Arthur Vicary gave a pre-arranged interview—which had been cleared with the principal—on Radio Grimethorpe. The subject was the administration and management of education. During this interview Mr Vicary said:

> Of course, the big problem is that education managers get very little training. Usually they are successful teachers or academics who get promoted to managerial positions —and then sometimes spend the rest of their working lives making a mess of their institutions. Not a million miles away from Grimethorpe, for example, an able teacher and academic in a managerial capacity is busily destroying an institution by demonstrable incapacity to manage course development . . .

DOCUMENT A

Extract from a memorandum marked 'Confidential' to J Bluthal from M Strickland, 6 November 1980.

> . . . and, therefore, while appreciating your request for a further member of staff and more secretarial support, in the light of current resource constraints, I am unable to give my support. You may, of course, pursue the matter further but since I am responsible for course and staff development, and, moreover, advise the institutional committee to which such requests must be sent, you will appreciate that your time will better be spent in actively persuading your department to meet course development deadlines and, in short, to benefit us all by acting within the constraints which afflict us.
>
> As to the promotions to which you refer, you may pursue them as I have intimated above. However, I cannot see that Mr Vicary or Mrs Tomkins will ever rise above the SL level unless the former gets out of the broom cupboard and does some work rather than indulging in his endless disruptive political practices, and the latter a) teaches someone something, and b) actually attends the Institute in a capacity other than producer of dramatic entertainments . . .

DOCUMENT B

Extract from a memorandum to M Strickland from J Bluthal, 7 November 1980.

> . . . not only can I not accept the sentiments, tone, aspersions, and constitutionality of your memo of 6 March, but I can only imagine that it stems from pique, malice, and a wish to blame others for the failure of policies for which you are responsible. I wish, therefore, to make the following rebuttals:
>
> 1. It is accepted that your responsibilities as vice-principal make you an appropriate person to advise the Staffing and Policy Sub-committee, but I have searched the Instrument and Articles in vain to ascertain that you have the right to act as its dictator. You are clearly acting *ultra vires,* and I shall make representations to the sub-committee accordingly.
>
> 2. My Department has always endeavoured to meet developmental deadlines. Your statement is an unwarrantable slur upon the professionalism of my colleagues, and I demand a retraction. Any delays and failures to meet deadlines are largely resultant from the lack of clarity and direction stemming from yourself as course development co-ordinator.
>
> 3. Your statements concerning Mr Vicary and Mrs Tomkins are most unfair. That, as

NATFHE Branch Treasurer, Mr Vicary has a great deal of union business to attend to is in the nature of that office and also, I might add, is a situation doubtless exacerbated by managerial incompetence. Certainly his teaching timetable has been light of late, but this is due to the lack of current work for him to do. He is a researcher, and a teacher of research methods. He will be extremely busy as soon as we get the masters' degree, and that is why I want him promoted. Thus his current comparative teaching inactivity is rather more your fault than his.

As you are well aware (see, for example, my memo of 23.9.80) I have arranged a light timetable for Mrs Tomkins in the current academic year out of consideration for her state of health following her maternity. The Institute ought to be grateful to her for continuing her interest in the Drama Society, and the benefits which her productions bring to the Institute. Such productions also stimulate local interest and are, I believe, excellent recruiting pitches for her short courses. Her short course work was disrupted by her maternity leave; she has made great efforts to stimulate recruitment since her return, and the fact that the financial climate is against her is scarcely her fault. I believe that we should continue to offer her courses, and my reasons for wishing her to be promoted are to reward her for her endeavours and to encourage her in the future, and also to demonstrate the importance which the Institute places upon this particular service which it offers to its local community.

In short, your charges are unfounded and your behaviour disgraceful. It is small wonder that there is friction and disruption in this establishment when it is pervaded by the kind of moral leprosy which can be directed against staff as unfairly as it is without justification. You will learn in due course of the steps which I propose to take. In the meantime, I suggest that as a matter of managerial policy, gratuitous malevolence be excised from the conduct of affairs.

DOCUMENT C

Letter appearing in the *Grimethorpe Evening Gazette.*

Sir,
We have been told by the Chairman of the Education Committee that the Grimethorpe Institute is a 'centre of excellence'. We support this 'centre of excellence' from our rates. If the Institute is so excellent why is it that the Council for National Academic Awards has not allowed it to begin masters' degrees, and why is it that the manager apparently responsible continues to draw a salary of over £15,000 without the Education Committee even murmuring? There are a lot of people in Grimethorpe subsidising through their rates a management which makes even BL look good.
Yours despairingly,

Disgusted Ratepayer (name and address supplied)

DOCUMENT D

Extract from *Staff Memo*, February 1979.

. . . While I recognise the necessity for academic freedom in debate, and the enhancement of life in education brought about by the free exchange of views, in the current climate of uncertainty regarding the future of higher education institutions, I feel that the Grimethorpe Institute can only be harmed by the various leaks and squibs which have recently found their way into the columns of the local press. It is, therefore, with regret that I must insist that from now on all press releases must first be submitted to me, and that there be no unauthorized dealings with the press. It remains desirable that we obtain favourable publicity for the Institute. I will, therefore, sanction on application requests to speak to the press but I must insist that any matter likely to cause controversy must be discussed only with my express permission. No doubt those colleagues responsible for the recent leaks were either duped or acted in the light of motives which were well intentioned, but misplaced. However, that practice must cease forthwith.

H Block
Principal

.

DEFAMATION: A BRIEF DIGEST

Defamation is spoken or written publication of matter which may entail an individual suffering hatred, contempt, ridicule or being shunned by reasonable people.

Slander, because it is spoken and therefore transient, is a civil matter. The person defamed must prove special damages – actual financial loss capable of valuation. The exceptions are: implication that a woman is unchaste; assertion that a person is culpable of an imprisonable offence; statement that a person suffers from a disease infectious or contagious and thus unfitting for his or her presence in decent society; disparagement of a person in his or her employment, even though the words do not refer directly to conduct in that capacity.

Libel – written defamation – is a civil or, very occasionally, a criminal offence. An offer of amends may be made where the defamation is innocent and accidental. As with slander, an apology may suffice.

Defamation is actionable as soon as the offensive matter has been published (ie, is shown/spoken to some person other than the complainant).

Defences: that the matter is true in its entirety; that it is fair comment on a matter of public interest; privilege.

Absolute privilege applies only to parliamentary speeches and reports, statements made in courts and other tribunals recognized at law, fair and accurate newspaper reports of judicial proceedings, communications between officers of state during duty.

Qualified privilege applies to reports, written or verbal, in the execution of a public or private duty, provided that they are made without malice (ie, absence of right motive).

To claim privilege, the defendant must believe the statement made was true at the time.

EXERCISE

The discerning reader will notice that this exercise owes something to a theatrical device employed by the Scarborough playwright, Alan Ayckbourn: the basic plot can be developed in several directions according to the whim or choice of the actors. This means that the outcome is not wholly predictable. This may be pedagogically dangerous. So is life, especially the managerial and litigious varieties thereof.

The only stipulations are these:

(a) Roles developed must be consistent with the characterization provided, and any previous/mitigating events invented should not be such as would destroy the basic plot.

(b) Something must happen, somewhere. The atmosphere of the Institute is clearly highly coloured (some might maintain overdrawn; others that it is no more than perfectly healthy institutional paranoia). It is unlikely that everyone involved will quietly settle down, pretend that nothing has happened and address themselves to mundane tasks such as teaching. This, of course, may be the reaction of the majority — or so Mr Vicary's publicly proclaimed theory of the intertia of majorities would have us believe.

(c) If the action develops in ways not covered in the course so far, it will be stopped or diverted, or else sufficient explanation will be given to allow it to continue. This decision will be taken by the deviser of the exercise, but appeals are allowable.

FORMAT OF THE EXERCISE

(a) Roles will be allocated or chosen, and persons and parties will then negotiate and develop the action.
(b) Course books/handouts are available for legal guidance.
(c) Stage 1 of the exercise will be operated in two parallel groups. The most interesting/relevant case or action to develop will be taken to Stage 2, and the other Stage 2 roles will then be allocated.

ROLES: STAGE 1

Dr Henry Block
Ms Mary Strickland
Mrs Judith Tomkins
Mr Arthur Vicary
Dr James Bluthal
Union advisers: AVPC (Association of Vice Principals of Colleges)
Union advisers: NATFHE (National Association of Teachers in Further and Higher Education)
LEA officers.

The last three groups of personnel are interchangeable according to client approach.

ROLE DETAILS

Henry Block, MSc, PhD, MBIM
b 1928; educ Liverpool and Cambridge; m, two children; mathematician; taught in advanced FE; taught in schools; LEA officer; HMI 1968-70; vice-principal college of education in North England 1970-74; principal Grimethorpe 1974-. Member of NATFHE. Interests: fell walking, baroque music. Publications: *A Better Way to Teach Mathematics*, 1967; *Quantitative Analysis and Educational Administration*, 1973. Block is a shy man, conscientious, academically able, has difficulty in delegating, prefers subordinates to carry out their functions independently and justifies his lack of guidance as allowing individuals freedom to express their abilities. Very conscious that he was appointed to save the Institute; worries a great deal; a very happy home life. Finds confrontations with staff highly upsetting, and seeks to avoid them. Critics accuse him of being kind to his enemies, and unkind to his friends.

Mary Strickland, MA, PGCE
b 1934; educ Oxford; single; studied English; taught in schools (three yrs); taught in colleges of education; vice principal Grimeville College of Education 1974-75; principal 1975-77; vice-principal Grimethorpe Institute (course development; staffing) 1977-. Member of AVPC. Interests: reading; opera; travel. Publication: *Jane Austen, the Peerage, and the Art of Regulated Hatred*. Ms Strickland is forthright, brusque even, confident of her ability but finds herself in a world which does not accommodate the style she developed in her college of education days. Her administrative approach is authoritarian, and all the more so when she feels threatened. She has few friends, and none in Grimethorpe; her milieu is more metropolitan; she makes a distinction between professional and personal relationships. Difficult to alter her opinions or to dissuade her from a decided course of action. Friends find her humour delightful; an able conversationalist; wealthy.

Judith Tomkins, BA, PGCE
b 1942; educ Leicester; m, one child; studied history and English; registered for PhD; research topic: Socialism and Oscar Wilde; taught in schools 1964-68; taught in adult education 1968-72; taught in college of education 1972-75; Grimethorpe Institute 1975-. Appointed to Grimethorpe to teach certificate history, rapidly redeployed in the 1976-77 diversification onto short course/in-service work, displaced on the award-bearing courses by persons redeployed from the Grimeville College. Member of NATFHE. Interests: drama; anti-blood sports. Conscientious and dedicated but frustrated by the assaults of fate on her career; feels she has to run very hard just to stand still; finds her greatest expression in her drama pursuits; usually level-headed but recognizes a career threat when she sees one; attracted to the rebel element in the Institution but not totally identified with it; tolerant but inclined to take a very determined stance on occasions; very popular with the students; dislikes pomposity; very much her own woman; recent health problems have put her under considerable strain.

Arthur Vicary, BSc(Econ), MA
b 1946; educ Bristol and London; single; sociologist; research assistant and subsequently polytechnic lecturer, London, 1969-77; Grimethorpe Institute 1977-. Publications: *Cargo Culture; The Dynamics of Disadvantage; Man, Myth and the Question of the Zip*. NATFHE branch treasurer. Interests: jazz, cinema, speedway. His last publication, a novel (1970), achieved a certain sub-cult following but did not give him an income sufficient to write full-time; he still hankers after an author's life but enjoys the political opportunities and personal relationships afforded by academic life. Irreverent; a wit; courts disapproval; often provocative—believes this stimulates action and revelation; uses ability as a protection; politically active (broad left); friends accuse him of using Grimethorpe as a field study; essentially a loner; abstemious; a class warrior; capable of the quixotic action; unpredictable; hard-working when he wishes; evokes strong responses; terrier-like when pursuing an objective; usually acts in a premeditated fashion. Co-respondent in divorce action 1978.

James Bluthal, MA, PhD
b 1934; educ London; m; historian; taught schools and subsequently colleges of

61

education; head of history, Grimethorpe Institute 1974-77, and head of humanities 1977-. Publications: *The Chamberlains; Yalta and After*. Interests: twentieth-century history, *papier mâché*. Bluthal was once attacked by Vicary at Academic Board thus: 'My honourable friend, the Member for Humanities Going West, is known to us all as a frank writer of incautious memos, but it would come as a welcome relief if he were occasionally to consider his opinions before he voices them.' Bluthal is short tempered, conscious of his dignity, fiercely defensive of his department; anxious to behave in an open manner with his departmental colleagues; a limited but effective institutional politician; liked in a somewhat protective manner by his students; stubborn but with a warmth in his personality which is attractive—even if those attracted ultimately regret their involvement. Self-consciously busy; responsibilities weigh heavily; ultimately impatient of the time-consuming nature of administration; at his most irascible by mid-term when he realizes that, yet again, he is falling behind in his research work. Suffers fools not at all but is uneasily conscious of his own ability sometimes to appear foolish. Tenacious, but has a tendency if thwarted of victory to seek martyrdom. Drinks heavily but appears able to control it; socially convivial.

ROLES: STAGE 2

Plaintiff(s) (or complainant(s)/applicant(s) before relevant procedural body)
Defendant(s)
Friend(s) (or counsel)
Person responsible for the conduct of the case(s)
Witness(es)
Members of judicial/quasi-judicial body
Observers

It will be appreciated that the scope of the exercise is wide. The presentation issue—that of defamation—is not proven in any of the simulation papers. In almost every instance, even though the lines are fine, something further would probably need to be provided to convince a court. The defences of truth, absence of malice, fair comment, and qualified privilege would all probably be upheld. Thus the simulation depends very much on the reaction of the participants, and the main characters have many possible routes to follow, most of which will cause reaction in the other participants.

Opportunities to institute grievance procedures are open to Strickland, Vicary, Tomkins and even Bluthal. Tomkins may wish to make out a case of constructive dismissal, to claim breach of the legal provisions relating to maternity and sex discrimination, or even to claim that she has been slandered by Strickland. While acting *ultra vires* may be hard to prove against Strickland, she may well have a claim that her tenure is being unfairly jeopardized.

In the most interesting operation of this simulation, Vicary, having stirred matters up, ran true to form in avoiding a final confrontation. Tomkins, despite strenuous efforts by her union official to provoke her to action (because the official felt it necessary to inflict a defeat upon the management) decided to lie low; but Strickland, failing to secure an apology from Bluthal and any support from Block, took out a formal grievance procedure against Bluthal. A hearing took place before the governors. The governors disallowed the claim, but expressed the hope that Bluthal and Strickland would reconcile their differences, reminding them both that as senior employees they should exercise more restraint. The governors also decided that Block should be informed informally that his managerial conduct would have to be improved. In subsequent evaluation, the group felt that the exercise had not been too highly coloured, that the circumstances were realistic and, interestingly, since most of them had played the part of governors, that while in that role they had little alternative to act as they had done, they remained dissatisfied at their own decisions. In short, the group had experienced how necessary it is to tackle problems at their level of occurrence, and how blunt, insensitive or inadequate remedies at higher levels might be. There was a strong feeling that Block should never have been appointed, and weary recognition that such appointments were not as rare as might be hoped. Equally, it was appreciated that the Academic Board in the college was not functioning as effectively as it might, and that the obvious over-staffing in a time of contraction would lead to even more severe problems.

In both simulations quoted, the root of the exercise was to demonstrate that while humanity is capable of infinite variety, a very close attention to procedural appropriateness is necessary at the base of the organizational pyramid; and that, once begun, legal processes do not necessarily lead to comfortable conclusions.

Biographical note

Dr Ian Waitt lectures in education management at the Anglian Regional Management Centre/North East London Polytechnic. He has been a research historian, school teacher, college of education lecturer and writer. He has contributed a variety of articles to the education press. His most recent book is *College Administration,* NATFHE, London, 1980, of which he was the editor and prime contributor, and which won a commendation in the Library Association's 1981 McColvin Awards for the reference books of the year. He is a co-ordinator of the Technical Education Research Centre, Government of the Republic of Korea/North East London Polytechnic curriculum development project; and has undertaken recent consultancy in India, Egypt and Singapore.

Ian Waitt
Anglian Regional Management Centre
Duncan House
High Street, Stratford
London E15 2JB
England

6. The SORTHAM OUT simulation – a school management case study

John V Taylor-Byrne

Abstract: This case study looks at the reasons underlying the preparation of the SORTHAM OUT simulation, the issues involved and how they are presented, the debriefing and evaluation. It is designed to provide insights for members of the teaching profession and educational administrators into the problems associated with decision-making in committee.

The simulation highlights the problem of identifying objective and subjective issues that feature in management discussions. The setting for the simulation exercise is a staff meeting where the matter for discussion is the possible termination of employment of two of the six temporary contracted part-time teacher colleagues in response to staffing cuts.

The debriefing discussion suggestions include role-play experience, hierarchical status role play experience, the identification of issues and the identification of lines of argument. Evaluation techniques are considered and the main evaluation results are reported.

The conclusion presented is that both educational and management simulation aims may be achieved through this simulation exercise.

Introduction

A simulation exercise in the area of management might be seen in the same light as simulation in other areas – that of gaining insights through non-direct experience. Within the area of education, there are certainly management simulation exercises, such as outlined in Powell (1981). These tend to be 'In-basket', 'Timetabling' and 'How to cope with difficult parents' simulations for headteachers and deputy headteachers. For those lower down the scale there tends to be little offered – apart from pupil management, which is after all one of the basic skills in the teacher's repertoire. What seems to be missing is a range of simulation exercises in educational management that give insights for the newly qualified or intending teacher as well as the experienced or higher status teacher/administrator.

I would argue that the inexperienced teacher, along with those of experience or in posts of responsibility, should be aware of and concerned with the process of educational administration. Members of a school staff should be knowledgeable about the functions and organization of schools, not simply the day-to-day decisions but issues of wider importance.

The functions of a school are those fundamental aims concerned with the direction and focus of the pupil's education. A secondary school in a rural area may consider the inclusion of rural studies in the curriculum offered as being important in reflecting the vocational openings in the locality. A town school may concentrate more on wood and metal crafts or secretarial studies to meet this need.

The organization of the school is very much related to, if not based upon, the agreed functions the school intends to implement. Aspects such as staffing, timetabling and finance allocation are examples of the organization that the staff must consider.

The process of attaining these organizational elements of the school is through decision-making in committee, though some headteachers make these decisions with little or no consultation. The SORTHAM OUT simulation has as its setting a staff meeting where an issue of school organization is being discussed. The participants are mainly senior members of staff and the issue under discussion is the termination of the contracts of part-time teaching staff.

Issues of influence

My years of teaching in schools, the latter years in posts involving management responsibility, alerted me to a number of issues that influence the way decisions are arrived at. The central theme of the simulation SORTHAM OUT is a consideration of how far professional lines of reasoning influence decision-making. All members of a committee or meeting bring to it their own personal knowledge and convictions. In some cases the knowledge can be out-of-date or simply inadequate. Their convictions are shaped by their own background, their promotion aspirations, their friendships. I am not suggesting that either the states of knowledge or conviction can be done away with. It is possible that their state of knowledge can be improved or that the individual can be made aware of these states and respond accordingly.

I suggest that the issues influencing decisions may be considered as lying on a continuum, with objectivity at one end and subjectivity at the other. One example might be the issue of setting homework for pupils. This issue may be viewed objectively by considering the value in terms of increased learning through consolidation and preparation. Equally it may be considered subjectively in terms of the extra time required in selecting, collecting, marking and returning this work which would greatly impinge on the teacher's evenings and weekends. A teacher, making a decision with this issue, may be swayed by the more objective, professional reasonings or the more subjective, personal reasonings.

Where subjective reasonings can be identified and discarded, thus allowing decisions to be based upon the more objective, professional reasonings, then these decisions may be more readily accepted.

The SORTHAM OUT simulation

THE PACKAGE

The package provides materials that make up the organizing tutor's booklet, the nine participants' booklets and observer's booklets. The tutor's booklet contains details of the organization of the simulation, copies of each of the participant's booklets and guidelines for drawing out the learning objectives of the simulation. The participants' booklets contain information about the geographical and historical setting of the Sortham Comprehensive School, the headteacher's memo calling for the meeting, the participant's views of the six part-time staff and a particular viewpoint to be expressed in the discussion. Each viewpoint lies at some point along the continuum of objectivity/subjectivity and each participant sees the part-time staff in different ways, having quite different strengths and weaknesses.

The observer's booklet contains only the basic information of the school and the nature of the staff meeting. No further information regarding the staff is included. Guidelines are provided for the role and action of the observers during the running of the simulation and the nature of their contribution to the debriefing session.

THE SETTING

The setting of the simulation is a secondary school staff meeting of senior members plus some invited junior members. The meeting is called in response to a request from the headteacher for an indication of the considered opinion and feeling of his staff in order to guide his comments at a future governors' meeting. This governors' meeting is called to consider which of the temporary part-time staff shall have their contracts terminated in order to meet the cut-back in staffing levels brought about by reduced allocation of monies based on the falling number of pupils. Two part-time staff must go—the problem is, which two?

THE PARTICIPANTS AND THE ISSUES

Nine members of staff are involved in the staff meeting. Each sees the six part-time members of staff in a different way.

1. The Headteacher is concerned to meet his parental and colleague views. He will keep on a teacher of an 'important' subject such as mathematics, and will be more willing to release a teacher who cannot keep discipline.
2. The Deputy Headteacher is concerned with promotion and hence the 'good name' of the school. A part-time teacher who is involved with successful examination subjects clearly will be retained.
3. A Head of Faculty who is concerned about the career teacher is inclined to retain the male, bread-winner teacher and the single female teacher. Teaching, he sees, is their career and not simply a second family income.
4. Another Head of Faculty who is concerned with the able teacher equates ability with maintaining good discipline. Other than that he would ensure that his faculty does not lose a part-time member of staff.
5. A third Head of Faculty attempts to consider the overall curriculum balance for the pupils. The part-time teachers to be retained would be those in subjects that would give this balance.
6. A Year Group Co-ordinator has ideals of education being concerned with problem-solving and not pure rote memory. He favours those teachers who are stimulating the pupils' minds into original thought.
7. A subject teacher is invited to the meeting because he holds a professional union post. The viewpoint here is concerned with union membership and recency of appointment.
8. A Department Head who fears a dilution of her future specialist teaching if the part-time teacher in this department is retained. Personal reasons are important here to the point of suggesting that the part-time teacher should be released.

9. A Department Head who wishes to retain a part-time teacher to enable examination classes to continue. Without this part-time teacher, the present examination classes would have to end and so a drop in status — perhaps even of the department itself — would follow.

Nine quite different perspectives are thus brought to bear on this central discussion, ranging through (i) good for the school, (ii) good for the pupils, (iii) good for the profession and (iv) good for me and my future. Some participants combine two, three or all four of these perspectives.

THE DECISION

The decision in the simulation discussion to be arrived at is the naming of the two part-time staff who are considered, for whatever reasons, to be least required. The guidelines in the headteacher's booklet suggest that a vote may be carried out to achieve this.

The organizing tutor can see from the notes in the tutor's booklet that three of the part-time staff are the most likely candidates for contract termination. In practice the final selection of candidates may be a function of the force of personality of the participants, the power and skill of their arguments or possibly the total adherence to the character guide suggestions.

Debriefing

The section of the organizing tutor's booklet concerned with drawing out the learning objectives of the simulation suggest four major areas. They are:

(a) role-play experience
(b) hierarchical status role-play experience
(c) identification of issues
(d) identification of argument lines.

Which single learning objective or combination of learning objectives is centred on depends largely on the previous experience in role-play of the participants and the particular reasons for which the tutor selects this simulation.

ROLE-PLAY EXPERIENCE

Where participants have had no previous experience of role-play in such simulation exercises, the tutor may concentrate discussion on the adoption of a role in circumstances to gain particular ends. It may be argued that all levels of educational management require roles to be played — if not acted. The intending teacher may gain insight into placing his or her feelings aside and 'be' a different person. A teacher, for example, may be totally amused by some prank of a pupil, yet have to reprimand that pupil in apparent sincerity — or at least go through the motions in order that honour is saved on both sides.

HIERARCHICAL STATUS ROLE-PLAY EXPERIENCE

Role-play of a status different from, and particularly higher than, the present one can alert the participants to issues and behaviours that they would not normally meet. What issues would concern a departmental head? Are issues different in nature or of more importance for the head of faculty as opposed to a head of department? What issues concern the deputy head and the headteacher, and to what extent do these agree and differ? What attitudes and behaviours are expected by those above and below in the hierarchy?

ISSUE IDENTIFICATION

The issues planned for in the character guides of the participants are those of strengthening the curriculum by either reducing or increasing the subjects to be offered, maintaining individual or departmental status, reflecting the requirements of parents and others significant in the area, ensuring continued employment for the career teacher, and the nature of a 'good' teacher.

ARGUMENT IDENTIFICATION

This simulation exercise includes the possibility of non-participant observers as an in-built feature and booklets are provided to achieve this. The observer may select a participant character or characters and attempt to identify the central element or bias in their argument, to judge the validity of these arguments and to see how far the arguments influenced the final decision. This experience may 'tune up' the ability to see through the words in order to find out the real standpoint of a participant in a discussion. This ability to stand back, even when involved in discussion, to determine the fundamental standpoint of others can be a most useful one.

Evaluation

The SORTHAM OUT simulation has been run with two different groups of participants. Firstly, it has been run with initial teacher education students who have completed their final teaching practice and so have some 'feel' for the wider issues of teaching. Secondly, it has been run with full-time and part-time in-service courses for practising teachers ranging from those with only a few years' teaching experience or management responsibility to those with many years of experience or with considerable management responsibility.

In each case the focus of the exercise was aimed at debriefing discussion areas pertinent to their interests, experience and the nature of the course being followed. The initial teacher education students had previously engaged in the SORTHAM COMPREHENSIVE simulation which gave them some experience of role-play, though with a different subject content.

Evaluation of the simulation exercise was attained through tape-recording debriefing sessions, follow-up seminars and tutorials. The verbatim reports were analysed according to responses related to:

(a) role-play experience
(b) hierarchical status role-play experience
(c) identification of issues
(d) identification of argument lines

The in-service groups, many of whom had no previous experience of role-play in simulation exercises, commented on the value they saw in taking a role, perhaps alien to them, and gained insights in this activity. The teachers with little managerial responsibility stated that they had gained insights into the wider issues that face their administrative colleagues. The headteachers found 'retreating' to a more humble role frustrating, when they realized how little influence this role appeared to have.

The objective/subjective reasons underlying decision-making in management discussions were clearly identified. Some of the intending teacher participants were appalled that personal issues should be brought to bear and questioned this inclusion. The experienced teachers confirmed the need for this element to be included, bemoaning the fact that it seemed to be a major influence in some decisions to which they had been witness. Two features that promoted much valued discussion for both groups were in the area of the dividing line between objective and subjective viewpoints, and also what constituted a 'good' decision.

One further response that emerged was a criticism made by the younger teachers. They suggested that, although interesting, enjoyable and valuable in identifying issues for concern and thought, the exercise was not really true to life in that such discussions were never held in their schools. This led on to a furious debate—no doubt the subject for a simulation exercise in the future— relating to the desirability or otherwise of open staff discussion in such sensitive areas as staff contract termination.

Conclusion

From the educationalist's point of view, the SORTHAM OUT simulation may not necessarily simulate accurately staff discussions of the particular issue. It certainly *does* promote questions, and this thirst for further knowledge, rather than relying on present and no doubt limited knowledge, is a major aim of education. As a non-direct, dry run simulation, SORTHAM OUT does highlight the problems facing educational management—the balancing of many pressures to arrive at the most reasonable solution based on sound objective reasoning.

This simulation fosters an appraisal of how decisions are arrived at and what influences can be brought to bear in such discussions. The personal and possibly selfish viewpoints are shown to be undesirable yet potentially powerful in influencing what should be sound professional decisions. It is therefore suggested that those involved at *all* levels of educational administration and organization will benefit from using this simulation exercise.

The simulation exercise is available in kit form or ready to use from the author. The kit provides mastersheets of the basic literature which may be photocopied and made into booklet form. Advice notes dealing with booklet assembly are provided.

References

Powell, L (1981) Resource list: Simulation and gaming in education management. *Simulation/Games for Learning* 11 2

Taylor-Byrne, J V (1979) *SORTHAM COMPREHENSIVE simulation.* Brighton Polytechnic, Mimeo

Taylor-Byrne, J V (1980) *SORTHAM OUT.* Brighton Polytechnic, Mimeo

Biographical note

John V Taylor-Byrne holds an MSc in Educational Research (Surrey), a Diploma in Education (London), ACP and Certificate in Education (Worcester College of Education). At present he is Senior Lecturer in Education at the Eastbourne campus of Brighton Polytechnic, being concerned with initial and in-service teacher courses. Seven years in lecturing follow twelve years teaching in infant, junior and secondary schools in the Kent and London area.

J V Taylor-Byrne
Brighton Polytechnic
Eastbourne Department of Education
Trevin Towers, Gaudick Road
Eastbourne
Sussex BN20 7SP
England

7. CYBERDRAMA

J M Antia

Abstract: This paper describes a simulation technique for studying power in organizations. It can be used for therapy, teaching and research. The technique is based on cybernetic principles and uses drama as a vehicle. Application of the technique is illustrated by two case examples from therapy contexts. The paper also reports some preliminary findings about the operation of power and its implications for training and management development.

Definition

CYBERDRAMA is a simulation technique based on drama for studying management processes of communication and control.

It focusses specifically on power, its use and abuse in the governing of people.

Significance of power

We distinguish at the outset between authority and power. Authority may be defined in a management context as the right to require action. Power on the other hand is the ability to get action. Since a manager's role is to make things happen, power lies at the heart of this role. The quality of leadership and consequences for the organization and the people who work in it are profoundly affected by the way power is used.

Power has fascinated the minds of leaders over generations and in fact without power little can be accomplished. President Reagan has as his motto: 'There is no limit to what a man can accomplish provided he does not care who gets the credit for it.' This is a profound thought which highlights a very important aspect of power — namely, not needing to care. It also defines the limits to power set by accountability and legitimization by one's subordinates and followers. No one understood the significance of this legitimization more than Lord Bute, prime minister of England during the reign of George III, about whom Lord Macaulay said that he seemed to lead because he was sure to follow. The importance of appealing to the hearts of followers has been underscored in no uncertain fashion by the contrasting experiences of two recent prime ministers. On the one hand, Edward Heath could not carry the day in confrontation with the miners. On the other hand, Harold Wilson managed to secure legitimization through his concept of 'social compact'.

However, there are other elements that go towards establishment of a leader's power. The emotions aroused by the espousing of a cause or the need to close ranks against 'the enemy without' are generally recognized as potent elements. The other elements appear to be possession of the ability to purvey rewards and punishments, both tangible and intangible. The operation of these, however, is complex and whether they lead to power may well depend on such factors as whether followers and subordinates care, or whether they can be made to care, and how far the leader is free from guilt and shame.

While it is possible to think of social relationships as systems, it is as well to recognize explicitly that social interaction is not an intellectual or rational process. It is largely an emotional process, and a social situation will be mediated through personalities involved. Decisions may be evaluated objectively, analytically and intellectually. They are, however, made on the basis of emotion. This seems to be the lesson of business, family and public life.

If personalities mediate social situations, the focus of power and the power outcomes may well depend upon what combinations of personalities are thrown together and the purpose to be achieved in the face of threats, risks and opportunities present in the operating environment. Feelings experienced by each individual will be the crucial factor in what he or she decides to do.

Over the years, we have managed to evolve a number of paradigms of organizations such as bureaucracies, cells, matrix structures, free form. These structures constrain behaviour through procedures, rules for clearance, restrictions on spending limits, information systems, staff roles, and so on, while permitting a limited measure of discretion. Whether certain personalities will thrive in this environment may well depend upon the needs of the individuals. Burns and Stalker (1961) found that mechanistic structures were inhibitive in innovative organizations and Litwin and Stringer (1968) came to the conclusion that achievement-orientated individuals tend to be alienated in bureaucratic organizations unless there is built in rapid feedback on performance.

Another important aspect of organization structures is that they tend to foster dependency. This may be seen in the family as well as in the work organization. In addition, there is the demand for performance and a competitive situation often full of injustice. Powerful emotions of anger, jealousy, envy, greed and fear divide as well as unite people within organizations. It is within this context that the individual has to function at work.

How do managers behave in these settings? What kind of personality thrives and what kind is crushed? How should a subordinate with a leadership bent behave *vis-a-vis* a manager who is a powerful person? In organizations stuffed with god-like managers, crown princes, favourites and *personae non grata*, what is appropriate behaviour for the company savage? These are important issues in any programme of management development.

71

The need for a different approach

Answers to many of these questions may be found in the works of Jay (1970), Korda (1979), Bacharach and Lawler (1980), Likert and Likert (1976), amongst others. However, when it comes to learning to use power and to counter power, the acquisition of such cognitive knowledge by the individual may not be an effectual way of changing behaviour. A person can acquire knowledge but may not learn. This need occasion no surprise as learning is not an intellectual and cognitive process. Rather it is an affective process. An individual's perceptual style develops early in childhood and gets frozen into habits of life. As de Bono (1977) points out, we are all prisoners of our concepts. Before any change in behaviour can take place, knowledge has to be internalized. For knowledge to be internalized, it has to be experienced. And it has to be experienced as alternatives and their consequences. This cannot be done vicariously. The experience needs to be personal to each individual. It is only by experiencing error-actuated feedback on results of behaviour that a person learns about the value of alternative options.

A vast range of therapies have been developed aimed at personal growth, and a lot of work has been done in the field of organization development aimed at team-building and enhanced co-operation through integration and resolution of conflict. However, some of the proposed norms for behaviour in organizations, such as candidness, confrontation and assertion, may be inconsistent with continuing membership of the organization at particular stages of its development, and in certain situations of conflict and negotiation. In everyday life one has to work amongst people at varying stages of personal development who all have their scripts, wear their masks and armours and are still busy with their unfinished business. We need a non-threatening learning environment for providing competence in acquiring a feel for the situation and responding in a way consistent with the ethos of the organization on an 'as is' basis, while maintaining the joy and integrity of the individual.

There is a high risk to the individual's sanity if he receives contradictory feedback from his personal growth therapist and from the organization. The way out of this *impasse* may well be to leave the organization. However, if the individual has given hostages to fortune he may find he cannot afford to leave.

But there are alternatives to flight and there are ways of ensuring that the person does not get trapped. It is possible to learn about power, how to use it and how to protect oneself against its abuse. How to play politics is not a dirty subject for study. It is a reality of organizational life. Power is its main ingredient. We need to learn about leading and following, with alliances and isolations; about resolution as well as creation of conflict; about the art of negotiation; about disciplining and about acquisition, dispersal, and containment of power by managers and subordinates. For all these purposes we need an effective learning environment. CYBERDRAMA has been developed as one such technique.

The Antecedents of CYBERDRAMA

In the author's money counselling sessions the issue of power was raised by clients time and again. For them power was a threatening subject and they needed to deal with it. The need for a non-threatening and effectual learning environment that would enable a client to learn effectively led the author to experiment with drama. Moreno (1952) had developed drama to deal with personal growth issues. Since then drama has attracted a substantial following amongst therapists. However, the writer is not aware of any previous attempt systematically to develop drama simulations as a learning environment for the study of power in organizations, and for providing the individual with internalized coping mechanisms for survival and growth without taking the flight option.

The logic of CYBERDRAMA

In CYBERDRAMA the medium of drama is used in an environment that permits 'cybernation' to take place for the individual. The term is derived from the Greek *kubernetes*, which means steersman. Cybernetics is the science of management control. Essentially, this science sees the management world as a complex system — a black box. The system receives inputs and produces outputs. When the information on output is fed back to the homeostat (a manager), the latter compares it with some norm. After evaluation of the significance of any deviation from norm, he takes action to change inputs to restore control. It is thus a learning process.

The axiom of CYBERDRAMA is that a person learns and relearns more effectively when deeply reliving a crucial scene in his or her life than if he merely talks about it or is advised. He enacts the scene. He experiences the action. The very act of enactment gives feedback which can be compared with the desired result. Options can then be explored to modify behaviour to accomplish the purpose. In CYBERDRAMA action is primary. It takes precedence over analysis. There can be no analysis or interpretation without action. In this situation, the resolution of a person's pain and dilemma does not require an extensive analysis or interpretation. The pain takes place *in situ*. The feedback and learning take place through action. The individual discovers that his or her behaviour is counterproductive and hindering achievement of goals. When cybernation brings the person to this crucial stage, new options and strategies can be tried and can be internalized when they succeed. The process is cyclical and escalation of its intensity is entirely within the control of the individual undergoing the process.

Attitude

The author has used CYBERDRAMA with some success as therapy in the context of student counselling and money counselling. Work is now in progress on developing a teaching module on power using the CYBERDRAMA techniques. A simplified description of the therapy mode of this technique is as follows:

THE ESSENTIAL ELEMENTS

(a) *a cyberprotagonist*
 — the person who presents for resolution a crucial problem he or she is involved in
(b) *an interpersonal power conflict*
 — the point of departure

(c) *supporting cast*
  — to play either props or *betes noires* of the cyberprotagonist
(d) *a stage or any open space*
  — to provide freedom for acting out problems
(e) *a facilitator*
  — who creates conditions for simulation of the real-life situation.

THE ETHOS

The cyberprotagonist is the subject and star of the show. She or he must live and relive the situation according to the mental picture of an important scene in her or his life. This picture will necessarily include past and future projections of important events going on in the inner drama. All time states will be brought out into the open through the state of the person. The mode of the enactment of the problem scene is important and it is crucial to the technique that the star is allowed to enact the scene, create the arena of operations and that the supporting cast play roles as directed. If a group is not available, then the facilitator may have to play these roles. In either case, the cyberprotagonist is both star and director. The role of the facilitator is merely to set the stage for action. He or she must not direct the action. In particular it must be ensured, at all times, that there are no attacks on the self esteem of the cyberprotagonist, originating either from the group or from the facilitator. The facilitator must ensure that no analysis or interpretation takes place before the actual enactment of the scene.

For these conditions to develop it is useful to have a warm-up session before the scene enactment. During this session the facilitator may describe the rules of behaviour, and invite a person to work on a problem. After acceptance of the invitation the person would be asked to say a few words about the problem, his expectations, and about himself.

After the enactment, expressions of empathy and support from the group are entirely appropriate as preliminaries to wider discussion. Here, the facilitator has to channel the discussion to avoid put-downs or other kinds of punishments, especially with failure-oriented individuals.

In the experience of the author, the most fruitful line of approach is to ask the star to say what was done in the situation and what responses he or she obtained. The person can then be asked whether his or her behaviour was doing any good. If he or she declares that the behavour was counterproductive, then it provides an opportunity for the facilitator, with or without the group, as the case may be, to help the person work out new options. The options suggested are not likely to be accepted without some doubt but progress will have been made if the person agrees to give them a try. It is useful to commit this agreement to paper, both as a reminder and as a message to our star that someone cares. Care feedback is a crucial element of the system.

Follow-up

In later sessions, our star would be asked to name the occasions when the contract was honoured and occasions when it was not. Gallons of praise should be bestowed for each occasion on which the promise was implemented. There should however be no punishment for failure to honour, nor should any excuse be accepted. Instead, there should be firm and unequivocal insistence that the contract is honoured. In addition, when the contract is honoured, the star should be asked to say whether the new strategy did any good. The feedback should come from him or her if cybernation is to take place.

When well advanced into therapy, the facilitator could get involved in the real world of the star and be in an actual operational situation with him or her. The reasoning behind this approach is that it is impossible for anyone to relive any situation exactly. Observing the person operating in a real situation can then provide a basis for further exploration of strategies. The author can confirm that, on each occasion when this opportunity has arisen for him, significant change in client's strategy has been proposed and implemented by the client.

Application

Two extracts from the case notes of the author illustrate the use of CYBERDRAMA in therapy.

A mature student on an advanced course sat dejectedly at the coffee table. In the course of conversation he said he had money worries associated with his broken marriage. His worries were affecting his studies and, according to him, lack of money meant that girls were no longer attracted to him. He had grown a beard so that he would look more manly. He continued to open up, indicating that a particular student in the class was the object of his attention. He said he felt so powerless in dealing with people, his wife, his children, his classmates and teachers. He agreed to be counselled.

At a warm-up session, he enacted a scene with his children. The author was directed to play his eldest child as a sulky disobedient brat. Father shouted and threatened to hit him but the child just continued to disobey. Father banged the door and left the room.

Asked to say whether what he did had produced the result he desired, he recognized that his behaviour had been counterproductive. He then proffered the information that it was not the child he was angry with but his wife. She was to blame for all his troubles. When it was suggested to him that an alternative strategy might be worth considering, he said he needed time to think about it.

A week later he returned and asked if he could enact the home scene with another woman student in his class. The scene began with his ordering his wife to tidy up the house but soon developed into a wrangle over money and an accusation by the wife that he was no man. Our cyberprotagonist ended the scene by leaving the room and slamming the door.

Asked what he was seeking to achieve, he said he was seeking to make his wife love him, but his efforts always ended in failure. When invited to consider what he really wanted, he said he wanted to move on to a new life but had no energy. It was pointed out to him that he had just shown a lot of energy in his angry outburst and would he consider channelling this same energy into his studies. He said he would and we drew up a programme for catching up on his assignments with due dates for submission and for budgeting his cash.

Three days later, when his first assignment was due he was asked for it. He said he had not finished it because he had to see his children over the weekend. The author simply insisted on his dropping everything and honouring his promise to deliver the assignment. It came in two days late but he was praised profusely for his achievement. The next assignment was produced on time and earned more praise. The third assignment was a day late. Again no excuses were accepted. There was uncompromising insistence that he met his promise. The fourth and fifth assignments were on time, earning gallons of praise.

A few days later, our subject turned up clean shaven and announced he felt much better. He said he had rediscovered how to pull girls and no longer felt inferior. He further stated that he had managed to learn how to get help from his classmates and that he now enjoyed his studies. He had also got himself a part-time job as a barman, and his cash was under control.

The next case concerns Fred, a young skipper. The case was referred by the managing director of the company for whom the author had acted as a money counsellor. The company had its headquarters in England but operated in Africa. A power struggle had developed between him and two other skippers. Fred was the blue-eyed boy of the managing director, whose sister-in-law he was engaged to. He had an outstanding record as a skipper over three years and the managing director had hoped to put him in charge of the entire African operation.

For some inexplicable reason Fred had a bad season. Clients complained about him; his staff sent letters to the managing director asking for transfers to other skippers; the other skippers treated Fred with contempt and derision when they had their regular fortnightly meetings, and he became moody, withdrawn, and very aggressive. The final crunch point came when he threatened violence against a fellow skipper.

A meeting had been called to discuss problems associated with the new season. It was the week before Easter and the new season was about to start. Just before the meeting was called to order one of the other skippers confided to the author that Fred was a coward and unfit to continue in command. A range of operational problems relating to maintenance were discussed at the meeting. Fred sat through the meeting sulkily and was not very forthcoming. At lunchtime the meeting agreed to reconvene that same evening to talk through some of the difficulties of maintaining communications and supplies.

That afternoon in the boat and away from the rest of his colleagues, Fred dealt with the charge of cowardice. He said it was unfair of the others to brand him when he had actually behaved in a very proper manner. Asked to elaborate, he said that he and his Italian girlfriend had been out walking in the mountains when they were set upon by two men. His girlfriend was violated. He could do nothing: he had been held with a knife in his back. Now he felt helpless and very angry. His girl no longer wished to see him. The gossip in the restaurants also bothered him. Most of all he felt that the other skippers were trying to blackmail him. If only there was a way out.

That evening, after much hesitation, Fred agreed to enact the fateful scene with a girl who was a member of his crew and two skippers, one of whom was the one who had made the charge of cowardice. The rest of his colleagues were in the audience. Fred enacted a scene that was very violent. At the end of it he burst into a flood of tears.

Asked whether he cared that everybody now knew about his cowardice, he said he did not and, in fact, felt fine. He also said he no longer felt guilty about his girlfriend. That same night he took charge of all social activities which hitherto he had boycotted. That season Fred performed as an outstanding skipper.

Warning

The above case studies illustrate one way of using CYBERDRAMA in everyday situations. It is vital to realize that the facilitator role is a very difficult role and demands affective as well as cognitive competence. It is not enough to know about the technique or about behaviour. The facilitator himself needs to be secure in his self esteem, free from worry about rejection and free from feelings of guilt and anger. He needs to be a caring and worldly-wise person. It is also very necessary to have knowledge of other techniques of therapy and to have experienced some of them. The author would like to warn very strongly against inexperienced and untrained persons embarking on that role as there can be serious risk of harm to participants. Furthermore, in the opinion of the author, this technique is not sufficiently developed to deal with seriously disturbed persons and should not be used in such cases.

Some preliminary conclusions

The author would like to report some very preliminary findings from experience of using power simulations based on CYBERDRAMA.

As a learning technique it has much to recommend it. There seems to be no need for extensive analysis and the subjects seem to discover for themselves what is bugging them. This discovery is accompanied by anguish. The inner drama is not evident to the observer though the visible anguish may be its high point. What has surprised the author is the speed and the suddenness of change when it comes.

A comparison of the before and after situation of subjects suggests that a person's striving for power is frustrated by energy being diverted towards negative emotions. When they give up anger and fear, they seem to open themselves up to dealing with reality. A further hypothesis is that it is the damage or possible damage to self esteem that leads to diversion of energy towards negative emotions. Laing (1977) has shown how a person's concept of self is formed by what feedback others give him. Organizational settings in power situations are full of feedback damaging to an individual's self esteem. Likert (1961) was perhaps alluding to this phenomenon when he emphasized the importance of supportive relationships. If this analysis has validity, then it must also follow that attainment of personal power is a precondition for attainment of power in organizations. As a corollary, attacks on a person's self-esteem by persons significant to him may be the most effective way of destroying an individual's power in an organization.

Implications

Assuming that the above analysis is sound, then several implications arise for the design of school and college curricula and for in-service training of managers, teachers and the helping professions.

In course design it could be useful to introduce the subject of power implicitly. Teachers should be willing to discuss techniques of manipulation and how to respond effectively. Inhibitions about the subject of power are not appropriate as the welfare of future generations is affected. It would also be desirable to make use of therapy. For every person who loses personal power represents a loss of resources to the organization and to the nation.

The above remarks also apply with some force to family situations. CYBERDRAMA may prove more effective than other methods of family therapy which are currently used.

Finally, it would be appropriate to offer CYBERDRAMA simulations to the helping professions, including nurses, health visitors, probation officers and social workers. Apart from its value as therapy, it could prove a very useful tool in their work.

References

Bacharach, S B and Lawler, E J (1980) *Power and Politics in Organisations.* Jossey-Bass: San Francisco

de Bono, E (1977) *PO: Beyond Yes and No.* Pelican: London

Burns, T and Stalker, G M (1976) *The Management of Innovation.* Tavistock: London

Jay, A (1970) *Management and Machiavelli.* Pelican: London

Korda, M (1979) *Power!* Coronet Books: Sevenoaks, Kent

Laing, R D (1977) *Self and Others.* Penguin: London

Likert, R (1961) *New Patterns of Management.* McGraw-Hill: New York

Likert, R and Likert, J G (1976) *New Ways of Managing Conflict.* McGraw-Hill: New York

Litwin, G H and Stringer, R A (1968) *Motivation and Organizational Climate.* Harvard University: Boston

Moreno, J L (1952) *Who Shall Survive.* Beacon Books: New York

Biographical note

Jim Antia is principal lecturer in Management Information Systems at the Anglian Regional Management Centre.

After qualifying as a chartered accountant, he spent a number of years as a professional accountant, and before taking up academic life, he held a number of executive positions in several industries. His research interests cover money counselling, motivation and management information systems. He has written simulations for management and several micro-computer-based psychological tests.

Jim Antia
Anglian Regional Management Centre
North East London Polytechnic
Danbury Park
Danbury
Essex
England

8. Case study simulations in the teaching of land administration

Martin Wynn, John Overall, Roger Smith, Peter Totterdill and John Taylor

Abstract: This paper considers the use of case studies and case study simulations in the professional training of surveyors.
A case study of a real urban development, which is developed as a simulation – THE COFFERIDGE CLOSE GAME – is described in detail, and the benefits which accrue from involving students in exercises of this type are considered, especially in relation to the experiences possible therein, which restrictions on access would make unavailable in real life.

Introduction

In our increasingly complex society, the pressures on the professional surveyor are greater than ever before; practising under the media spotlight as he often does, the surveyor is expected to act with an ever increasing degree of excellence. It has thus become of paramount importance that the surveyor should appreciate the perspectives and viewpoint of the politician, the planner and other public service practitioners, as well as those of the general public and the clients served. In the design of undergraduate courses, therefore, one is faced with the problem of how best to prepare the student for a professional career; more specifically, how can the teaching of different subject areas be most effectively integrated to give students a valid informed overview of the land administration process? This article, through providing a detailed worked example, attempts to show that case study simulations can play a valuable role in providing students with this broader awareness.

Antecedents

The case study teaching units currently being devised at the North East London Polytechnic combine two important educational techniques – the case method and gaming simulation. The case method is, of course, long established in higher education and much of the stimulus for the current work came from the earlier efforts of Cresswell (1929), McNair (1954) and Moore (1973).

To elaborate slightly, it must be recalled that Cresswell's classic *Honeywood Files* were fairly light-hearted serial accounts of how an architect running a job might improve his contract management from lessons drawn from the pages of a fictitious correspondence file. McNair's work documented the more serious-minded Harvard Bunsiness School's approach to training executives through the use of real world 'case' material, whilst Moore's work with estate management students at the University of Reading adopted this approach to provide background material for mock runs of public inquiry proceedings.

Similarly, the use of simulation exercises in the teaching of land administration is far from new. Early pioneering work by Duke (1964) and Feldt (1966) was followed by the development of urban games in the United Kingdom in which the dynamics and growth of urban systems were simulated. Simplified representations of reality provided environments in which students could experience something of the real-world dilemmas of decision-making.

Although the development of such simulations has suffered from a general lack of evaluation, one major criticism has been that urban games are poor in their definition and description of the planning environment (Romanos, 1978). This is largely because such games usually try to simulate development at the city or metropolitan area level; as a result, games tend to be either extremely complex in their design and execution, or else over-simplified to such a degree that whilst they help the student to appreciate theoretical principles at a high level of generality, they are in many respects remote from contexts within which real-life decision-makers operate. One way of ensuring both realism and manageability is to build the games around tightly defined local case studies.

In devising these games it is assumed that traditional teaching methods will provide students with an elementary understanding of the activities of the various practitioners involved in the land administration process at local level. The value of the case study gaming exercise is to take this one stage further by providing an authentic structure which defines the role of each actor and his or her capacity for action. We are talking here, then, about what Lester and Stoil (1979) term 'role-specific' situations, in which 'the roles assumed by participants directly correspond to a specific real world equivalent', rather than 'role-generalized simulations', which do not. An appropriate simulation exercise, therefore, is one which both clearly defines the parameters within which each role is played, yet leaves each actor with scope for individual initiative to pursue the particular goals which he or she has been given. By acting out these roles, the students become aware (to an extent not easily achieved through other teaching methods) of the inter-dependences and dilemmas that confront the key personnel in the land administration process. Nevertheless, it should be stressed that we are not suggesting that case study simulations constitute an alternative teaching method on which undergraduate courses can be based. Rather, we see them as a new application of gaming simulation which can be set alongside other teaching methods and other types of simulation in the teaching of land administration.

Example: THE COFFERIDGE CLOSE GAME

A good example of the type of case study well-suited to the simulation exercise described in the previous section is Cofferidge Close, a small commercial development in the old market town of Stony Stratford, now part of the designated area of the new city of Milton Keynes in Buckinghamshire. The plan for Milton Keynes, produced by the Milton Keynes Development Corporation (MKDC) in 1970, argued that Stony Stratford should contribute an element of historical identity and character to the new city, while providing a wide range of district shopping facilities and other services. But the commercial life and environmental quality of the town had suffered from progressive deterioration, and there was an urgent need for extensive revitalization.

The MKDC was the authority with overall responsibility for implementing the proposals for the new city. An *ad hoc* body set up under the provisions of the New Towns Act of 1965, it had extensive powers to plan and to promote the growth of Milton Keynes, including the ability to undertake the commercial development of particular sites where appropriate. However, all major proposals and capital expenditure by MKDC had first to be approved by the Department of the Environment, which expected certain financial returns and planning achievements. Relations between MKDC, and the local authority within whose boundaries the designated area of the new city fell, were generally constructive, though sometimes marked by a difference in outlook characteristic of the two sides; MKDC was naturally concerned with the growth of the city and its success in meeting regional objectives, while the local authorities were more interested in ensuring that local needs were adequately represented in the process of change.

As part of the improvement for Stony Stratford, the Central Planning Unit of the Corporation proposed that one and a half hectares of semi-derelict backlands located behind the High Street be redeveloped (see Figure 1) as a shopping and social centre. It appears that there was little real debate about whether the development should go ahead or not: there may have been genuine consensus about the need for the scheme, or it may be that the powerful position of MKDC inhibited any direct opposition. However, the question of how the site was to be developed was resolved only after prolonged efforts by the various protagonists. A number of organizations and departments participated in the preparation and implementation of the scheme, each with its own discrete areas of concern.

Disputes concerning the conflicting stakes and interests of the different participants were not uncommon. There was, for example, a continuous struggle to produce a design which would satisfy the objectives of both the Planning and Finance Departments, within the procedural requirements of the Estates Department. Should more offices be provided to increase the financial return on the scheme? Should housing for disabled people be built on the site? Was there enough money for a public hall? These issues had to be resolved in the face of pressure from the local interest groups and the need to persuade central government of the merits and viability of the scheme.

Moreover, the set of constraints faced by each group was not a static one: the process took place against the background of a falling property market, and uncertainty about the financial contribution to be made to the scheme by Buckinghamshire County Council. Changing requirements for the location of the health centre and library also necessitated substantial revisions at an advanced stage in the design process.

COFFERIDGE CLOSE, then, represents a consensus building exercise, resulting in a compromise solution which dilutes the returns expected by each participant from the scheme. It also identifies substantial external constraints as being major determinants of the final outcome. It was our intention that the framework of interdependence in which each participant was located should be recreated as realistically as possible, giving students an insight into the limitations of plan implementation through an experience of real life.

The COFFERIDGE CLOSE CASE STUDY SIMULATION has so far been used with classes of 20 to 35 students divided into two groups playing independent games. The game duration has normally been six and ten hours, sometimes spread over two teaching days.

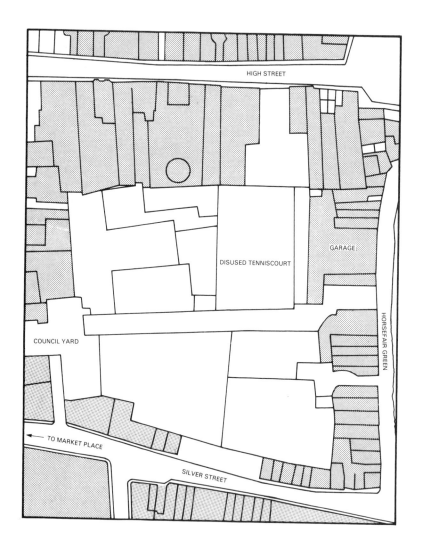

Figure 1. *Cofferidge Close, 1970*
(Shaded areas show existing buildings in 1970.)

ROLES

The following role descriptions are given to students:

The New Town Development Corporation Design Team:

Chief Architect and Planning Officer who is anxious to see the maximum number of houses provided, but especially disabled persons' dwellings. The officer is also anxious to see the provision of community facilities, eg, a public hall. He or she prefers small shop units to supermarkets and is concerned with the overall quality of the scheme, including landscaping and public open space. The officer has the final veto on proposals of the design team, and is also a member of the Executive Management Committee (see below).

Planning Assistant and *Design Assistant*. These are responsible for detailed design and planning work on the scheme.

Executive Management Committee (EMC). This is a co-ordinating committee of the chief officers; in particular it is responsible for the approval of all developments proposed by the Chief Architect and Planning Officer, before their submission to the Department of the Environment. (The teacher/game manager plays the DoE.) The EMC comprises:

(a) *Chief Architect and Planning Officer* (see above).

(b) *General Manager of Development Corporation.* The chief officer of the Development Corporation and chairman of the EMC, is concerned with the broad overview of the scheme, eg, financial returns and good planning. But the General Manager is also concerned with the overall prestige and good name of Milton Keynes. This entails a concern with newspaper reports and public opinion.

(c) *Chief Estates Officer.* This officer has responsibility for land purchasing and negotiations, and also advises the design team of the financial implications of their land use requirements. He or she should work closely with the design team to ensure that the land bought meets both financial and planning objectives. This officer can use Compulsory Purchase Orders (CPOs) subject to the approval of the EMC if necessary but it is Development Corporation policy to try to acquire land voluntarily.

(d) *Finance Officer.* His or her main concern is to maximize returns on the scheme. After all costs have been met, the scheme ought to show a profit of +10 monetary units (MU) in order to satisfy the Department of the Environment (see below). However, the DoE might be prepared to accept less if there are substantial planning and social advantages.

The Property Owners

Mr James. Owner of garage (non-conforming use) on periphery of side and adjoining land. Willing to sell if price is right.

Mr White-Bread. Owner of bakery and adjoining land and representative of other shop keepers. Does not really want to sell back of his yard, but sees some advantage in gaining access to rear of premises.

Wolverton Urban District Council. Own a council yard and adjoining land for which they have no use. They are keen to sell, provided the price is right, suspecting that the Development Corporation would not use CPO against them. (Public authorities are reluctant to use a CPO against each other although in law this may be possible.)

Stony Stratford Civic Society (SSCS):

Lt Gen Frogsmorton MC (and Bar). President of the Society.

Ms Vanessa Castells. Secretary of the Society, and lecturer at the Open University.

Mr George Grubbit. Local and long established shop keeper. He is frightened that new incoming firms would rob those like him of custom.

The Society is concerned that the Development Corporation will ride rough-shod over the interests of the indigenous community and will rob Stony Stratford of its distinctive identity, but some argue that the Development Corporation could provide new opportunities, such as a community hall and new housing.

The Society agreed at its last AGM to press for a new community hall at Cofferidge Close. They were suspicious that the Development Corporation would want to develop it on a less accessible site.

Reporters:

Two reporters. Their job is to get information as and when they can from the other actors, and to give their own opinions, through editorials. These will be posted on the notice board. The main channels of communication will be through the press. The reporters will also be expected to undertake case studies of the exercise and present them at the debriefing session.

Each player is given a badge to show his role, and each group (ie, Design Team, Property Owners, etc) is given its own area in the classroom or studio (a designation label is given to each group). A map of the Cofferidge Close area prior to development is shown (Figure 1), plus photographs, diagrams, etc, which will give the students something of the flavour of the area and the use and state of existing buildings, as well as the ownership patterns of the land. Each student is also provided with a diagrammatic version of the site set out on a 10x10 squared grid (Figure 2).

THE DESIGN BRIEF AND DEVELOPMENT VALUES

All the students are provided with the design brief issued to the Design Team. This states that the area is to be developed as a shopping and social centre to serve the new neighbourhood of Stony Stratford. The plan, therefore, should attempt if possible to provide:

(a) Enhanced shopping facilities in terms of small shops or supermarkets. (One shop covers one square on the grid; a supermarket must cover at least two squares on the grid.)

(b) Offices. (One office covers one square on the grid with total office development covering a maximum of six squares, a factor dictated by the Government's location of offices policy.)

(c) Community facilities in the form of a library and a health centre (covering a minimum of two and four squares respectively).

(d) Some housing for the disabled (half a square represents one disabled person's house).

(e) Some executive housing (one house covers one square).

(f) Public open space.

The plan should also get rid of the garage because it is an eyesore and because it is noxious, but as far as possible keep existing buildings intact.

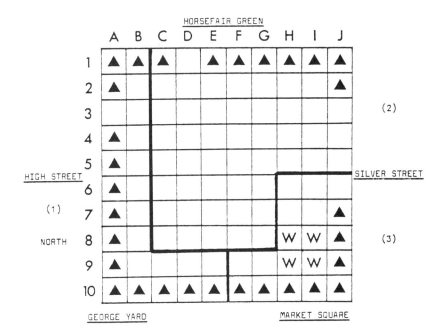

NB   Thick lines represent the boundaries between different land ownerships. Area 1 is owned by Mr White-Bread, a baker whose shop is located on square A 4. Area 2 is owned by James's, who run a rather dilapidated and noisy garage on square C 1. Area 3 is owned by Wolverton Urban District Council, who use the squares marked W as a yard for the Technical Services Department. Existing buildings on site are marked ▲.

Figure 2. *THE COFFERIDGE CLOSE GAME Board*

For simplicity's sake the planner will do the design work on the grid plan. Roads and parking space do not have to be shown on the plan, but have to be calculated on the basis of one road square per five developed squares (including buildings but excluding green spaces). The number of road and parking squares must, however, be allocated somewhere on the grid plan. Financial constraints are incorporated into the planning process. The monetary values are calculated in monetary units (MU) per grid square. The most profitable use of land is for office development. Each square of office development yields seven MU/sq. Other values are as follows:

— Library (occupying a minimum of two squares): + one MU/sq
(paid for by Buckinghamshire County Council, therefore some profit to MKDC)

- Health Centre (occupying a minimum of four squares): + one MU/sq (paid for by Buckinghamshire County Council, therefore some profit to MKDC)
- Green zones: —one MU/sq (an expense for the MKDC)
- Shop (occupying one square each): + three MU/sq (commercial rent for MKDC)
- Supermarket (occupying a minimum of two squares each): + four MU/sq (more profitable than ordinary shops and therefore rent yield greater)
- Executive houses (occupying one square each): + two MU/sq (rent gain to MKDC)
- Disabled people's houses (two per square): —two MU/sq (subsidized by the Development Corporation and therefore constitute a loss for MKDC)
- Roads and parking spaces: —one MU/sq.

Land prices must also be taken into account, and so the rate which the Development Corporation has to pay the landowners, by either voluntary or compulsory purchase, for each square, will have to be deducted from the Design Team's profit estimates. Before the game starts, all the players are told that James's land is the most valuable and that Wolverton UDC's is the cheapest. Developed land is more expensive than undeveloped land and land prices in the area have recently varied between 0.5 and 1.5 MU/sq.

Should the Development Corporation wish to go for compulsory purchase then, once the decision has been made, the teachers/game managers will act as district valuers and inform the Development Corporation that the values of James's land are 1.2 MU/sq undeveloped, 1.4 developed; White-Bread's land is worth 1 MU/sq undeveloped, 1.2 developed; and Wolverton UDC is 0.8 MU/sq undeveloped, 0.9 developed. Unless there are compelling social reasons, the Department of the Environment will not give permission to the Development Corporation to go ahead with the plan unless it shows an overall profit of +10 MU. Consequently the Design Team must match commercial viability with social need.

GAME PROCEDURE

If we assume that role assignment and familiarization with the design brief are over by 10.00am, the game can proceed, under the overall direction and co-ordination of the game managers as follows:

(a) The Design Team prepares a plan.
(b) Members of the Executive Management Committee consider the financial parameters.
(c) Property owners decide on their selling prices.
(d) The Stony Stratford Civic Society produce their plan—with emphasis on the social value of their scheme, even if it makes a financial loss.
(e) Newspaper reporters try to get statements from the involved parties and make their own editorial statements. Ideas in note form are pinned upon press notice boards.

10.45am: The preliminary design is submitted to the EMC for discussion. The

SSCS and the property owners are subsequently invited by the General Manager to participate in the latter stages of the meeting. The EMC then discuss the reactions of the SSCS and the property owners. The design team is then brought in to make any modifications considered necessary. The draft plan is issued and preliminary negotiations for land purchase begin. It is possible that at this stage some or all the necessary land is purchased, subject to DoE approval. This depends upon whether an amicable agreement with the various parties can be made. The press, after sounding out general opinions, reacts. The Development Corporation may at this stage start thinking about compulsory purchase procedures.

12.30pm: Summary of game so far. Lunch.

1.30pm: Circulate notes indicating a shift of policy on the part of Buckinghamshire County Council: the library scheme is withdrawn and the health centre has to be located on squares 9FG and 10FG (simplifying what really happened— see above). Game participants react, considering the implications for the design of the area. Shortly after, the collapse of the property market is announced (simplifying a general trend which took place during 1974).

The value of office development falls to +2 MU/sq, supermarket to +3 MU/sq, shops to +2 MU/sq, and the public hall from −2 to −3 MU/sq. Land prices also fall to vary from 0.3 to 1.1 MU/sq. These figures are made generally available. If land has already been purchased, the Development Corporation has to try to recuperate its losses by adjusting the design content accordingly. If no land or only some land has been purchased at this point, then negotiations will be revised. Should compulsory purchase be necessary new instructions will be given as follows:

— James's 0.9 MU/sq undeveloped, and 1.1 MU/sq developed
— White-Bread's 0.7 MU/sq undeveloped, and 0.8 MU/sq developed
— Wolverton UDC 0.5 MU/sq undeveloped, and 0.6 MU/sq developed.

The Development Corporation now revises its plans and draws in participants for discussion and negotiations as it thinks fit.

The plan is then submitted to DoE and, through the press, the SSCS reacts.

DEBRIEFING

The debriefing may take place at the end of the first day or at a later date. The development of the real case study is recounted by the game manager and at critical points the explanation is halted and the members of each game are asked to comment on the differences between the real case study and the two simulated versions. These comparisons have proved invaluable in stimulating discussion about the functioning of the planning system. Having worked through the case study, the students are then asked to write down what they have learned from the exercise, thus clarifying their own thinking and reinforcing the learning experience.

Subsequent discussion in tutorial groups can then lead towards a critical evaluation of both the students' responses within the game and of the political, economic and social context within which the land administration process operates.

Concluding remarks

In summary then, it needs to be said that the design and running of such case study simulation puts certain demands on both the lecturer and student that are not normally found in the lecture hall. As Vincent (1976) has said, the teacher who uses the case study approach must shift attention from himself to the class. He must allow the pupils to explore and create, yet at the same time he needs to provide guidance and clear overall direction through the welter of information presented in the case.

Experience suggests, however, that such extra effort is well worthwhile for two major educational reasons. Firstly, there is always the danger that the students may not have acquired an adequate sense of reality. Limited access to local authority files means that students are often given little opportunity to examine tangible evidence of real-world land administration decision-making in a favourable academic setting. Even when such files are available for discussion, spare copies and direct access are not often possible for reasons of confidentiality or political sensitivity. Furthermore, it is freely acknowledged that such files are only a partial account of a process. Obviously it is possible to see the files as a one-sided story, lacking both depth and balance.

Secondly, and connected with the above, we are concerned that new ways should be tried to improve the integration of learning in different subject areas. The world of land administration is a fine blend of law, economics, politics, planning and professional doctrine, and student feedback has suggested that case study simulations such as THE COFFERIDGE CLOSE GAME can successfully highlight the overlap and interdependence of different disciplines and professions, and reveal the linkages between different strands of what is often a complex administration process. Such games, then, can provide students with a stimulating framework for integrating knowledge gleaned elsewhere on their undergraduate course, resulting in a heightened awareness of their own and others' roles, and their improved performance as practitioners in years to come.

References

Cresswell H B (1929) *The Honeywood File.* Architectural Press: London

Duke, R D (1964) *Gaming Simulation in Urban Research.* Institute for Community Development, Michigan State University: East Lancing, Mich

Feldt, A G (1966) Operational gaming in planning education *Journal of American Institute of Planners* January

McNair, M P (1954) (ed) *The Case Method at Harvard Business School.* Harvard University Press: Cambridge, Mass

Moore, V W E (1973) Documents to be used in conjunction with audio-video tape of a mock planning inquiry. College of Estate Management, Reading University

Romanos, M (1978) Undergraduate planning—is gaming the answer? *Simulation and Games,* 9 1

Vincent, M (1976) Gaming and simulation with particular reference to the case study: how well do you use the case method? *Educational Studies* 2 2

Biographical notes

Dr Martin Wynn is research fellow in the department of general surveying and construction, North East London Polytechnic. His special research interests include planning and development in southern Europe and participatory teaching and training methods.

John Overall is head of the above-mentioned department. His research interests include course design and computer applications in higher education.

Dr Roger Smith is reader in the department of town and country planning, Trent Polytechnic, Nottingham, and Peter Totterdill is research assistant in the same department.

Dr John Taylor is Head of Bretton College, Wakefield, North Yorkshire. He pioneered the use of Land-Use Game Simulation (LUGS) in this country in the early 1970s.

Acknowledgement

Grateful acknowledgement is given to DECD, UNESCO and RICS (Royal Institute of Chartered Surveyors) for support in related research areas.

M Wynn
Department of General Surveying and Construction
North East London Polytechnic
Forest Road
London E17 4JB
England

9. Simulation in the sandbox – not just a game

Heinz D Naetscher

Abstract: The sandbox is a cheap and simple medium for teaching and learning, whose potential for simulation has been recognised for at least 150 years. Its uses are demonstrated by reference to a simulation game LOCATION FACTORS–SIMULATED IN THE SANDBOX, developed by the author for the teaching of economics. Details of the game's operation are described and evaluated.

Introduction

Only on rare occasions, and all too seldom, do educationalists point to the sandbox as a teaching and learning medium. For most of us it is an association with carefree pleasures of childhood and the ideas of playing, building castles, or baking cakes. The sandbox is usually taken to mean exclusively a children's toy, and it is part of the basic equipment of public and private playgrounds – and not only because of the relatively low cost of acquisition and upkeep. Educational considerations favour the sandbox too. Children gather sensory experiences in it, with a material whose mastery they seek to acquire through building the most diverse structures. They practise creativity through play.

Adults too can profit educationally from using the sandbox. Armed military forces used the sandbox from an early stage on, as an educational instrument. In 1824 von Reisswitz published a textbook on sandbox war games, for the training of officers. Terrain orientation, drawing up battle plans, and decision-making practice in case of war are facilitated by the use of a sandbox for demonstration purposes.

Police and fire services also use the sandbox in connection with site plans and models to teach strategy. For industry too, the sandbox is not a toy in the ordinary sense of the word, but a necessary planning instrument. The accurately sealed, reduced technical layout represented in the sandbox is necessary to reduce as much as possible excess costs and constructional faults.

The advantage of the sandbox as a medium for simulation can be outlined at several levels. The most impressive fact is the enormous educational value of presenting a three-dimensional structure with a relatively simple medium. The sandbox does not require any operating with highly breakable gadgets, nor does it need any wiring for electricity. The flexibility of the sand provides its dynamic possibilities and educational opportunities. It is easy for sandbox players to construct, rebuild or rearrange structures or models in the sand. Most users recognize in the sandbox a familiar medium from their childhood, and one of its specific features is its flexible use for many-sided possibilities. Also cognitive learning targets experienced in the sandbox through reception, clarification and ordering of insights and everyday experiences should be noted. Users gather through play creative, practical knowledge and they develop sensitivity.

The pedagogic uses of the sandbox for demonstration derive not only from enjoyment, but also from its value in allowing the demonstration of imaginative ideas. Experimentation in the sandbox before planning and constructing a new living area is an example. Its main advantages are in its ability to be modelled into an accurate representation and its ease of construction—you only need a box strong enough to hold sand, and the sand itself. Both box and sand can be obtained relatively cheaply. The additional playing materials, as described later, can be altered according to educational aims. Teachers can, of course, let their students play this simulation game without a box, in the open air, either on the beach or in sand in the corner of a public playground.

Although the simulation game LOCATION FACTORS—SIMULATED IN THE SANDBOX is intended to be played in economics classes, the use of the sandbox as a learning medium is not restricted to any age group. A survey in North Germany showed that the sandbox is primarily used in schools in local geography and history lessons. Some teachers use it for introducing map-reading or for clarifying basic geographical concepts. Equally, it has proved useful in teaching aspects of history. When a two-dimensional picture is no longer sufficient to gain comprehension of a concept, a sandbox construction can illustrate the situation. With the specialist advice of the teacher, prehistoric graves, places of worship and fortifications appear in the sand. Students can also construct realistic models of Hadrian's wall or a medieval town, castles, various types of settlements or the three-field system.

The current position regarding the use of the sandbox in school can be characterized as a little sand in the gearing of the school system! This article attempts to show the sandbox as a practical teaching and learning medium and to explain methods of application. The sandbox is by no means obsolete as an educational device, and simulation in a sandbox is not just a children's game.

The simulation game LOCATION FACTORS—SIMULATED IN THE SANDBOX should inspire use of the sandbox as a learning medium in economics classes. Pupils learn the factors which have a role to play in the search for location, they see the combined effects of individual decisions, and have to deal with economic and social problems. Furthermore, players handle the material creatively. They are engaged in shaping and fashioning it, and together they plan, advise and make decisions. The teacher can introduce the game into the practical part of the lesson and use it to ensure that learning objectives have been met. The number of players is not fixed, nor is the age level of the participants. Using a variety of materials, the teacher can adjust the game according to the capabilities of the students. As in all simulation games, every student should participate.

The game begins with the room being arranged in accordance with Figure 1. A group of tables for the working materials stands in the middle of the classroom. The sandboxes are grouped at a convenient distance, and finally a semicircle of chairs is formed around the blackboard.

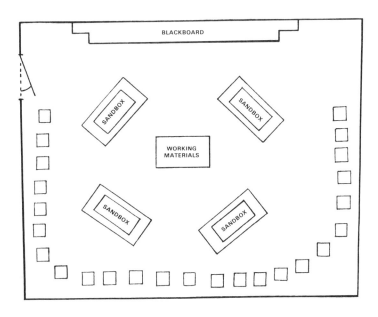

Figure 1. *Arrangement of room for*
LOCATION FACTORS— SIMULATED IN A SANDBOX

To prepare the students, who are sitting around the board, for the sandbox game to follow, the teacher hands out the working materials and roles. He or she divides a class of, say, 20 participants into four equal groups and chooses a leader and reporter from each group. Each team is then assigned a sandbox and the leader takes the game folder as well as the simulation case (see below).

Sandboxes, made of unbreakable Acrylglass, allow building constructions to be seen from the side. The only criterion for the height of the edges is that each player should be able easily to reach the middle. The material which fills the box

91

should be clean, fine-grained sand. Equal grain sizing makes the sand easier to use. A grain size between 0.09 and 0.6 mm is recommended. The players can maintain a certain degree of dampness by spraying the sand with water. An alternative to sand has recently become available: lighter than sand, it is a workable mixture of sand-coloured sawdust and synthetic materials.

The game folder consists of different coloured badges for the leader and reporter. Also, for each player there is a reporter's sheet as shown in Figure 2. The report sheet is filled in with key words during the course of the game. If the teacher so wishes, a completed report sheet could be used as an example.

The simulation case contains working implements (sand moulds, coloured pens, scissors), models (buildings, vehicles, animals), and materials (cardboard, aluminium foil, polystyrene).

Using the game materials gives the students an understanding of spatial relationships and orientation. Players have to think logically, recognize alternative ways of approaching a problem and find justifiable solutions. In these processes they have to speak to each other. The necessity to explain one's ideas to the other participants and to work as a team breaks down barriers and has a socially integrating effect; it also helps to develop language skills.

The economics-orientated simulation game LOCATION FACTORS— SIMULATED IN THE SANDBOX is divided into two stages of game events.

In stage 1 each group forms a landscape in the sandbox according to their own wishes. For this, the teacher explains to the game leaders, reporters and participants their special functions and introduces them to their roles. The leader co-ordinates ideas, and if a clash of opinions occurs has the right to intervene as referee.

The reporter in stage 1 controls the transactions of the group participants and notes down observations. The participants receive their instructions: build a landscape just as you like. (See Figure 3 on p94.)

Formation of landscape

The players choose whatever aids they want from the simulation case and form a sandlandscape. Students of the University of Mainz built (as Figure 3 shows) hills, lakes, forests, etc. At this stage the wealth of imagination of the participants develops visibly. Hollows in the sand are covered in foil and filled with water to make rivers or lakes; from coloured pieces of polystyrene tree clusters are formed, matchsticks represent fences, painted little strips of cardboard symbolize roads. At this stage players have the freedom to work from their own experiences and observations. In so doing, they practise handling the sand, explore its capacity to be shaped and test their own manual dexterity. Particular demands are made on the creativity of the participants. As a team, players strive to build an original landscape, which serves as the basic model for stage 2.

After the expiry of a pre-arranged period of building time all players begin to fill in the report sheet. According to inclination or talent a drawing or detailed description of the landscape is made. The leader then explains stage 2: the task of establishing an enterprise and searching for a suitable location for it within the landscape formed in stage 1. To facilitate the task, the teacher with the help of the players lists the considerations, which can be set out on the blackboard as shown in Figure 4 on p95.

```
              R E P O R T   S H E E T
        Location Factors – simulated in the sandbox


Name:                          Date: ...............

    player: ......................................

    reporter: ....................................

    other participants: .........................
```

Course of Game Events 1

Drawing of ladscpae or detailed description:

Course of Game Events 2

Type of enterprise: ....

Factors discussed

General atmosphere of game and noteworthy incidents:

Figure 2. *Report sheet*

Figure 3. *A landscape formation in the sandbox*

As a further part of the game each group specifies the nature of its enterprise and discusses suitable sites within the existing landscape in the sandbox. Groups are allowed only to make such changes as would be possible in reality. For example: the construction of an artificial lake, drainage or extension of a river, land levelling, the building of a tunnel, or the construction of an airport.

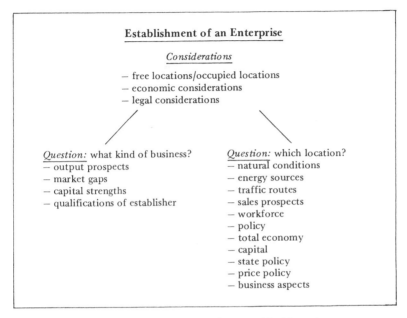

Figure 4. *Notes to be written on blackboard*

Players use the materials in the simulation case to adapt and elaborate their landscape in accordance with the rules. In one test of the game, a group of students placed signposts in the sand pointing towards nearby cities, to indicate the sales markets. They had to make the signposts themselves: they took wooden sticks and bits of cardboard from the simulation case, stuck them together and wrote on the card. Thus, within a short time, a little imagination and dexterity had produced important new definition in their landscape. It is part of the game to justify each change made in the landscape and this has to be recorded on the report sheet.

In the search for locations, the reporters play a constant role. They observe all changes and note them down. They watch particularly to ensure that participants do not demolish arbitrarily existing formations. They intervene in the discussions and present arguments in the public interest. They make sure that the rules of the game are adhered to and note every deviation on their report sheet.

After a further pre-arranged period of time the teacher breaks off the game. Each group places a symbol of its enterprise in the chosen position in the sand. Then each participant fills in a report sheet. All the players inspect each others' achievements. The group leaders in turn explain the course of events in the game in their sandboxes and the group members recount their experiences. In addition, the reporters report their impressions and then finally give a critical commentary about the decisions reached in the game.

At this stage the task of the teacher consists mainly of starting a discussion about insights gained, uncovering mistakes and working out suggestions for improvement. In doing so he or she uses the sandbox as a demonstration medium.

At the end of the discussion the players sit down again and the teacher goes through with the participants the findings gained from the sandbox game. The concluding discussion reinforces what was learnt from the game.

The simulation game LOCATION FACTORS— SIMULATED IN THE SANDBOX can be easily extended or reduced according to the number of participants by increasing or cutting down materials and subject matter or by altering length of time for play. Also, the teacher can introduce new problems at any time into the game with the help of suggestion cards. These cards include, for example, keywords such as bankruptcy, expropriation, natural catastrophe, interest rates raised, building ban, epidemic. Also incidents from the daily newspaper could play a part in the extended game. Such suggestions can encourage groups to choose new locations, and again they have to justify their decisions.

The combination of sandbox and simulation game in class achieves several learning targets, such as types of location factors, their interaction and the resulting clashes of interest as well as related social problems. It does this realistically, in searching for acceptable alternatives and in selecting reasonable solutions.

For a clarification of some specific learning functions, it is worth comparing here the simulation game ISLE OF WIGHT (Naetscher, 1980) with LOCATION FACTORS— SIMULATED IN THE SANDBOX. In ISLE OF WIGHT the task is also the establishing of an enterprise, location factors being taken into consideration. A map in simplified form consists of important orientation points on the Isle of Wight. The island is divided into four parts and players try to find a suitable location for a language school. However, changes in the landscape brought about by construction, demolition or a shift in location cannot be demonstrated using only maps, and here the sandbox has much to offer as a suitable teaching method. Participants have their ideas realized immediately as they build structures in the sand, and then extend or rebuild them as they see fit. In doing so they learn to handle sand and develop other manual skills in the preparation of the additional game materials.

Players recognize very quickly, with support from other members of the group, ideas which are unrealistic and therefore impossible to put into practice. The simulated reality of the sandbox provides innumerable insights and an opportunity for the creative imagination of the participants to flourish.

Emotional-affective learning objectives, such as development and encouragement of persistence and patience as well as attentiveness and concentration, are all present in the sandbox game. These attributes are well demonstrated by participants on occasions when subsidence of the sand makes rebuilding necessary. Communication and social skills are also learned. Shy and reserved students will contribute without embarrassment to the decision-making. In the game students learn to discuss, accept other points of view, show consideration towards each other and make compromises with their fellow participants. The group work has an effect on co-operative behaviour and stimulates team spirit. Comparing the handwork of other participants with their own achievements encourages tolerance, competitiveness and a capacity to reach judgements. Learning to resolve conflicts in the game is an important element which translates to the everyday lives of the players.

The learning game LOCATION FACTORS – SIMULATED IN THE SANDBOX has two elements: work and play. Scheuerl (1973) counts the building with sand as play in its formative character; he recognizes that work and play are not opposites, and that interaction of play and work in lessons should arouse motivation and encourage readiness to learn. For it is the combination of work and play that makes learning fun. The return of the sandbox in schools would be a great contribution to teaching and learning.

References

Naetscher, H D (1980) *Simulation als Lehrform und Entscheidungshilfe zur Berufswahl in der Schule.* Hochschulverlag: Freiburg
Scheuerl, H (1973) *Das Speil.* Baltz: Weinheim

Biographical note

Dr Heinz D Naetscher is lecturer in the Education Department of the Johannes Gutenberg University of Mainz (West Germany).

He studied economics in Vienna and Giessen and first came across simulation in a management game session. After graduating he undertook research work in the field of simulations and games, which led to a book *Simulation zur Berufsfindung,* published in 1980. At present, he is working on a research project concerning the application of simulations in teacher training with particular reference to economics, and is preparing a video film about the use of simulation as a didactic tool in lecturing.

Heinz D Naetscher
Johannes Gutenberg-Universität
Schillerstrasse 11 (Schonborner Hof)
Postfach 39 80
6500 Mainz
West Germany

10. The business game and teaching English as a foreign language

Derek Wright

Abstract: This article is intended to be an introduction to the problems of using games in TEFL (teaching English as a foreign language). A study is made of the background against which such teaching work is done, together with a presentation of the reasons why games have been so infrequently used up to now in this field. It is also hoped to show the non-TEFL-specialists why games are so useful in language teaching, and a short illustration is given on the ways in which one very well-known game —MONOPOLY— can be used in the teaching of business English. The question is also raised of the competence of TEFL teachers to teach business, and to design business games, in that any course in business English almost inevitably requires some basic knowledge of how the business world works. The final question posed is whether TEFL specialists should try to design their own business games, or simply adapt what already exists, with the help of specialists from the different areas of business studies.

Introduction

Although the business game as such has been in use for some considerable time, its regular use in TEFL is a relatively recent phenomenon. Too often it has been relegated to the role of a filler-in, the sort of thing to be used at the end of term, on a rainy day, or even to jazz things up a bit! In a sense, this is a result of the background against which we are working, where game-playing is somehow not a serious occupation, and certainly not one which should appear in the classroom. In addition, as in other areas of teaching, there is almost inevitably an apprehension on the part of many teachers about launching themselves into this field, even though the benefits may be obvious. The need to adapt the material to the class stops some from trying the method, while others feel that they are falling between two stools: they feel they are teaching neither English nor business, and indeed many feel that they are not competent to teach the latter. It is a fact that on occasions the need is felt for advice from a specialist colleague, but this should be an encouragement to develop games rather than to abandon them.

Another difficulty in TEFL is that there are not many, if any, business games designed specifically to teach English. If you are not a language teacher, you may say, 'Does this matter?' The answer, indeed, is, to some extent, 'No'. However, it must be borne in mind that since we are supposed to be teaching English, there are elements in any existing business game which need to be looked at very closely before the game can be used to greatest effect in the teaching of English. And yet, if the teacher of English writes his own business game, he runs the risk mentioned above of either producing a game too clearly aimed at language teaching, or one which does not ring true, since he is not a business studies specialist.

For those readers who are not language teachers, it should perhaps be mentioned here that at one time it was felt to be enough to drill students in commercial/business vocabulary and give them enough expressions, and then, as if by magic, students would suddenly know how to speak business English. English was often taught like any other academic discipline, and the method's efficiency was checked by means of dictation and translation, with a short oral to see how things were shaping up. Whilst this was, and perhaps still is, a valid method at university level with students whose main area of study is the language itself, it does not take account of the needs of the business studies student, for whom language is by no means the major area of study. The idea of encouraging students to talk and to make mistakes, to use the language in context is quite a recent development.

It came to be realized that the language element had to be a secondary one, that the first thing was to get people talking. To do this, the classic language class was useless; what was required was a situation in which the students would not only have to use their English, but one in which they would want to use their English. Like any new development, this has been seen as gimmicky, and I would go along with some of this criticism. But the results—non-specialist students holding long and complex negotiations in English—really do give the lie to such comments. Students with a mathematics or economics background are notoriously bad at English: something drastic and new had to be done.

Having said this, games alone are not enough. The language element obviously cannot simply be dropped, but at least with games it finds its role better defined than with the standard specialist approach. At the level at which I am working (A-level, plus second, third, and fourth years) students have already gone through the classic secondary teaching of English, and do have some idea of the basics of the language. What they are incapable of doing is putting into practice what they have learned, such as grammar and vocabulary. This is where the game comes into its own. It puts the student in a situation where English is simply the vehicle by which his or her ideas are expressed. For most students it is an inadequate vehicle, for they have neither the depth of language nor the feeling for its use which they require in order to convey what they have to say. This is where the teacher/facilitator enters, and this is where the greatest difference with standard teaching practice appears, for now the teacher is needed only for purposes of advice and correction.

I say 'only', but in fact this is an enormous task, which involves not just advising students, but also going through matters such as complex grammar and demanding vocabulary, while at the same time, as always, trying to stay in the background as much as possible.

In any game, situations arise where students have to express their opinions, negotiate and comment on what is happening. This exercise is tremendously beneficial for them, just as is having to say things like 'Hang on a minute!' and 'He's cheating!' and 'It's your turn'. This type of thing seems pretty banal to someone not involved in language teaching, but for the specialist such comments include vocabulary and grammar with which students often have problems in France. In addition, the need to react spontaneously, which is so very hard to do in another language, is encouraged. And by getting the students involved in the running of the game, attention is drawn away from purely linguistic questions and placed squarely on the communications element of language. For business studies students this is essential, for they are learning that what can be done in their own language can also be done in English.

When one talks of business studies, one thinks immediately of the mathematical aspect of the work. This is an inevitable and of course essential part of any such degree course, but it is one which gives the TEFL teacher quite a headache. Learning to count and use numbers generally in another language is one of the great difficulties the foreign student has. If in addition we try to use business games, with the usual mass of figures, then another problem is brought up. In this case, I think one has, if not to admit defeat, then to accept that in some cases calculations are going to be done in the native language. However, I do not think this matters: once again, one has to be pragmatic; we are teaching non-specialists, and we cannot demand the same language levels as with specialist students. Providing that the final details are transmitted orally in English, I don't think one should worry unduly.

A further factor to be considered is that of the relevance of the game to the work in hand. This is an obvious point, but one well worth mentioning, since errors are still being made in this direction. I would not for a minute, as part of my programme, dream of using Shakespeare with my business studies students, even though I like Shakespeare myself and would very much like to see my students take a greater interest in fields other than business studies. Similarly I would not as part of a regular course in English literature, use simulation games such as EXECUTIVE DECISION or ELASKAY. My point here is that part of the teacher's job is to fit the game to the students, not *vice versa*. The need for adapting material is often forgotten, at all levels. It is not only subject matter, but also the degree of difficulty which matters. This is more important than is usually realized, for students who would be prepared to tackle some games, baulk at others because of lack of knowledge or complexity of operation.

The last two points put together (the importance of calculations and the degree of difficulty in most business games) lead me to pose two further questions: is it possible to produce a valid business game in which numbers are not predominant? And secondly, is it possible to design a game in which the degree of difficulty can be modified by the facilitator? My reasons for asking are simply that these are two areas in which I find the greatest problems, although they are sometimes almost equalled by the complexity of explanation required by some games before the students can start playing! Once again, remembering that I am talking about non-native speakers, I think that the non-specialist reader will see the sort of snags we have in getting some games off the ground.

MONOPOLY and language teaching

To illustrate my point, let us take the game of MONOPOLY. Everyone knows and most have played this game, and have fought with the fairly realistic problems which arise of buying property and developing it, collecting rent, negotiating with other players, obtaining a loan from the bank and so on. Although it might be worth noting here that, in purely business terms, it is surprising to learn how often business studies students fail to understand that if you borrow £100, at 15 per cent compound interest, after five years you will have repaid exactly double the initial loan! However, to return to the language element of the game, you may say 'OK so we make sure the students have all the specialized vocabulary they need. Then they can get on with the game.' It is true that students need to know what a loan is, what rent is, what a deed is and so on, but, in addition, they also need to have assimilated these words so as not to have to keep asking how to pronounce a particular word. They must be capable of counting out the numbers on the dice: a simple operation for a native speaker, but one which still creates difficulties even for people who have been studying English for seven or eight years. They have to know how to say: 'It's your turn', 'Wait a minute', and 'I'd like to buy Mayfair'. These are so obvious and so simple — if you are a native speaker. *You* don't have to think about what you say, but a non-native speaker does. What he or she has to learn is how to say these things spontaneously, without searching for the words and above all without using his or her own language. And because games are reflections of what happens in real life, the students are put into a situation where their English is the only means of communicating their needs, requests and requirements.

To appreciate fully how hard this is in another language, try playing any game you know in French, German or Spanish, and you'll get the point soon enough, especially if you lose £10 as a penalty every time you use your own language.

To illustrate briefly the problems involved and to show how MONOPOLY can help the language teacher, here is a short and far from exhaustive list of what you need to know when playing what is, after all, a fairly simple game:

(a) how to count simple numbers from one to 12;
(b) basic commercial vocabulary (rent, purchase, loan, interest, profits, deed, mortgage, property, etc);
(c) how to interrupt play with statements like 'I'd like to buy this property', 'Excuse me but I'd like to build a house here', 'You owe me rent for Mayfair';
(d) how to comment on play: 'He's cheating' (and not 'He cheats', as French students often say, since the use of the continuous present confuses them), 'It's my turn' (with the special intonation needed, and stress on *my*), 'Just a minute', or 'Hang on a minute' (again with special intonation);
(e) how to negotiate a loan (If I borrowed £200 at 15 per cent, how much would I have to pay back?);
(f) how to draw up a simple balance-sheet (a useful exercise being to stop the game after an hour or so, and ask each team to evaluate assets and liabilities, and explain them to others);
(g) how to buy at an auction, a delicate exercise in view of the numbers involved;
(h) how to stay polite ('I'd like...' rather than 'I want...', 'Could/can you pass me...' and not 'Pass me...').

It is clear even from this brief list that a lot can be gained linguistically even from as simple and well-known a game as MONOPOLY, yet how many people use it? Good preparation by the teacher is required, and clear explanation too, so that all rules are well understood at the start (especially if one introduces forms of payment by results such as the fine for speaking their own language). Bearing that in mind, and providing that the students are aware of the linguistic gains to be made, I see no reason whatever for not introducing all types of games into the classroom, whenever the context demands active participation by students. Since this is 80-90 per cent of the time, then it is clear that games have a great role to play.

In language teaching terms, games give people the chance to use their English and to check this usage. Some distinctions between words, the context in which some of them can and cannot be used, the way to express different feelings and desires, are all part of the language learning process, and the learning is enhanced by the use of games.

In all of the above reflections, I have deliberately avoided one rather delicate question, but one which I can no longer avoid mentioning. How does one define the word 'game'? Without getting into a lengthy discussion about the difference between games, role-plays, simulations and so on, I will say that, for me, role-plays and simulations *are* games, but I recognize the need for some sort of working definition of the terms. In my above comments, it was not necessary to saddle myself with a long series of complex definitions. Yet part of the answer to some of the questions raised may well depend on such definitions.

Whatever the answer, I think it worth pointing out that whereas a language teacher can usually produce a fairly acceptable case study involving some form of role-play or simulation, he or she is usually far less successful playing games like EXECUTIVE DECISION. Once the numbers start to creep in and experience of real-life production schedules and runs, investment plans and profit margins, is required, then the language teacher can rapidly find himself or herself in very deep and murky water.

Design or adapt?

When it comes down to actually designing a language-based business game, we often have to produce something simplistic or risk getting out of our depth.

A basic question facing teachers of English as a foreign language arises when you want to motivate 19-24 year-old French business studies students, with an economics or mathematics background, who have little spoken English, who have been through the classic secondary methods of being taught a foreign language, and who for the most part are not specialist students of English. What is to be done?

This seems to identify a basic problem, whatever the nationality. For such students, English is already of secondary importance behind accountancy, marketing, economics, etc. They are imbued with the grammar-mistake syndrome, whereby a sentence must be grammatically correct before it is worth saying. They have invariably learned that the written language is more important than the spoken language (because most exams are written). Trying to persuade people with this type of profile that they, too, are capable of putting across what they want to say, and that they can learn to understand most of what the other person is saying, is the hurdle we have to cross.

I think that by analyzing their needs, in the context of their background, and by working backwards to see how we can suit our teaching of English to their requirements, one comes very quickly to see and appreciate the value of business games in TEFL. If one starts with the premise that the student comes first, then the role of the game is quite clear in teaching business English. What we do need is the help of colleagues in other disciplines in getting the basic context of games clear and in clarifying debatable points.

In the business schools, the need for games is clear, even though they are not used everywhere. Elsewhere, things are not at all clear. For some reason, pragmatism sometimes seems to be a dirty word in higher education, whereas what we are talking about is, in fact, merely putting the knowledge we have to best use, and optimizing the learning opportunities for the student.

Conclusion

Whilst it is often true to say that language teachers often know precious little about the business world, even though they may work with business studies students, it is also true that with motivation, language teachers can understand how business works sufficiently well to be able to teach the language in context. Perhaps all that is needed is for language teachers to adapt and, where necessary, modify and even simplify existing games intended for specialists using their own language. However, we have a need at present in our school, for example, for a good game in the export field, and another in personnel management. Such games may in fact already exist, but whatever the situation I should be pleased to hear from anyone with ideas in these areas. This is after all one of the strong points of SAGSET: bringing people together from many different fields. In this particular case, we can handle the language side, but we need your help with the rest.

Reference

Ellington H I and Addinall E (1978) POWER FOR ELASKAY — a learning package on alternative energy resources for use by science teachers. *School Science Review* 59 209: 747-50

Notes

EXECUTIVE DECISION is published by The Avalon Hill Game Company, 4517 Harford Road, Baltimore, MD 21214, USA

MONOPOLY is published in the UK by Waddington House of Games Ltd, Castle Gate, Oulton, Leeds LS26 8HG; and in the USA by Parker Bros, Salem, Mass 01970

POWER FOR ELASKAY is published by the Institution of Electrical Engineers, Savoy Place, London WC2R 0BL

Other games which can be used in language teaching, providing the students are interested in business-orientated studies, are the following:

BUSINESS STRATEGY and STOCKS AND BONDS, both published by Avalon Hill at the address above

FORTUNE 5000 published by Pressman Toy Corporation, 200 Fifth Avenue, New York NY 10010

NORTH SEA CHALLENGE: three case studies concerning the discovery, development and ultimate exploitation of a North Sea oil field. For students with a good level of English the special language pack is not absolutely necessary. It is published by BP Educational Service, Britannic House, Moor Lane, London EC2Y 9BU

Biographical note

After completing a BA in French (Leeds 1968) and an MPhil in French semantics (Leeds 1973), Derek Wright went back to France to work in the French Business School network. After a year in Dijon Business School, he moved to Le Havre. He has used role-play, simulation and video during this time. As one of five English teachers in the Le Havre Business School, he works mainly at advanced level with both students and adults on in-service training. This team is involved in developing and publishing new material for TEFL and ESP (English for special purposes), and in seminar work on the use of role-play simulations and video.

D W Wright
English Department
Ecole Supérieure de Commerce
1 rue Emile Zola
76090 Le Havre Cedex
France

Part 2: Reflections: Theory, design, use and evaluation of simulation and gaming

11. Real time company simulation for management development

Peter Woolliams and Derek Moul

Abstract: In the traditional business game, course members spend a series of periods in decision-making activities. The decisions are then entered in a computer at a particular time equivalent to, say, a month end. They are then acted upon by a symbolic model in the computer program to produce subsequently printed management (end of period) reports. The authors had previously attempted to minimize the artificial nature of such situations by a series of technical improvements, for example, user-friendliness, 'what iffing?', using the computer to aid decision-making rather than recording (and processing) decisions, and by an open systems methodology. However, the corporate model is essentially frozen until operated upon each period. Thus a major problem of credibility exists because life is not like this. Sales come into an office daily and machines run continuously according to schedules. Decisions are required when trends and circumstances demand them—not when a computer demands them.

The authors have recently developed computer software and associated teaching methodologies whereby the dynamic continuity of the real world can be reflected in simulations. Thus in the 'real-time' models, the computer (ie, each VDU) is continuously displaying actual results (against budgeted results) as they happen. It is the *rate* of change of these factors that is influenced by the decisions of the course members. A comprehensive 'real-time' simulation has already been written and evaluated in the teaching situation (named DYNAMO) and will be described. Positive benefits can be demonstrated from the 'real-time' simulation concept although, interestingly, they are different from those that might have been predicted.

Introduction

This research has attempted to develop new computer software techniques and associated teaching methodologies whereby the dynamic continuity of real world companies can be reflected in simulations for management development.

In the traditional business simulation, as used for management development purposes, the course members spend a series of periods in decision-making activities, which are acted upon by a symbolic model in the computer to produce subsequently printed management reports. Previous attempts at developing comprehensive simulations to embrace all aspects of a company by an open systems methodology have already made a significant contribution to management development. However, the corporate model essentially is frozen until operated upon each period and thus detracts from the situation in which the manager operates.

In real life, sales and operations are continuous, whether the management are in decision-making meetings or not! It is necessary to attempt to model this continuity of activity (eg, throughout a five-day residential period). Thus, each (competing) company's visual display unit will be continuously displaying orders and the consumption of raw materials and finance. The *rate of change* of these factors would be influenced by the decisions of the course members.

A major problem of credibility exists in the traditional business game in the fact that decisions have to be entered in the computer at a particular time, eg, the end of a month, before the model 'comes alive' and acts upon the information. Life is not like that. Sales come in to the office continuously, raw materials are consumed daily, machines run continuously according to schedules, providing they are maintained. The world does not stop, awaiting the decisions of managers, before the business leaps into action; the management of enterprises is a continuous, hour by hour, day by day, week by week activity. Decisions are made when trends and circumstances demand them—not when a computer demands them.

The unique nature of DYNAMO

DYNAMO is a real-time simulation of a packaging company, which has been created especially for management development, and has a number of strategic features in its design which overcome most of the historic problems described above, but in addition it is the first dynamic simulation ever developed on a multi-user micro-computer that recognizes the continuing and changing nature of the management situation.

From the time the micro-computer-based model is set in motion the days tick by—of course, in a one week programme the passage of time has to be condensed—and about every nine minutes the new daily sales and production figures change together with all the other variables that make up a manufacturing and sales system. The manager is therefore in a position to receive and interrogate the computer and get the absolute up-to-date information he or she needs in order to make decisions whenever they are needed, at any time of the month or period.

In addition, DYNAMO incorporates the following original features:

☐ it is entirely micro-computer based
☐ course members with no previous computer experience can easily use the visual display unit
☐ course members can use the computer to help make decisions as well as recording decisions
☐ different groups, with their own VDUs in different rooms, can all access the same micro-computer for different purposes simultaneously.

Simulation methodology and DYNAMO

To put simulation methodology in the perspective of management development processes, it is useful to take the flight simulator as an analogy. A flight simulator is a full-scale model of the flight deck of an aircraft. Through various computer-based programs it is possible to simulate practically all of the conditions that an aircraft is likely to be faced with in operation.

In it, the flight crew are trained to cope with the many simultaneously varying factors that relate to an aircraft in operation—without risk to property and passengers.

The ultimate in management simulations would be somewhat similar: following in-depth research of an organization, a computer model would be built to reproduce accurately the conditions that do and can exist in its markets, factories, administrative systems, etc. By taking managers away from work and providing them with the facility of such a simulation, called a SIME (simulated management experience), they have a powerful opportunity not only for improving their ability to manage but also for experimenting with corporate change, without risk to the enterprise.

The degree to which reality can be simulated in a SIME, for training purposes, is limited by:

☐ the numbers of managers that can be released simultaneously, and
☐ the amount of time available to use the SIME.

In this respect, therefore, DYNAMO has been tailored to meet the needs of a course with between 12 and 40 members over several days. However, it must be recognized that management and, therefore, performance development, is not just getting involved with a simulation. The SIME embraces DYNAMO in an open systems methodology which embraces the real-world sales negotiations for major accounts, the results of which contribute, quite naturally, to corporate performance.

The simulation phases

The simulation is based on several phases:

PREPARATION

The tutor executes programmes to reset the data base for the number of companies competing and defines which companies are operating at each remote VDU.

REAL-TIME SIMULATION PERIODS

These are the equivalent of the decision-making periods of the traditional business game but act in real time. Sales and production are continuously updated, while simultaneously, with the use of the VDU by each company, budgets are prepared and amended and decisions continuously amended and refined.

ACCOUNTING PHASE

At the end of the 'live' real-time period, the tutor executes accounting programmes to convert the accumulated sales and production data to management information.

PRINTOUT PHASE

Printouts are obtained and circulated to companies in preparation for the next real-time period.

Multi-user systems

The facility of a real-time competitive interactive simulation requires the provision of several VDUs on-line, and thus a multi-user system is required. Current low-cost computer technology provides several types of solution:

MULTI-USER BASIC

In this approach, the computer memory contains one copy of the BASIC interpreter and a machine code program called the task controller, and the remainder of the available memory is divided up amongst the users. Of course, input/output interfaces have to be provided for each user's VDU, and appropriate input/output character routines have to be provided for each, including initialization procedures. Each VDU (user) thus has its own allocated area of memory in which resides the program currently being executed by that user, together with any numeric and string variables involved in the computation.

The task controller causes the computer to execute a given number of instructions for one user before jumping to the next and performing the same number of instructions for that user. The computer thus works on each program in turn. Before leaving a user, the controller has to 'remember' the stage that the computation reached in order that it can continue from the same point when it returns. Similarly, before re-starting with the next user, it has to restore the position it reached last time around, so that it can continue. The number of instructions that the controller is set to perform for each user can be set as a parameter. If the value is set too high, the VDUs not actually being serviced appear to go dead and response time is apparently poor. If the value is set too low, the computer spends most of its time saving and restoring the status of each user (generally known as 'thrashing') and little time performing any computation. For any particular specific application there will be an optimum value of this instruction count parameter because of the relative amounts of input/output and computation. It is important that the operating system is 'tuned' for any such specific application. For general purpose applications, in which the system may be called on for a whole range of programs by each user, the multi-user system tuning will inevitably be a compromise.

In order to achieve user-to-user communication other than by writing to and reading from discs, a proportion of memory may also be reserved as a common area. Users' programs can store and retrieve values with this area (by PEEKs and POKEs) and thus pass data between users.

However, using this method only enables hexadecimal values to be continuously converted to and from hexadecimal. As the number of users increases, the memory space available for each user of course decreases and response time becomes poorer. For practical purposes (but depending on the traffic intensity) the number of users is normally limited to eight.

The North Star Horizon can be operated in this way using NORTHSHARE but it requires input/output and other personalizing routines to be provided by the user. A similar system was available for the Cromenco but has been withdrawn in favour of the bank-switch version (see below). The SWTPC 6800 can also be set up in this mode for four users with maximum of 4K for each user under the FLEX operating system.

BANK-SWITCHED OPERATING SYSTEMS

This method requires the capability of being able to turn on and off banks of memory. At any one time, the processor sees only one bank of memory (ie, the one that is on). All other memory is effectively isolated from the processor.

When control is passed to the next bank (user) then it in turn is turned on and the others turned off. Thus, each user is provided with a bank of memory containing a complete copy of the BASIC interpreter as well as that user's programs and variables. A small amount of memory is always left switched on and contains the task controller which performs similar functions, as described above. However, transfer of control from one user (bank) to the next is usually initiated after a given period of elapsed time by an interrupt being generated, rather than after a given number of instructions have been executed. Thus, a hardware clock is used to control the bank-switching. There may be less flexibility for system tuning and this method requires more memory. In other respects this method is more effective since it enables each user to execute different types of jobs. For instance, one user could be running in BASIC and another in PASCAL because each user has effectively total control over the processor in a unique memory for a given period of time. User-to-user communication may be more difficult, unless additional areas of memory are provided which can be used to pass over data from one bank to the next.

The MS16800 micro-computer can be run under SDOS in this mode by using an extra serial interface clock to control the switching. However, this configuration gives poor results, being based on the Motorola M6800 microprocessor which has only one index register. Systems based on the M6809 can be expected to perform better when they are further developed. The Z80-based North Star Horizon and Cromenco family of micro-computers can be set up in this way with excellent results and are based on modified DOS systems.

MP/M is a multi-user/multi-tasking version of the ubiquitous CP/M (control program micro-computer) operating system and potentially provides a transportable system. However, as it is based on the 8080 micro-subset of the Z80 it does not perform as fast as dedicated genuine Z80 systems, like the Hotel Microsystems North Star multi-user re-entrant system.

MULTI-PROCESSOR SYSTEMS

There are a variety of 'network' systems under development in which several separate micro-computers are connected together and share common files/disc drives. For example, CP/M net can be set up to control a master 8080/Z80 micro-computer, connected to several other micros running under CP/M. Another approach, typified by the Cambridge Ring, is where 'packets' of data/instructions are sent around the ring destined for a particular user plugged into the ring.

Various protocols are used to identify senders, recipients and status information. Similar ventures have enabled experimenters to connect APPLEs, RM 380Z micros and others. The MUPET system is somewhat similar and enables several Commodore PETs to be connected to common disc drives via the IEEE bus.

The main advantage of such systems is that each separate user is provided with a complete and separate micro-computer. However, it is usually necessary to dedicate one complete computer to act as the master controller, as this cannot usually perform this function as well as acting for a user. The number of users that can be connected to a 'ring' is only limited by the number of bits in the data packet (by its requisite variety).

Real-time simulation controller

In addition to providing the multi-user operating system, a control program must be written (eg, in BASIC) which performs control operations for real-time simulation based on the following principles:

CLOCK

A simulation software clock, ie, a continuously looping program, exits the loop every period. For a real-time simulation of a 20-day working month in a three-hour session, this would mean a 'clock tick' every nine minutes, approximately. The controller must know which program each user is running (passed over via common memory area) and when or if each user is in an idle condition (flags set): for example, a user, having displayed the current operating plan, is thinking about it rather than actually entering response or amendments. When a user is in such an idle condition, the program controller notes the position of the cursor on that user's VDU and then proceeds to display in a (known) blank area of that VDU the updated dynamic display. Whilst the controller program seizes control of a company's VDU, the controller sends a keyboard lock signal, preventing the user affecting the VDU whilst the controller is producing the dynamic part of the display.When the controller has sent directly to the VDU the appropriate dynamic part of the display, the controller then sends a signal to return the cursor to its position before control has been seized and then sends a keyboard unlock signal.

The above happens virtually instantaneously of course, and, from a user's point of view, there is effectively no interruption in use. The user then either remains at an 'idle' position or makes responses to request other information. During these activities when the user's VDU is actively receiving data directly from its own program/memory area, the controller does not interrupt the transmission because it knows that the VDU is busy. The busy/idle protocol is provided separately for each company's VDU and makes the real-time simulation concept a practical reality.

DYNAMO HARDWARE

The version described herein has been developed for NORTHSHARE but versions are now being prepared for other computer operating systems and environments.

Simulation in management development

There was a time when popular management development programmes generally took one of three forms. They were workshops, a *pot-pourri* of generally related seminars, activities and guest speakers. They focussed on an enhanced understanding of some aspect of management from finance to human aspects, or they were of the 'how to do it' variety —interviewing, negotiating, problem solving, etc. Many such management development programmes are still being mounted, and indeed well attended, but increasingly professional opinion tends towards the view that, although such programmes can be interesting and enjoyable, their main value is that course participants are given the opportunity of a complete change of environment and changed social circumstances, in which to share a new experience.

Something over 10 years ago fashion dictated that all management development programmes should have objectives. These generally took the form of establishing that at the end of the programme the course participants should know something that they did not know beforehand, that they had acquired a deeper understanding or that they had acquired one or other set of skills. Increasing efforts were made to be more precise with respect to the ways objectives were set and objectives tended to start to be differentiated between cognitive and affective varieties. A direct result of the setting of objectives for management development programmes was the move to measure results. Tremendous efforts and a wide variety of techniques from Kelly's repertory grid, through factor analysis and attitude surveys were used to try to determine the effectiveness of the programmes.

The setting of precise objectives, structuring and designing programmes to meet these ends and making efforts to measure results are still seen by perhaps the majority of management development specialists as being fundamental to success.

Unfortunately, all management development programmes where groups of managers are gathered together for a few days or a few weeks away from the workplace suffer from a number of fundamental deficiencies.

THE PROBLEMS OF TRANSFER

No matter how professionally a programme is designed and run, no matter how well the performance of the participant improves whilst on the programme, no matter how much more he or she knows and understands, the fact remains that these accomplishments are related to the course environment and not to the work environment where a job has to be done in difficult circumstances. Revans (1980) has laboured over the years to emphasize that only through action learning in the work situation and reflection on the experience gained can the problems of transfer be overcome.

The practice of management, and the ability to apply what is known to the

work situation, is situational and is contingent upon these peculiar facets that operate on and in the manager's environment. The manager has to apply his knowledge and skills in special circumstances at work, having to deal with a variety of dynamic systems, each of which relates to a greater or lesser extent to each other, and each of which may be the result of a number of variables operating at different periods and with different intensities.

On a management development programme, although probably the same principles of management pertain, the ways in which knowledge and techniques are applied are dependent upon the people and the environment of the programme. They are heavily dependent upon these influences, which are very different from those they have to deal with at work. They are different in pace, level and nature of stress, social relationships, formal and functional relationships, political emphasis, and so on.

Thus what is learned on programmes remote from the workplace can only marginally and conceptually be applied on the return to work, and then only if circumstances are perceived to be such that personal benefit can accrue through their considered application.

WHOSE OBJECTIVES?

What are the objectives of a programme designer, and how do they relate to those of a programme participant? The primary objectives of a professional programme designer may be to make a profit, to enhance a reputation, to obtain job satisfaction or to raise the status of his or her department in the organization as a whole. The secondary objectives of the developer will probably be associated with the interests and performance of the course participant and then only as he or she perceives them. This may seem somewhat unkind to programme developers, and yet it may well be reasonable when one considers how difficult it is to determine the real management needs of a group.

Each manager on a programme has different abilities, different experiences, different strengths and different aspirations. It is not conceivable that, on a programme centrally associated with improving performance, objectives can be set by the programme developer which will satisfy the needs of each participant. What can be done is to design a programme around a model that gives a very wide range of opportunities for managers on the programme to improve in their individual and different ways.

Simulation-based management development

Professionally designed and executed short management development courses have much to offer, and in no way are the preceding comments intended to be unduly critical of the conventional methods. However, our own view is that it is somewhat presumptuous for course designers to emphasize what they feel the experienced manager will achieve on such programmes. Certainly, experienced professionals with a knowledge of their market, and a general knowledge of the educational and training needs of their clients, should set some generally achievable objectives for their programmes, but to try to specify in detail what will be learned is very ambitious.

A more useful basis for course development lies in the use of models as a basic concept of the activity of the course. Action-centred leadership courses based upon John Adair's (1973) leadership model were notable for taking such an approach. A model is selected which is widely recognized as being a useful aid to managers. Then a programme is developed whereby the course members can gain practice in the use of the model and identify, through the experience, areas of personal strengths and weaknesses. Models such as John Adair's leadership model, various problem-solving and decision-making models, planning models and a whole range of behavioural models provide an overall coherence to the activities embraced by the course, give the course member an opportunity to use and validate such models and provide an excellent basis for analysis and diagnosis of areas of strength and weakness.

In addition, and perhaps most usefully, such programmes, designed on the basis of management models, provide each course participant with the opportunity of learning across a wide spectrum of competence. Indeed, managers commonly find that they have learned something in an area of whose existence they had not previously been aware. Frequently they also have significant learning experiences that were not foreseen in the development of the programme (ie, revelatory paradigm). Fundamental to the design of such model-based experimental programmes is the inclusion of as wide a range of feedback techniques as possible, whereby enhanced understanding and reinforcement of learning can take place. Video and peer feedback are powerful tools in this respect, provided they are used effectively.

Experience has shown that reflective learning is an important feedback device. Managers can develop the discipline of reflecting on their experiences on such programmes and be sure that this is one technique they can take back to the workplace with them. If this is combined with the commitment to use models adopted on the programme, this provides a powerful combination which can help bridge the gap between the course and the workplace requirements.

Real-time company simulation

This then provides a learning environment for the basic process of management, that is, planning, organization and control. By preparing budgets and receiving continuously varying and up-to-date information on sales and production, course members can experience 'real life'. By monitoring planned results against actual results, participants are led to variance analysis, and thus the opportunity to refine continuously decisions in the light of variances not previously possible in the traditional business game.

References

Adair J (1973) *Action-centred Leadership.* McGraw-Hill: Maidenhead.
Revans R (1980) *Action Learning: new techniques for management.* Blond & Briggs: London

Biographical notes

Dr Peter Woolliams is a principal lecturer at the Anglian Regional Management Centre having been recently appointed following a period in which he was seconded to ARMC as a computer consultant/lecturer. He has worked extensively in both further and higher education in the management application of computers and as a management consultant in computer based applications. His particular interest has encompassed corporate model building and has more recently developed corporate models for nationally known companies including Berger Paints and Bowater Containers.

Derek Moul is a principal lecturer in strategic planning and improving manager performance at the Anglian Regional Management Centre. Before joining ARMC in 1970, he had been in functional and executive management in the power generation, automotive and medical products industries for some 24 years. He has worked in Canada and the USA, India and Europe on both permanent and assignment bases. He has consulting experience in a range of national international and small companies, in the area of strategic planning and corporate model building.

Peter Woolliams
Derek Moul
Anglian Regional Management Centre
North East London Polytechnic
Duncan House
High Street, Stratford
London E15
England

12. Approaches to designing games which simulate real life organizations

Chris Brand and Terry Walker

Abstract: Maxim Consultants specialize in developing games to aid management training and development and organizational problem-solving. Several games have been designed to simulate the operation of real-life organizations, in both the public and private sector. It is essential that such games capture the essence of the real-life organization and individual players should recognize and experience the actual organization in the game. This paper examines the various approaches used to translate an actual organization into a playable game while retaining its central characteristics.

Introduction

An increasing number of games are being developed to simulate the operation of specific real-life organizations or particular processes within them. They normally aim to aid management training and development, and to facilitate the solution of organizational problems amd the formulation of policy. Maxim Consultants Ltd is a management consultancy specializing in developing such tailor-made games. Clients have come from many backgrounds, including central and local government and private sector companies in financial services, computing, packaging, retailing and catering. Diversity of client backgrounds is

114

indicated to stress that gaming is essentially a technique applicable to widely differing situations. The game designer does not require expertise in the area encapsulated within his games. At the outset, relevant knowledge and expertise normally reside in the client organization itself, or can be brought in.

This paper concentrates on three areas where the game designer's skill is crucial. These are:

(a) Organizational research. The designer must research the 'game area' to acquire relevant knowledge, understanding and expertise to achieve the simulation's objectives.
(b) Creation of an organizational model. This must capture the essence of the organization.
(c) Creation of a viable game form. The organizational model must be translated into a game.

Organizational research

PURPOSE

Games successfully simulating a real life organization need to capture its essence, both quantitatively and qualitatively. For example, when games are designed to aid problem-solving or policy development, participants must recognize the crucial issues, have realistic information available, and experience dilemmas, ambiguities and political pressures similar to those they would experience in the actual organization. In this respect, games have several advantages. They can identify and test potential options without incurring costs of implementing them, generate strategies and options which more traditional analytical processes are unlikely to identify, and predict reactions of individuals to various situations. Decision-making within games also takes place in a low cost environment, away from the pressures of the actual situation.

The game's actual role is as a communication medium. It helps develop participants' understanding of a situation in terms of options, key relationships, major factors, potential consequences, problem areas and priorities. Games do not usurp the decision-making role or organizational management, and predictions made by a game may not occur in practice. This does not undermine their value, but it is necessary to appreciate their proper role and limitations.

RESEARCH PROBLEMS

The central research problems are fairly clear. Organizations possess bewildering amounts of data, much of which is irrelevant or misleading. Information is collected, used and presented without consideration of the game designer's needs. Personnel hold varied and often controversial views, depending on their particular position in the organization. The willingness of individuals to divulge information (even with authorization) and to express value judgements varies tremendously.

The question of confidentiality almost inevitably arises. Maxim Consultants attempt to resolve the issue by stating information needs in advance and ensuring the game is authorized by an executive with power to release it. This does not always solve the problem. Managers often under-estimate how deeply researchers need to probe key issues. They are surprised when important issues are uncovered that they did not want revealed. They are suspicious of researchers' motives, particularly in controversial areas, and question the need for extensive cross-checking to ensure accuracy. Particular problems arise when individuals realize the extent of information revealed in circumstances where they do not understand its precise use. Clear statement of the project's purpose and needs helps to resolve confidentiality issues, but reference upwards is often the only solution.

It is difficult to specify the duration of intra-organizational research. There is a trade-off between the duration (and therefore potential depth) of research and its costs. A medium sized, fairly homogeneous organization could be researched in approximately a week, with additional time required to examine policy statements and operating documents. Geographically dispersed, heterogeneous organizations offering many products and services require greater research effort. Clearly, successful research requires stringent selection, an ability to orientate material towards potential game models and an economy in cross-checking.

Orientation of research

Game research is not 'academic' in nature and rarely requires repeated observations and rigorous testing. The game's designer is rarely seeking precise relationships, exact procedures or aiming to produce a single deterministic model. He is attempting to capture the organization's essence. This involves determining:

(a) major decision points and factors influencing them;
(b) action triggers and their mode of operation;
(c) decision-making levels;
(d) key elements in control systems;
(e) patterns of interrelationships and points of interaction, areas of congruency and conflict in organizational perceptions;
(f) areas of clarity and areas of ambiguity;
(g) the pattern of organizational politics.

The actual list and its overall shape varies with the game and its objectives. Many issues are not defined precisely. The game designer's skill is to get a feel for the organization and incorporate it into the game. This will be supplemented by the attitudes, values and perceptions that participants bring into the game when they play it, and this presents a major constraint in the development process.

Preparation

Stringent selectivity and limited time-scales make it desirable to undertake as much preparatory research outside the organization as possible. There is a surprising wealth of published material available. For example, one game related to a furniture manufacturer. Though the industry mainly consists of small organizations there is no dearth of data. Advertising brochures, price lists, census of production data, company accounts, *Financial Times* reports, and Department of Trade statistics make it possible to construct a fairly realistic picture before entering the company. It is possible to determine its approximate size, turnover, market segment, product range, potential competitors, profitability and approximate wage rates. This provides a useful foundation for in-house research and helps to identify potential game issues. Public sector organizations, being subjected to continuous scrutiny and debate, are often even more fully documented.

In-house research

The success of this research depends on choice of people interviewed, access to relevant documents and careful preparation.

Choice of personnel presents problems because the game designer is at least partially reliant on the client's advice. At an early stage it is desirable to gain an overview, to identify and clarify issues, and to determine areas for further investigation. Chief executives, finance directors, business planners, personnel and training managers can provide this.

Choice of operating documents and reports is also problematical. Key documents like budgets, financial reports, corporate plans, etc, are particularly useful because they illustrate the manner in which financial data are presented, highlight key managerial issues and give a breakdown of costs. The actual existence of other relevant papers and reports may be difficult to determine, unless the author or a person directly affected by it is interviewed. Once identified, most reports are made readily available. Discovering their existence is the major problem.

Distilling the essence

It is necessary to construct a model of the organization before detailed design work is commenced. Potential game formats, possible problems and game issues are considered in the initial design brief, and ideas are modified by research findings.

In most games the final game is very different from the original concepts, and reflects the model of the organization which aims to capture its essence.

Central features of essence are incorporated into a fairly simple quantitative and qualitative model of the organization. Simplicity is vital. The game designer must cut through the mass of research data to produce a limited number of key statements, which reflect and summarize the organization.

Maxim Consultants normally make such statements in value-laden terms so organizational personnel can respond to them. Empirical statements about size, product range, structure, and breakdown of manpower may be accurate, but they are flat and do not capture its essence.

The initial model consists of three elements.

(a) A list of key statements about the organization.
(b) A thumbnail statistical sketch.
(c) A statement of the major constraints affecting the organization.

The example below illustrates the process. A game is being designed for a local authority-run welfare agency where overall policies are determined nationally. Research focussed on a number of county services and the list of key statements below relates to one such service:

(a) Variety. The county provided many services, often in very different ways.

117

(b) Inconsistency. The same service was offered differently across the county.
(c) Written policies. The service had attempted to formalize its policies through a series of papers and working party reports.
(d) Implementation gap. The service had not resolved the problem of translating policy into action.
(e) Autonomy. Areas within the county attempted to maintain autonomy.
(f) Tension. The service operated with considerable tension between its regional and service type components, and between managerial and professional ethics.
(g) No clear priorities. Despite the existence of written policy, priorities were viewed very differently at operational levels.

The thumbnail statistical sketch consisted of a summary budget, percentage cost breakdown and statistics indicating workload trends by major category. Constraints were associated with central and local funding, the role of central government and the service's accountability.

Creation of a viable game

There is no simple formula for translating an organization into game terms. The solution depends on complex interactions between:

(a) The client's needs. These include game objectives, issues to be raised in the game, the potential target audience, confidentiality considerations, time availability for play, and use of material generated in the game.
(b) Organizational characteristics. A large homogeneous organization, marketing and producing a single financial service, needs very different treatment from an organization selling many different products and services to several markets. Public sector, non-market organizations present different game issues from organizations selling goods or services.
(c) Game considerations. Game variables include the core game frame, participant decisions, methods of interaction between participants, provision of feedback, and role of game controllers.

The game designer is attempting to achieve a 'best fit' between these three areas.

Case studies

BACKGROUND

This section provides a case study which illustrates the problems of creating a viable game. It concerns a large financial institution providing a wide range of financial services and credit packages to companies and private individuals. The game covers a division of the organization which markets and supports these services through a chain of high street branches. The concept of a game arose when the measure of accountability and performance of branch managers was changed from turnover to profitability. Managers required a complete reorientation in approach. They did not really understand how factors which they could influence affected profitability. These included the marketing and sales mix, labour deployment, product mix policy, and presentation of particular packages. The game's objectives were to enable participants to explore their area of decision-making discretion, and to help them understand how factors affecting profitability operated. They also needed to explore the range of options available. The game, therefore, helped managers to formulate branch policy.

The central problem was how to translate branches into a game. Market conditions varied by product type, managers controlled over 150 products, while some sales required headquarters' authorization.

RESEARCH

The research attempted to explore a manager's key decisions affecting productivity, and to construct a quantitative and qualitative model of a typical branch. Key decisions included:

(a) Selection of target market group. This had two dimensions. The first covers type of client (whether industrial, service, or consumer) and the second, product types on which credit packages were based (for example capital equipment, buildings, or consumer durables).

(b) Selection of geographical area. Some geographical areas were inherently more profitable than others.

(c) Choice of promotional media. Some forms of promotion generate business more cheaply than others. Options include local press and radio advertizing, mail drops (either generally or to identified groups) and provision of material at points of sale.

(d) Deployment of salesmen. Within limits, managers could employ salesmen and their deployment affected both business and profitability.

(e) Product mix choice. There was a conflict between services which were easy to sell and those which were most profitable.

All of these factors had a direct impact. Others operated less clearly, for instance, size and breakdown of staff affected costs and profitability: if too few staff were available, clients were processed ineffectively, processing was delayed, interests costs to the branch increased and administrative problems were generated.

DEVELOPMENT OF GAME

The research showed that a traditional management game format, with decisions orientated around the above areas, was appropriate. Problems were centred around the simplification and construction of models.

SIMPLIFICATION

The branch was far too complex to model in detail in a reasonable time span. Each area of its operation required considerable simplification. For example, 150 products was far too many for a game. The solution was to take six products reflecting the main managerial options and the main business areas. These gave a sufficient range of its options to capture the central marketing problems. Branches used detailed analysis of staffing, interest, bad debts and overhead costs.

In each case the real-life situation was simplified and cost headings grouped together. For example, non-selling staff were treated as a single group and a single equation (based on workload statistics) used to determine their productive capacity. Each market model underwent a similar simplification process in order to concentrate on major issues.

GAME MODELS

The first problem revolved around the geographic model. A branch required a realistic geographic location with supporting socio-economic demographic detail, and industrial, agricultural and commercial description with associated trends. The current breakdown of business across the geographic area was necessary. This was resolved by examining a number of branches stated as being 'typical' by the client, and producing a fictitious geographic location incorporating characteristics from each.

As target market groups, promotional policies, product mix policies and deployment of the sales force affected turnover, costs and profitability, detailed models were needed which reflected their operation and impact. The company maintained only limited information about each area and did not analyse it in any suitable format.

Available data did enable very broad tolerances to be determined, and the game designers constructed their own models within these.

As a result, a critic might argue that the final game models were rather crude and imprecise, giving a rather inaccurate reflection of reality. This ignores the game's objectives and the information limitations available to real life managers. The game succeeded in helping managers understand their business more effectively. It raised central issues, exposed key relationships, and confronted managers with their own (often implicit) assumptions. The game exposed existing information limitations and the manner which assumed that relationships could affect turnover and profitability (not necessarily with justification). The game can also be modified at a later stage to reflect more accurate information when it becomes available.

The lack of a competitive model is an important omission. This factor was agreed with the client. They argued that variables and factors within the organization's own control were more important than competition, and that it was not necessary to include it to meet the game's objectives.

Situation-based games

Games which examine a particular process such as negotiating or budgeting within a private sector organization and those which simulate public sector, non-market organizations rarely have market models of the type described above. In some cases they might use cause and effect-type models, relating, for instance, to productivity of particular factors, consumption levels or the interplay between economic variables. In other cases they may be based on a situation which provides an initial powerful constraint, but after that players can have relative freedom of action and manoeuvre, and participants' later patterns of play may be dominated by their interactions within loose or even non-existent controls exerted by umpires. For example, in the public sector welfare simulation cited above, participants playing the role of the management team have considerable freedom in determining the review's conduct, the contributions of roles lower down the hierarchy, and the form that participants' decisions should take. The game umpire's role is limited to establishing deadlines, and inputing additional information, though he has a mechanism for intervention if participants are not proceeding with the task.

Conclusions

Games designed to simulate the operation of real-life organizations provide a stimulating challenge for the games designer, and are likely to become a powerful tool in management training, organizational policy development and problem-solving. This development is not restricted to the area of management: parallel activities are taking place, which examine actual political, environmental, social, planning and economic problems through games. As design skills are improved, games are likely to become an increasingly important input in policy-making and problem-solving.

Although such games are similar to other games in style and format, they do present special design problems. Live research is required to capture the essence of a particular organization, and the requirements of this process are difficult to quantify. The game must use a proper and appropriate game frame, and at the same time be realistic to those playing it. The purpose of the game must be remembered. It is essentially a communication device for exploring issues, identifying options and considering consequences. It is not a substitute for managerial decision-making.

Biographical notes

Chris Brand and Terry Walker are currently directors of Maxim Consultants Ltd, a company which specializes in the design of bespoke management games. In the past both authors were senior lecturers in the Management Centre at Brighton Polytechnic.

C Brand and T Walker
Maxim Consultants Ltd
19a Queens Road
Brighton
Sussex
England

13. Managing games and simulations: the user's skills

Lynton Gray

Abstract: This article examines the surprisingly neglected question of the skills and attitudes needed by successful users of games and simulations. After considering published opinions on the competence looked for in simulation users, the relationship between teaching competence and the skills of the simulation user is examined. It is suggested that the skills required by the latter should include organizational, listening, evaluative and political skills, as well as a capacity for detachment. The article concludes by examining the particular problems of group-managed simulations and the training of trainers.

Introduction

Amongst the growing wealth of literature on the uses of games and simulations, there is a surprising lack of discussion of the knowledge, skills and attitudes required by teachers and trainers using gaming and simulation, in generic rather than specific terms. And the little material that is available tends to be of the 'tip for trainers' variety, based on the hunches and prejudices of game designers. This article attempts to stimulate some initial ideas on the types of skills, knowledge and attitudes needed by the competent user of games and simulations. Reference is made particularly to simulations and games in management education and training, but the analysis is at a sufficiently general level to be applicable to their uses in other contexts, or at least to suggest some guidelines whereby the skills, knowledge and attitudes required in contexts very different from management education might be considered.

The article is arranged in four parts. The first considers the available literature on the capabilities expected of the teacher and trainer, and its applicability to the user of games and simulations. The second focusses upon the requirements sought by games designers in games users, and the capabilities implied therein. The third looks more specifically at simulation management in two kinds of situation — where a single teacher or trainer is using a simulation, and where the simulation is managed by a group of trainers. Finally, some suggestions are made on ways in which simulation users might be prepared, trained and developed to ensure their competence in the testing tasks of managing games and simulations. The emphasis throughout is upon the simulation *user*. There is already a wealth of advice for game designers (for example, Shirts, 1975; Megarry, 1976; Mitchell and Schmid, 1980; Ellington and Addinall, 1977) and the article tries to keep out of that territory. It does, therefore, make the basic assumption that, although many teachers and trainers are both designers and users of simulations, quite different capabilities are employed in the two activities.

Teaching skills and the simulation user

Enthusiasts for and designers of games and simulations have long urged their uses as significant parts of programmes of learning. As has frequently been pointed out (for example, by Boocock and Schild, 1968) initially such exhortations were based on no more than a blind faith that they would improve the learning process. This was later qualified by some disillusionment that a panacea for all teaching and learning problems had not, after all, been discovered, to be followed by a more realistic estimation that some benefits are likely to accrue from the use of games and simulations. However, attempts to evaluate just what these benefits might be seem to date to have been even less successful than attempts to evaluate outcomes of other forms of teaching and learning. In consequence, the early enthusiasm for research and evaluation in the field of games and simulations seems to have evaporated, although Stadsklev (1981) does suggest that interest in evaluation is growing again in the United States. In general, evaluation exercises have usually identified a high level of enjoyment engendered in groups using games and simulations, but there has been little evidence that such recreational benefits have been matched by educational ones.

A central problem has been the absence of measures whereby the competence of the simulation user can be assessed. Designers of games and simulations have, in exhorting their uses, assumed either that users will be competent teachers and trainers, able to add simulation to their existing repertoire of teaching skills, or that simulation can be employed by anyone, because it is, essentially, a learning process rather than a form of teaching. This is in line with the prevalent attitudes to preparation for teaching and training, which, until very recently, have given little thought to any capabilities expected of a teacher or trainer other than the cognitive ones of knowledge of the subject to be taught. Hence it is only in the last decade, and in spite of considerable opposition, that we have begun to require that all new entrants to the school-teaching profession in maintained schools in England and Wales should be professionally trained. It is still possible to teach in private schools—and indeed in certain 'shortage' subjects in maintained schools—without any training at all. Only a minority of teachers in universities, polytechnics and further education colleges in England and Wales have received professional training, and in industrial training organizations, trainers are rarely trained in any formal sense other than the time-honoured method of 'sitting next to Nellie'.

As recognition that initial training is necessary before letting teachers loose upon students is still largely confined to the maintained school sector, it is not surprising that there is, as yet, little consensus as to the corpus of knowledge, skills and attitudes which characterizes the successful teacher. It is only within the last decade that teacher-training institutions have attempted to identify these at all in anything more than restricted cognitive terms. Some programmes of professional training have been developed, both in Britain and in the United States, which are based upon the systematic development of specified teaching skills. In support of these, skill acquisition techniques have been developed, such as micro-teaching (Brown, 1975). Simulations and games have themselves been extensively employed in the development of such skills, through the use of role-play exercises, simulated classrooms, in-basket and critical incident techniques (see, for example, Taylor and Walford, 1972; Wragg, 1974).

Examination of the teacher-training literature, while hardly prolific in its analyses of pedagogic skills and capabilities, would seem to permit the identification of some basic skill areas. In view of the multiplicity of theories of teaching and learning, it might be anticipated that an equivalent profusion of appropriate pedagogy would result. However, the issues most fiercely debated by protagonists of one or other of the currently fashionable ideologies tend not to concern the skills used by teachers. Rather, they focus upon either the deployment and purposes of such skills—goal issues—or on the measurability of such skills—assessment issues.

Thus, the controversy surrounding the competency-based teacher education movement (CBTE) in the United States in the 1970s focussed primarily upon whether the identified teacher 'competencies' were measurable, and could be related to specifiable learning outcomes. Even the fiercest opponents of CBTE did not take issue with the capabilities identified by its advocates as basic to the process of competent teaching. Indeed, it is difficult to take exception to these basic teaching skills, so generally are they cast.

Weigand *et al* (1971) identified seven basic skills—preparing performance objectives, question asking, creativity, sequencing instruction, evaluating student progress, assessing intellectual levels, and human interaction. Allen and Ryan (1969), in preparing the Stanford micro-teaching programme, recognized 14 teaching skills, but these have been simplified to five by Wragg (1974), namely

> *questioning* — fluency in asking questions, probing, higher-order and divergent questions
> *starting and finishing* — set induction and closure
> *interest and variety* — stimulus variation, illustrating and use of examples
> *communication* — lecturing, completeness of communication, non-verbal cues, planned repetition
> *sensitivity* — recognizing attending behaviour, reinforcement of children's participation.

Cohen and Manion (1981) note 11 aspects of instructional behaviour. These are the organization, questioning, clarity, structuring, use of praise, use of criticism, use of non-verbal approval, enthusiasm, flexibility and variety, personality and use of pupil ideas by the teacher.

It is difficult to disagree with a statement that a teacher or trainer ought to be able to undertake all of these behaviours competently. It is a very different matter to agree just what is meant by 'competence'. The complexity of attempting so to do was underlined recently in a study (Cruikshank *et al*, 1979) which took one of these behaviours, teacher clarity, and by the use of pupil responses, demonstrated that it comprised a very wide range of different teacher behaviour.

Not only is it difficult to identify teacher behaviour which demonstrates competence in particular teaching skills, it also does not follow that possession of such skills can promote learning success. Not only are cognitive aspects of teaching ignored, but it has been cogently argued that the key to teacher effectiveness is knowledge of the informal group dynamics amongst learners (Hargreaves, 1975). Another body of research has focussed upon teacher attitudes towards learners as the key to effective learning, shaped by teacher expectations (Rist, 1970).

A further weakness of the studies of teaching capabilities is that they have not been related to the different methods of teaching employed. Even where training programmes have included games and simulations, they have not assumed that those thus trained would necessarily have developed skills which enable them to make successful use of simulation as a mode of teaching and learning. There is no available evidence to suggest that any of the teaching skills indicated above are of particular relevance to simulation users. Nor is there evidence to indicate that those teachers and trainers considered competent in the skill areas above would, necessarily, be capable users of simulations. The congruence of simulation use and the application of other teaching/learning methods has not as yet been explored.

The expectations of simulation designers

One way of approaching this problem is to examine the expectations of the designers of games and simulations, to consider the skills expected in competent users to assure successful simulation operation. However, it would seem that designers have given little or no thought to issues of user competence. It is commonly assumed that the capable teacher is thus a capable simulation user. Or else it is considered that the use of games and simulations is a learning process whose effectiveness is reduced by teacher intervention, and which therefore makes no demands on teaching skills. Indeed, some designers suggest that teaching experience and competence can be antipathetical to successful simulation use. Thus Jones (1981, p66) states that:

> the first job of the novice [simulation] controller is to shake off any inappropriate habits or thoughts derived from the experience of teaching or instructing. The main part of every simulation, the interaction, is not taught. By training and by habit teachers interrupt, guide, explain, give hints, smile, frown, and in many subtle ways (including silence) try to help students learn. But if a teacher tries to do this in a simulation, it stops being a simulation and becomes a pseudo-simulation or guided exercise.

The implication here is that the successful simulation user needs very different capabilities from the successful teacher. However, closer examination indicates that this view derives from a very restricted concept of the teaching process and teaching behaviour. Stadsklev (1980) succinctly identifies the central problem:

> Many teachers are afraid to use simulation games and other autotelic inquiry techniques because they are fearful of giving control over to students; and as teachers they lack the skills and techniques necessary to conduct a simulation game experience and facilitate an effective and meaningful debriefing session.

Teachers whose capabilities are restricted to didactic modes of teaching are those who cannot cope with the demands made by simulation use. The skills required in the latter capacity are rarely spelled out, but Jones (1975) offers one of the more comprehensive sets of guidelines in his communication skills simulations for secondary schools, produced originally for the Inner London Education Authority. His controller's notes inform users that:

> Your role, as Controller, is easy. It is your job to introduce the simulation. Once this is done it develops a dynamic momentum of its own. You don't 'teach' the simulation, you don't take part in it, you don't interfere,...you should not teach, but allow participants to exercise full adult responsibility, and that includes making their own mistakes.

Jones gives further advice to teachers on organizational problems, coping with pupil misbehaviour, and the distinction between active learning through simulation and other forms of 'passive' learning.

It is clear that this is a modern and specific version of the age-old dichotomy between the teacher as pedagogue and fount-of-knowledge, and the teacher as facilitator and manager of learning. The qualities of the successful simulation user are prescribed at some length in a recent book on simulations (Jones, 1981). As specified they amount to little that would be challenged by any exponent of experiential teaching and learning. Detachment, observational skills, presentational skills, and timing are prescribed along with the 'teaching' skills needed for briefing and de-briefing. The only area of controversy would seem to be the claim (Jones, 1981, p11) that:

> a simulation is not teacher-student oriented. The participants have powers and responsibilities, and the controller has none of the attention and tension of teaching, but has a more relaxed function — well suited to observing what is going on.

Any suggestion that the use of simulations is a more relaxed, tension-free form of activity than 'teaching' does not accord with the author's experience or that of other experienced teachers who make extensive use of simulations!

In summary, it would seem that the simulation user requires the skills of the didactic teacher in the preparation and briefing of simulation activities, and the skills of interactive, experiential teaching in operating and debriefing the simulation. This is not particularly helpful unless the use of simulation is analysed more deeply, to discover whether there are more interactive teaching skills which are of particular importance for competent simulation management, and others, which need to be exercised at a higher level of competence in simulation use than in other modes of teaching. These questions are examined in the next section, in the context first of the single teacher or trainer using simulation, then of the larger-scale simulation operated by a group of trainers.

The teacher, teaching skills and the successful simulation

Analysis of the skills used by a teacher or trainer when using simulations would seem to some to be an unnecessary exercise. This is the view of Suddaby (1976), who claims that 'if a teaching technique is to be evaluated, its benefits must spring from its inherent structure, and not rely on the variable skill and expertise of the operators'. Hence his critical analysis of simulation games makes no reference to the capabilities required by users, in spite of his recognition of evidence suggesting that teaching effectiveness is due to the qualities of the teacher, rather than the specific teaching technique (Morrison and McIntyre, 1973). And of these qualities, enthusiasm would seem to be a prime requirement.

Is it enough, then, to look for enthusiasm in a teacher in order to ensure successful use of simulations? Experience, occasionally of the bitter variety, more commonly of a milder but still chastening form, would suggest otherwise. There do seem to be certain teaching skills, which, while desirable in most forms of teaching, are quite indispensable when using simulations. And there are other skills which are more likely to be required when using simulations than in other modes of teaching/learning.

In the first category come a range of organizational skills. While necessary in all forms of teaching, games and simulations make organizational demands of a peculiar intensity. The preparatory organization requires a particular thoroughness, if only because much of the impact of a simulation is dissipated, should interruptions and interventions become necessary in order to remedy organizational deficiencies. And the structure of many simulations requires the careful organization of environment, participating groups and materials—often of some considerable complexity—as well as the phased or selective distribution of materials and other resources during the simulation. Few, if any, other teaching techniques require, and are so dependent upon, the thoroughness of teacher organization, both before and during the teaching/learning experience. Jones (1981) describes quite graphically the disruptive impact of what, in other teaching situations, would be quite minor organizational hiccups—the loss of, or delay in obtaining a piece of documentation, or an appropriately arranged classroom. In management training such organizational skills are of vital importance when a simulation's success is largely dependent upon the acceptance by participants of the reality of simulation materials and close approximation of the simulation environment to the actual managerial world it aims to model.

Another group of teaching skills of especial importance in simulation and gaming are those which involve listening to and making use of participant ideas, opinions and perceptions. A particular sensitivity here is required, in that the success of many simulations depends in part upon the non-intervention of the controller-teacher for the action phase of the exercise, yet the final de-briefing stages are very largely dependent upon the ability of the teacher to have monitored discreetly the activities, views and intentions of participants. Management training simulations commonly involve the exercise in a safe and controlled environment of identifiable managerial capabilities. The controller thus needs to be able to have observed the ways in which the simulation facilitated the demonstration of such capabilities, in order to conclude the simulation successfully. Yet the trainer-trainee relationship in such exercises is sensitive to trainee perceptions of appraisal by the trainer, such that the effectiveness of the simulation is likely to be considerably reduced should such monitoring intrude upon the 'game reality'. Here again, while all teaching situations require sensitive use of trainee ideas and perceptions, these are not usually acquired as discreetly and as partially as in simulations, making particular demands upon the skills of the teacher.

A third area, where teacher and trainer skills are of particular importance in simulation and gaming, is that of evaluation. All teachers and trainers evaluate in some way the impact of their teaching, however subjectively or partially this might be. Simulations present real problems for teachers in this aspect of their work. The difficulties of evaluating outcomes have already been touched upon. Teachers do not have, therefore, the subjective and objective means for assessing outcomes available in some other forms of teaching. Lack of control over the learning process combines with ambiguous objectives and unclear criteria for assessment in this form of learning, to make it difficult for a teacher even to guess at the kinds of impact which the simulation has had upon participants. The enthusiasm commonly generated by simulations amongst participants can itself obscure the evaluative process. For a simulation's considerable success in meeting recreational objectives—intended or otherwise by the trainer—can make it all the more difficult to judge whether or not educational objectives have been achieved.

Long (1969) drew upon the work of John Morris at the Manchester Business

School some years ago, in drawing attention to the relationship between teaching methods and objectives. A spectrum of training objectives, from knowledge at one end, through skills, social skills and interpersonal skills, to self-understanding at the other, is juxtaposed with a spectrum of teaching methods and learning situations, from the printed word through lectures, discussion, simulation and T-groups to 'experience' at the other (see Figure 1). The areas of congruence between methods and objectives, while simplistic, are related to the extent of feedback in the teaching-learning process. The concomitant of this, however, is that those teaching skills which facilitate such feedback are more important in some teaching methods than in others; and this suggests a rationale for the importance placed upon organizational, listening and evaluative skills above. For

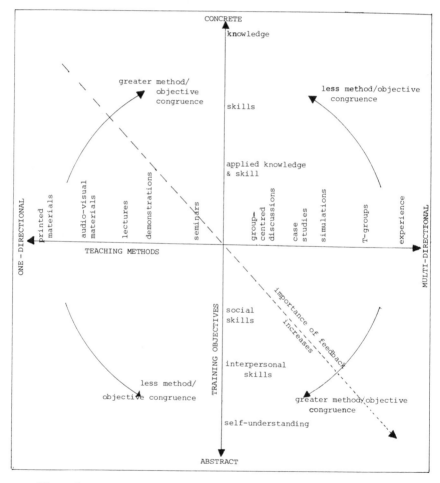

Figure 1. *Teaching methods, learning objectives and the significance of feedback (after Long, 1969)*

these are precisely the capabilities necessary to acquire and make use of such feedback as is a crucial feature of learning through simulations and games.

The second category of teaching skills referred to above is that of skills and qualities likely to be needed in using simulations, but not necessarily in other modes of teaching. Prime amongst these are the qualities of detachment, which enable teachers to relinquish control over the teaching-learning process during the course of the simulation, and thus for a significant — even major — part of the total time available for teacher-student contact. Such detachment is by no means a negative lapse into the 'relaxing, tension-free' period mentioned earlier. Rather it demands not only the self-control to resist all temptations to steer, encourage, alter and intervene in other ways in the development of the simulation, but also the readiness to allow learning activities to develop in directions never intended or even envisaged by the teacher, and, for school teachers at least, the acceptance of pupil noise and behaviour patterns that might well not be approved of by colleagues. For it is by means of such detachment that participants are freed from trainer control to manage their own learning. And it is through such self-management of learning that simulation is able to build upon the existing capabilities of participants, in order that they might acquire, practice, and reinforce new and higher levels of skills, in an environment where mistakes can be made safely and failures do not carry a cost. In management training, where the developing competence of participants cannot be pre-determined by the trainer, such detachment and participant independence is of crucial importance. For trainers the problem is compounded by the need to combine detachment with sufficient enthusiasm to ensure student motivation, given the earlier comments on teacher enthusiasm as a prime influence upon student learning.

The other important skill area demanded when using simulations, but not necessarily in other forms of teaching, is that of political capability. This is rather different from the communication and other interpersonal skills required by every competent teacher. The nature of simulation and gaming creates an atmosphere quite different from other forms of teaching and learning, in which participants can, in consequence of the very independence central to the process, feel unprotected, threatened and manipulated. The removal of dependence on the teacher throws participants into situations where they can become dependent upon, or attempt to establish dominance over, fellow participants. It is the responsibility of the teacher to ensure that participation is a beneficial experience for all, and that no individual is exploited in ways from which he or she might not benefit: a difficult and delicate task in view of the teacher's withdrawal from a position of authority.

Simulations share, to some extent unfortunately, the rather unsavoury reputation acquired by forms of experiential learning such as T-groups and encounter groups. Hauser (1977) has commented on the consequential ethical problems, and the fears of manipulation and destructive conflict. His solution was to seek a code of conduct for simulation gamers. Without decrying such an aim, it would not seem to address the central problem here, which is not that most simulation users are Machiavellian manipulators, taking advantage of the simulation to generate unhealthy conflicts; but rather that they lack the political skills to cope with simulations which manifest conflicts and exploitation, which inhibit effective learning by some group members. This is hardly surprising. The usual teacher-student or trainer-trainee relationship carries with it authority connotations which make the exercise of political skills unnecessary. However, as has already been noted, the exercise of such authority during a simulation exercise would normally be counter-productive. Hence the teacher needs to be both astute enough to perceive potential problems, and skilled enough to be able to defuse them, through persuasion, negotiation and related strategies. In management training, the use of simulations is a particularly likely source of potential dysfunctional conflict; while, given the ubiquity of political activity in the world of management, it is important that this is reflected in simulation exercises designed to model that world. It is even more important that trainers are able to cope with the consequences.

Group skills and simulation management

So far, the assumption has been that a single teacher or trainer is using simulations. However, there are many simulations, both in management training and elsewhere, which depend upon a team of trainers for their effective operation. One of the best known and most used examples is the Open University's social science foundation course summer school exercise SIMULATION OF AN INTERNATIONAL SITUATION, which must have been experienced by many thousands of Open University students. In exercises such as this, the team of controllers is assembled on the basis of complementary academic fields of knowledge. Yet the complementarity of skills and attitudes is, from experience, far more important. The success or failure of an exercise can depend less upon the simulation materials and structure than upon the team's skills and compatibility. A new range of capabilities now become important. Leadership and followership skills play a vital part in team effectiveness, for tensions within the controlling team are soon picked up by participants, usually with deleterious effects upon the simulation's success.

Without criteria for assembling a team with complementary skills, one response to resultant problems is to attempt to structure the simulation so as to minimize trainer autonomy. The Open University simulation referred to above evolved with an increasing body of instruction and advice for controllers, even to the extent of attempting to structure humour into the debriefing sessions. Needless to say, such a response is likely to be met by resistance, as controllers perceive that they are being de-skilled, to become technicians rather than teachers; and also perceive a threat to their academic freedom.

A more positive approach might be to attempt to use the accumulated knowledge of group dynamics (eg, Handy, 1976; Rackham and Morgan, 1977), and thus to assemble a team with compatible skills and attitudes. Thus Handy uses the categories of strong fighter, friend and helper and logical thinker when looking for the characteristic roles within an effective group, and this provides an indication of the range of capabilities which, if brought together, are likely to facilitate group effectiveness. The first-hand experience of working together within such a group can only facilitate the achievement of those simulation objectives which look for greater understanding of group processes— common aims of many management training activities.

Training the trainers — preparing for more effective simulation management

This final section looks at some of the implications of the analysis of trainer skills, and makes some proposals for training programmes for teachers and trainers, particularly in areas where it is assumed that a significant part of the teacher's work will involve the use of simulation and gaming. This, naturally, includes the preparation of those involved in management training.

An initial assumption is that any such training should be based upon the identification of the capabilities and qualities required of a competent teacher or trainer. Appropriate training techniques should then be selected to facilitate the acquisition, development and reinforcement of such capabilities. While this would not exclude cognitive inputs, the emphasis would be predominantly experiential, using the training model outlined earlier. And simulations and games would, naturally, play an important part in such training, both as modes of learning and as areas of study, although the learning model does not permit an easy distinction between the two in practical terms.

The organizational skills, the capabilities involved in listening to and building upon student ideas and perceptions, and the skills of evaluation should obviously be prime elements in any programme of teacher training. Equally, real, simulated and abbreviated (eg, micro-teaching) teaching experiences should be employed in developing the necessary competence.

The qualities of detachment and the political skills referred to earlier would seem to require rather different developmental approaches from the previous group. To some extent they run counter to the conventional teaching capabilities. Hence training approaches would need to begin by analysing existing trainee attitudes, identifying possible obstacles to the development of these distinctive teaching qualities, and using learning approaches which contain within them potent demonstrations of the value of such qualities. Inevitably simulation and gaming would form a major part of such training. One interesting example of the use of simulation in the development of political skills is Laver's (1979) attempt to develop a sequential series of games which 'distil some of the essence of...real political interactions'. While these deliberately ignore the ethical issues raised by Hauser (1977) and referred to earlier, it would be hard to envisage a training programme which, if it used these materials, did not have to face up to the morality of so doing. Similarly, the ideas and associated games of Christie and Geis (1970) in their studies of manipulative behaviour and 'machiavellianism' are of value only in the hands of a skilled trainer, who is able both to cope with the potential conflict and exploitation, and to heighten the sensitivity of trainees to the ethical issues inherent in such studies.

Any advocacy of reform should include consideration of the practicalities of implementation. Simulations and games are but one of a number of teaching approaches, each of which has its own advocates and enthusiasts. If users of games and simulations accept the argument here that particular capabilities are desirable in those who make use of these approaches, it still remains necessary to influence those with responsibility for the training and development of teachers and trainers. It would seem logical that the national and international professional associations and learned societies concerned with simulation and gaming, including SAGSET, have some responsibility here. Through dialogues with teacher-trainers, through directly provided workshops, through the provision of appropriate training materials, and through the encouragement of other providing bodies, it should be possible to improve the quality of initial and in-service training. Key objectives might be:

(a) that trainers should be able to identify when simulation and gaming is an appropriate teaching and learning approach;

(b) that they should be able to design or select appropriate simulation and gaming materials;

(c) that they should be equipped with the necessary capabilities at a sufficient level of competence to make effective use of such materials;

(d) that they should be aware, and able to make participants aware, of the ethical issues involved in the use of such materials;

(e) that they should be able to integrate the uses of simulation and gaming within a broader and coherent training programme.

The issues discussed here are by no means exclusive to the sphere of management training and development. However, it is in this area that there is a particularly acute need for some resolution to the problems implied above. The 'credibility gap' between trainer and practitioner is notoriously wide in management development. Trainer credibility is thus particularly dependent upon professional competence, measured through the perceived impact of training programmes and the demonstrable purposiveness of such provision. Managers and trainee managers are an acutely perceptive and critical occupational group. Simulation and gaming is a powerful tool in the training of this group, but its purposes need to be made obvious, its outcomes identifiable, and the competence of its users above reproach. These ambitious goals are only likely to be attainable if there is a shift in emphasis amongst those professionally involved with simulation and gaming, from design to effective use.

References

Allen D and Ryan K (1969) *Micro-teaching.* Addison Wesley: Reading, Mass

Boocock S S and Schild E O (1968) (eds) *Simulation Games in Learning.* Sage: California

Brown G (1975) *Micro-teaching.* Methuen: London

Christie R and Geis F (1970) *Studies in Machiavellianism.* Academic Press: London

Cohen L and Manion L (1981) *Perspectives on Classrooms and Schools.* Holt, Rinehart and Winston: London

Cruikshank D R *et al* (1979) Clear Teaching: What is it? *British Journal of Teacher Education* 5 1

Ellington H and Addinall E (1977) Systems Approach to Development. SAGSET *Journal* 7 1

Handy C (1976) *Understanding Organizations.* Penguin Books: Harmondsworth

Hargreaves D (1975) *Interpersonal Relations and Education.* Routledge and Kegan Paul: London

Hauser R (1977) The Ethics of Gaming. SAGSET *Journal* 7 4

Jones K (1975) *Nine Graded Simulations.* No.1 SURVIVAL, first published by ILEA, now published by Management Games Ltd: Bedford

Jones K (1981) *Simulations: A Handbook for Teachers.* Kogan Page: London

Laver M (1979) *Playing Politics.* Penguin Books: Harmondsworth

Long B (1969) A theoretical model for method selection. *Industrial Training International* 11

Megarry J (1976) Ten further 'mistakes' made by simulation and game designers. SAGSET *Journal* 6 3

Mitchell D and Schmid R (1980) Using instructional algorithms to design instructional games. In Race P and Brook R *Perspectives on Academic Gaming and Simulation* 5. Kogan Page: London.

Morrison A and McIntyre D (1973) *Teachers and Teaching* 2nd edition. Penguin Books: Harmondsworth

Rackham N and Morgan T (1977) *Behaviour Analysis in Training*. McGraw-Hill: New York

Rist R G (1970) Student social class and teacher expectations. *Harvard Educational Review* **40**

Shirts G (1975) Ten mistakes commonly made by persons designing educational simulations and games. SAGSET *Journal* **5 4**

Stadsklev R (1980) Why aren't teachers using more simulation gaming techniques? *Simulation/Games for Learning* **10 4**

Stadsklev R (1981) Evaluation revisited. *Simulation/Games for Learning* **11 1**

Suddaby A (1976) A critical analysis of simulation games. SAGSET *Journal* **6 3**

Taylor J and Walford R (1972) *Simulation in the Classroom*. Penguin Books: Harmondsworth

Weigand J (ed) (1971) *Developing Teacher Competencies*. Prentice-Hall: Englewood Cliffs

Wragg E C (1974) *Teaching Teaching*. David and Charles: Newton Abbot

Biographical note

Lynton Gray has worked at the Anglian Regional Management Centre since 1978, his career having progressed from teaching in various schools via college of education, and his areas of interest from geography, through educational technology to education management. In each of these phases he has been substantially involved, since the mid 1960s, in the design and use of games and simulations. Current concerns for the management of primary schools and of technical education have involved periods as lecturer and consultant in India, Egypt and the United States, and a major contribution to the NATFHE Handbook *College Administration*.

Lynton Gray
Education Management Division
Anglian Regional Management Centre
North East London Polytechnic
Duncan House
High Street, Stratford
London E15 2JB
England

14. Using the neighbourhood action packs

Tony Gibson

Abstract: The problems of communication between professionals and lay people have been tackled by the development of three-dimensional models, to provide a focus for discussion. These developed into resource packs, enabling groups to model their own environments and thus explore possible alternatives. Other simple devices involve the use of cards for exploring feasibilities.

Introduction

Gaming probably appeals more to those, like me, whose lives are spent partly in academic ivory towers, than to those who are working away at the coalface far below. I learned this early on when I was asked by the Department of the Environment to use techniques I had developed in schools, but to apply them as means to effect neighbourhood action, by residents of all ages, to improve the environment, consult with local authorities, and establish a working relationship in which different sections of the community could use a common language.

The language problem

The language problem was central. In the mid 1970s, when the Government was legislating to give residents a greater say in the management of housing estates, the formation of co-operatives, and participation in formulating local plans, both sides confronted each other across a 'communication gap'. The deputy director of a borough housing department told me, more in sorrow than in anger, 'I have redrafted this circular 12 times, and the residents still don't understand!' As for the residents, their response to invitations to participate was met by the establishment of innumerable talking-shops in which the professional talkers (mainly the local authority representatives) always won.

Techniques used

The techniques I had been developing made use of three-dimensional table-top models and layouts. The models portrayed everyday problems realistically: what to do about derelict space on an estate; how best to convert a disused pub into a social centre. A group could cluster round the model, see things as a whole, explore possibilities together. On the waste site they could arrange and rearrange scraps of card representing, on the same scale, the improvements they might want to introduce – zebra crossings, adventure playgrounds, access roads for refuse vehicles, police foot patrols, sheltered housing. The model pub had movable non-loadbearing walls, and there were clip-on additions to create kitchen hatches, fire doors, toddlers' toilets. These materials enabled people to *show* each other what they meant, not merely talk about it. You need very little command of words to back up your ideas when at the same time you can point things out, or make a physical rearrangement to illustrate what would happen if this or that innovation were to be tried. Earlier experience in some 200 classrooms in junior, middle and secondary schools in England and Scotland, using such materials over periods of up to a year, had shown that, to the 'surprise' and 'amazement' of many of the class teachers, the interest of the children and their staying-power were mobilised over a very wide age and ability range: from IQs of 135 to under 70, from nine year-olds to sixth formers. This seemed to be because the materials were a catalyst, turning a mixture of individual abilities into a purposeful compound. People were concerting ideas, pooling experience, saying things to each other with their hands as well as their tongues.

The resource packs

The first resource packs developed for use by tenants' associations and other neighbourhood groups were based on real situations which I had observed for myself. But for the users they were no more than dummy runs. The pack materials enabled a user group to put themselves in the shoes of people who had experienced a particular problem/opportunity, and then work out what they would have done. But one tenants' association in Dalmarnock, in the east end of Glasgow, decided that this did not go far enough. They wanted the 'try-out' directly related to their own neighbourhood, so that whatever they planned could be 'for real'. Between us we devised a pack which enables any group anywhere to make an instant model of their own neighbourhood, assembled in 2'x4' sections so that a layout around 8' square can represent half a square mile of their own immediate surroundings. On this can be deployed a range of different items representing the improvements they want to see effected.

In attendance by invitation there may be some of the professionals principally concerned—planners, housing officials, community workers, parks and recreation officers, police. These professionals are there to be consulted, but not to be in control. Their presence makes it possible for residents to test out their own ideas, and check on financial, legal and technical practicability. It still leaves them to say (and show) what their priorities are, and to negotiate possible trade-offs, with everyone concerned getting back to the model to shift things around into new patterns in order to see what might be involved. Since then we have published other packs employing similar techniques to show how the layout of a building can be considered and rearranged in order to convert it to workshops, a social centre or a teenage coffee bar.

Many of the traditional virtues of a role-play or simulation are preserved. People do get very hot under the collar, as they become emotionally involved; but they are not finally committed and can go back on an idea that went wrong, having seen what it might entail. People find buoyancy in working together informally—they egg each other on to try things out, and give each other encouragement and reassurance. But there are fewer rules than usually figure in gaming. The constraints that influence the situation can be quite easily recognized and accepted. People know, or soon learn, how traffic will affect the use of buildings or play areas, where the sewers run, how far apart pensioners and adventure playgrounds should be placed. In using the materials, people find that it pays to let everybody join in a free-for-all at first, putting bits and pieces on the model without much reference to each other. Commonsense then suggests a pause for stocktaking—do we really want 16 adventure playgrounds in one neighbourhood? If not, how many, and where? All those concerned with adventure playgrounds (including those who would rather not have one within a mile of them) withdraw to one corner of the room to sort out their ideas, periodically revisiting the model in order to try out the alternatives that seem most promising. No one had to assume a role, because those present, residents, officials, voluntary workers, are there in their own right and can draw on their own experience.

What results is not a final commitment. The very idea of anyone committing herself or himself may be premature. What has been achieved in a *feasibility study* in which a cross-section of all those who would be affected have been able to participate. In the process they have come to know each other, and have got used to considering problems and possibilities informally, without hierarchies, status symbols or personality traits getting in the way. It is interesting that the video recordings we have made of the PLANNING FOR REAL packs in use, in Nottingham, Sheffield, Manchester, Birkenhead, Islington and elsewhere, reveal a significant change in the eye-lines. In a conventional encounter where the emphasis is on talking, the contacts are usually eyeball-to-eyeball, and personalities often dominate. When there is common ground—the table-top layout of a three-dimensional model—the eye-lines converge on the subject matter and on the problems and opportunities it begins to reveal. People are talking to each other casually, out of the sides of their mouths, rubbing shoulders, gossiping almost, but with their gaze concentrated on the job in hand.

Parallel to such uses of very crude (and cheap!) model materials, we have found equally rewarding uses of scraps of card with perhaps two or three words on each, representing concepts, issues and particular problems or opportunities. They can be moved around by members of the group, using a very simple chart as a base. The chart may be divided into different 'working party areas' into which 'matters arising' cards can be sorted in order to share out the workload. Later they might be rearranged by each prospective working party on another background sheet divided simply into three horizontal columns NOW, SOON and LATER, and several vertical columns labelled, for example, EASY, NEEDS MORE INFORMATION, NOT CLEAR, NOTHING TO DO WITH US—PASS THE BUCK. The principle is the same. Move things around to show what you mean, but feel free to change your ideas as you proceed, because no one is committed and every possibility is 'up for grabs'.

Conclusion

A feasibility study, or 'try-out' is in one sense only a dummy run. It is not the real thing any more than a map is the real terrain. But you can use it purposefully to work out what needs to be done, and how to involve those who are needed to do it. It is a *run-in* to reality.

Biographical note

Dr Tony Gibson served a seven-year apprenticeship as a BBC staff producer in television and radio, and subsequently worked as a freelance writer and broadcaster, specializing in scripting and presenting educational programmes. He was director of the Audio-Visual Education Centre and the Television Research and Training Unit at Goldsmiths College, 1965-71, since when he has been at Nottingham University's School of Education, where he developed the Education for Neighbourhood Change programme, and associated publications, including the Neighbourhood Action packs.

Notes

Descriptions of the research and development of the techniques can be found in the following books by Tony Gibson:

Teachers Talking (1974) Allen Lane, Penguin Books: Harmondsworth
Resources and the Teacher (1976) Pitman Educational: London
People Power (1979) Penguin Books: Harmondsworth

A monograph, 'Decision-making and the Language of Manipulative Display' by Eric Lunzer and Tony Gibson (1979) and price lists of the resource packs based on these techniques can be obtained by mail order from Education for Neighbourhood Change at the address below.

T Gibson
Education for Neighbourhood Change
School of Education
University of Nottingham
University Park
Nottingham NG7 2RD
England

15. Flights of fancy – simulators for pilot training

John Rolfe and Wayne Waag

Abstract: There has been increasing emphasis on flight simulation as a means of achieving significant reductions in flying time within civil and military aviation. As a result, extensive efforts are currently underway to examine the training effectiveness of both current and future simulator facilities and programmes. Conventional reasons for employing flight simulators are examined and the assumptions made regarding training effectiveness which impact the actual design of systems are discussed. The need for realism is questioned and the point made that it is more appropriate to define fidelity requirements in terms of training objectives. Current simulation capabilities and utilization practices within civil and military aviation are discussed.

Introduction

Historically, simulators have been designed and manufactured under the concept that the effectiveness of a device can be equated to its realism. The goal has been to make the simulator equivalent to the aircraft to whatever degree possible. Such an approach to simulator design has been widely accepted for a number of reasons. First, it is a relatively simple matter to state design requirements. The aircraft and its flight dynamics represent a reasonably well-defined model about which to define simulator performance requirements. Second, it is relatively simple from the standpoint of evaluation. It is a straightforward procedure to have an experienced pilot 'fly' the simulator and make a judgement concerning its perceived equivalence to the aircraft. And third, it seems a necessity from the viewpoint of user acceptance. Since simulators are offered as ground replicates of the aircraft, it is small wonder that devices which fail to meet these expectations will be considered ineffective.

The issue of simulator fidelity

Despite these reasons for pursuing a design goal of maximum simulator fidelity, there are other considerations which cause us to question seriously the desirability of such an approach. One of the more important of these is costs. Increases in simulation fidelity typically lead to increases in cost.

Second, the ultimate in realism cannot be obtained. The aircraft moves in three-dimensional space while the simulator is bolted to the floor. And third, there are research data indicating that, for many situations, high fidelity simulation is not a necessary ingredient for effective training. Simulators of marginal fidelity, if properly used, have been shown to be highly effective training devices (Waag, 1979).

Thus, the user is placed in the dilemma of deciding how much fidelity is necessary. Before considering the various aspects of this problem, certain assumptions must be stated regarding the role of simulation in flight training. The goal of flight training programmes, whether they be civilian or military, is initially to acquire and subsequently to maintain the necessary skills for safe and effective airborne operations. The role of flight simulation must be considered in terms of its relationship to this goal. Flight simulation should be developed and utilized within the training programme only if it can be shown to make a positive contribution to the fulfilment of training and the maintenance of flying skill. As intuitively valid as this assumption may appear, its consequences are often overlooked in the development and evaluation of flight simulation hardware and programmes.

An excellent example of differences in requirements is given in trade-offs between physical and dynamic fidelity. In this case, physical fidelity refers to the similarity between simulator and aircraft in terms of cockpit layout, instruments and controls, while dynamic fidelity refers to performance and handling characteristics. At the one extreme are cockpit familiarization and procedure trainers which have limited dynamic fidelity but which replicate the cockpit layout. Such devices have been widely used in many flight training programmes. At the other extreme are research devices which have high dynamic fidelity but limited physical fidelity. Despite the lack of physical correspondence, there are certain applications for which the training effectiveness has been quite high (Waag, 1979). There are also effective training media with both limited physical and dynamic fidelity. For example, academic instruction and various learning centre media can provide effective training (Melden and Houston, 1975). The conclusion is that fidelity *per se*, whether physical or dynamic, may not be necessary for effective training. Instead, the critical issues are whether device capabilities will support specific training objectives and whether the training device simulates those cues which are necessary for effective learning of specific skills.

A second consequence concerns the utilization of the simulator in the flying training programme. The full fidelity model leads to the utilization concept that the simulator be employed like the aircraft. The student will fly a simulator mission in the same manner he would fly an aircraft mission. It is well accepted that the aircraft presents a very poor learning environment; to use the simulator in an equivalent manner does little to improve that situation. The view that the role of the simulator is to foster the acquisition of airborne skill implies that the device should be used in any manner whereby this goal can best be achieved. The designation of the flight simulator as a training device enables the introduction of training technology concepts, which, if properly applied, enhance the effectiveness of the training. There are certain benefits which result from the fact that the simulator is indeed different from the aircraft. These differences show themselves most clearly in relation to the instructional characteristics of the device rather than the simulated vehicle's characteristics. Some of the major benefits include: more control over the training task and the training environment; the opportunity for deeper and more objective assessment of performance; and greater flexibility in terms of the ability to vary the content, order, repetition and timing of training elements.

The argument that training effectiveness is a function of how the device is used as well as how the device is engineered introduces further aspects of the fidelity model. These dimensions are *operational fidelity,* which represents the extent to which the simulator is used as an aircraft substitute, and *instructional fidelity,* that is, the degree of correspondence between instructional procedures used in the simulator and aircraft.

Thus far, an attempt has been made to show that use of the fidelity model as a means of stating simulator design requirements is often inappropriate. There is much evidence to indicate that effective training can be obtained through the utilization of devices with limited fidelity. If one accepts the premise that the value of a flight simulator depends upon its impact on subsequent airborne performance, it follows that its design requirements should be dependent upon those training objectives it is intended to fulfil. Thus, fidelity requirements for visual and motion simulation cannot be determined strictly from the physical and dynamic models of the aircraft and the environment in which it operates. Of greater importance is a clear statement of the intended role of the simulator within the training system and the specific training objectives it will be designed to meet. Only when these are clearly defined does the question of fidelity requirements become appropriate.

Role of the flight simulator in the training system

Discussion to this point should make it clear that the flight simulator is only a part of the training system. Its role is determined by its relationship to other elements of the training system and, therefore, it cannot be considered as an independent and autonomous entity. Unfortunately in practice, there has been a strong temptation to ignore these interdependencies and treat the simulator in the same way as the aircraft and to attempt to follow similar definition and specification procedures. Miller *et al* (1978) concluded that often there was little correspondence between actual training requirements and training device functional capabilities and that frequently devices tended to dictate the structure of training. As a consequence, the maximum fidelity capabilities available often became the specification rather than the minimum required for effective training.

Another consideration in deciding the scope of training objectives to be fulfilled in the simulator is past experience. The research literature relating to the value of flight simulators is extensive. Reviews of the simulator training effectiveness literature are found in Orlanksy and String (1977) and Rolfe (1979), a review of current simulator substitution practices in Diehl and Ryan (1977), and a review of visual and motion training effectiveness in Waag (1979). In summarizing this literature, the following conclusions can be drawn:

(a) The flight simulator is an effective means of teaching and maintaining aircrew skills. This assessment is based upon a limited number of objective and controlled studies of simulator training effectiveness, the majority of which were undertaken in relation to initial training, and a large body of information derived from trials and evaluations.

(b) Substantial amounts of time in the air can be replaced by the use of simulators. It would appear that it is most correct to assume that skill training and maintaining activities will require at least as much time in the simulator as in the air. If savings are required, their most likely source will be in the reduction of the non-productive time associated with airborne training; for example, time spent positioning in order that the training detail can commence.

(c) The ease with which tasks can be learned in the flight simulator and transferred to the aircraft varies with the nature of the task. Providing the setting for the training is appropriate, procedural skills will transfer readily but will be forgotten unless practised regularly. Perceptual motor skills transfer less completely, because they are more susceptible to imperfections in the simulation of dynamic factors such as physical motion, visual and kinaesthetic cues and control forces. Nevertheless, while the level of transfer may be lower, rapid adaptation appears to take place in the flight environment. As a means of maintaining skill, simulators for procedural skills will be easier to provide than those whose task is to assist in the retention of perceptual motor skill.

(d) The effects of simulator training are most apparent in the critical period immediately after the student moves from the simulator to aircraft. Simulator trained students are likely to show high initial levels of proficiency on transfer to the aircraft with the result that student and instructor confidence is enhanced from the outset.

(e) Training effectiveness is not determined solely by the appropriateness of the training device to the training task. How the device is used can influence its effectiveness to an equal or greater extent. One very pertinent example is the strategy employed for allocating training time in the simulator. The bulk of controlled studies of simulator training show that simulators are most effective when the student is allowed as much time as he needs, with some maximum limit, to reach a criterion standard of performance. This strategy contrasts with the more frequently encountered policy of allocating fixed amounts of time for the purpose of learning task elements.

(f) Differences between the training and operational equipment and environment may be essential in order to achieve the most effective training. Training effectiveness can be improved by reducing the level of complexity in the training device, in order that the student can concentrate upon those elements of the flying task which are relevant to the task being trained. Many studies show that part-time training devices, systems and procedures trainers are very effective, within the limit of their defined roles. Secondly, changes to the equipment may be necessary in order to facilitate feedback between instructor and student, to provide the student with better knowledge of his performance, and to allow the manipulation of the training task using facilities such as freeze and replay. Thirdly, it can be beneficial if, particularly during the initial stages of training, instruction can take place in a more stress-free environment than that encountered in flight.

(g) Motivation is a key element in achieving effective training in a ground trainer. Effectiveness is highest when the instructor realizes and espouses the usefulness and relevance of the device, even though he or she may be required to teach around faulty capabilities or features. Students tend to reflect instructor attitudes. Further, where recurrent or refresher training is being provided to experienced trainees, with or without an instructor, an element of competition, or its equivalent, such as probability of success in combat simulations, tends to motivate trainees to better and faster learning.

(h) The degree of realism of simulation required will depend on the nature of the task, the level of experience of the students, and the level of proficiency the student is expected to possess at the end of the training device. For unskilled students there is considerable evidence that simple devices can be very effective for teaching basic procedures and skills. While far more complex devices may be required when the task is to develop and maintain the skills of operational aircrew, there may be valid reasons for employing some form of part-task trainer rather than a full simulation.

(i) The bulk of research data on the use of visual simulation concerns its effectiveness for transition training. With few exceptions, the overwhelming finding has been that visual tasks learned in the simulator show positive transfer to the aircraft. Successful use of visual simulation in training has been demonstrated, for fighter and transport fixed-wing aircraft as well as for rotary-wing aircraft. Few studies have been accomplished for tasks other than transition. This is due to the non-availability, until recently, of wide-angle visual systems necessary to perform certain tasks. Nonetheless, data thus far suggest that transfer can be obtained in visual tasks such as formation, refuelling, and surface-attack weapons delivery. For aerobatic and air combat skills, only a modest amount of transfer has been demonstrated.

(j) There is insufficient research data to make conclusive statements regarding the value of motion in the training context. Some research studies involving tracking tasks do show that the presence of good motion simulation produces operator control responses that correspond more closely to those recorded in the flight situation. However, such findings cannot be directly translated to mean that motion is essential for training simulators for conventional flight tasks. To date, studies of the training effectiveness of motion simulation have only addressed the contributions of platform motion cueing. Although there is evidence that motion cueing enhances performance in the simulator, in no instance was transfer to performance in the aircraft significantly improved. Since most studies focussed on training with centreline thrust aircraft, in which the role of the motion cues was to provide feedback to the pilot, the applicability of these findings to other situations is unknown. Because of insufficient research data, the recommended approach is to employ motion simulation when an analysis of the training tasks shows that it is needed for one or the other of two reasons. Firstly, it may provide those cues which are necessary if the student is to learn to perform the task correctly. Secondly, it can introduce features of the flying environment which can degrade performance and thus need to be experienced, so that compensatory strategies can be developed.

Assessment of simulator training effectiveness

In addition to defining training device requirements, an associated, but separate, activity is that of determining what contribution a flight simulator makes to training, that is, checking that the device does what it was bought to do. The term usually employed is training effectiveness. While this term is frequently encountered in the literature on flight simulation and training, it is a topic which is subject to misunderstanding and abuse. Training effectiveness should be concerned with determining whether or not a training device has an effect, either positive or negative, upon trainees' subsequent performance.

However, attempts to determine training effectiveness often rely upon user opinion, detailed assessment of the physical and dynamic fidelity of the simulation in comparison with the aircraft, or the measurement of how much the device is used. None of these measures is by itself a reliable indicator of training effectiveness. User opinion assumes that the user is able to assess accurately how much has been learned from the device. Assessment of simulator fidelity gives only an indication of a device's realism and not its training capability. The measurement of how much a simulator is used gives no indication of whether the device is being used effectively for all, or part of, the time.

Of the different approaches to the evaluation of simulator training effectiveness, the transfer of training methodology seems most appropriate (Rolfe, 1979; Caro, 1977). Transfer of training occurs whenever the existence of a previously learned behaviour and skill has an influence on the acquisition, performance, or relearning of a second behaviour or skill. Thus, if a behaviour learned in an aircraft simulator has influence upon the subsequent performance in an aircraft, transfer is said to have occurred.

A measure derived to meet the above requirements is the transfer effectiveness ratio (TER) developed by Roscoe (1971). The TER is calculated by dividing the number of training hours saved in the aircraft by the number of training hours in the simulator which are needed as a substitute. A TER of greater than 1.0 indicates that the training device is achieving the training objectives with savings in training time. A TER of less than 1.0 occurs when training in the simulator takes more time than the flying time which it saves.

An initial interpretation might be that simulators with TERs greater than or equal to 1.0 are effective training devices, while those with TERs less than 1.0 are not. This is not the case, as an important item to consider is cost. In all situations another measure, the training cost ratio (TCR), has an important role to play. The TCR compares on the same common baseline, for example pounds per hour, the costs of the training device with the costs of the actual equipment. If the two measures TER and TCR are considered together, a cost effectiveness ratio (CER) can be obtained as follows:

$$CER = \frac{TER}{TCR}$$

Values of CER greater than 1.0 will indicate that cost effective training is being achieved; values less than 1.0 will indicate that it is not.

For flight simulators the TCR is likely to be well below 1.0. Orlanksy and String (1977) found 33 cases in which the TCR between the simulator and the aircraft could be calculated. The median TCR in this study was found to be 0.116. This value supports the frequently made claim that simulator operating costs are in the region of 10 per cent of those of the aircraft represented. The importance of the above TCR data is that they indicate that, with the application of the CER, TERs as low as 0.2 may still be indicative of cost effective training.

Conclusions

This article has attempted to make the following points:

(a) The role of the flight simulator must be considered in terms of its relationship to the overall goals of the training system, that is, to the initial acquisition and subsequent maintenance of flying skill. Flight simulator development and utilization is warranted only if it makes a positive contribution to these goals.

(b) Simulator design requirements should be dictated by those training objectives the device is intended to fulfil.

(c) Specific cues should be simulated only if they are essential for the initial learning or subsequent maintenance of the intended training objectives. Fidelity requirements for visual and motion simulation are thus dependent upon the specific training objectives the device is intended to meet.

(d) The existing literature on essential cueing requirements for visual and motion simulation for specific training objectives is quite limited. Nonetheless, the available data indicate that of the two, visual cueing has a substantially greater potential for enhancing and extending the effectiveness of simulator training. Training effectiveness data to date have seriously questioned the value of platform motion cueing from certain applications.

(e) The transfer of training model is the most appropriate method for determining the effectiveness of simulator training.

References

Caro, P D (1977) Some factors influencing Air Force Simulator Training effectiveness. HumRRO-TR-7712: Alexandria, Va

Diehl, D E and Ryan, L E (1977) Current simulator substitution practices in flight training. TAEG Report No 43: Orlando, Fa

Melden, T M and Houston, R C (1975) Major changes in flight crew training: eight years of experience at American Airlines. Presented at AIAA 1975 Aircraft Systems and Technology Meeting: Los Angeles, Ca

Miller, R M, Swink, J R and McKenzie, J F (1978) Instructional systems development (ISD) in Air Force flying training. AFHRL-TR-78-59: Williams AFB, Az

Orlanksy, J and String, J (1977) Cost effectiveness of flight simulation for military training *Vol 1:* Use and effectiveness of flight simulators. IDA Paper D-1275 Institute for Defence Analysis: Alexandria, Va

Rolfe, J M (1979) The future of flight simulation: the impact of training technology. Research Note 10/79 Research Branch Headquarters Royal Air Force Support Command: Huntingdon

Roscoe, S N (1971) Incremental Transfer Effectiveness. *Human Factors* 13, 561-67

Waag, W L (1979) Training effectiveness of visual and motion simulation. AFHRL-TR-79-72: Williams AFB: Az

Biographical notes

Dr John Rolfe trained as an engineer with the Admiralty. After reading psychology at the University of Hull in 1959 he joined RAF Institute of Aviation Medicine undertaking research into a range of human factors/problems associated with the design and operation of civil and military aircraft. In 1969 he was appointed Reader in Aviation Medicine (Psychology) with relation to the Institute's teaching programme for the Diploma in Aviation Medicine. In 1976 he became Commanding Residential Officer at Headquarters RAF Support Command, where he is responsible for initiating and supervising research into factors influencing the operational efficiency of the Command.

Dr Wayne Waag worked with Dr Rolfe while on a scientific exchange posting from the United States Air Force Human Resources Laboratory, Williams Air Force Base, Arizona.

Dr J M Rolfe
Command Research Officer
Royal Air Force Brampton

Dr W L Waag
Research Branch
Royal Air Force Support Command
Royal Air Force Brampton.

16. How technologically-based simulation exercises can be used in management training

H I Ellington, E Addinall and N H Langton

Abstract: Simulation games and simulated case studies with a basis in science and technology have been widely used in science and engineering education throughout the world and have also proved useful in a number of other areas, including management training. This paper provides a rationale for the latter application, identifying three broad areas in which such exercises can be used. By way of illustration four specific exercises with whose development the authors have been associated are examined and their strengths as management training tools are assessed.

Introduction

Since 1973, staff at Robert Gordon's Institute of Technology (RGIT), Aberdeen, have been heavily involved in the design, promotion and evaluation of educational games and simulations with a scientific or technological background. Most of these are designed primarily for use in science and engineering courses at upper secondary and tertiary levels, and are now being incorporated into a large number of such courses in many parts of the world (Ellington, Addinall and Percival, 1981).

Several of the games have, however, found a wide variety of other applications, having been used *inter alia* as 'mind-broadening' exercises in non-science courses, in the pre-service training of teachers, in the in-service training of technical and scientific staff in industry, and in management training. This paper discusses the last of these applications, and suggests a number of ways in which technologically-based simulation exercises can contribute to the training of managers. It then illustrates the general rationale by describing four specific exercises with which we have been associated, showing how these have proved to be highly successful as management training tools.

Rationale for use of technological simulations in management training

We believe that there are at least three distinct ways in which technologically-based simulation exercises of the type developed in RGIT can make a significant contribution to the general field of management training.

First, they can be used to help bridge the 'two culture' gap by demonstrating the vital part played by science and technology in modern industrial society and providing the participants with an insight into such important technological issues as the energy problem and the nuclear debate.

Second, they can be used to give managers an overview of the industry or field in which they work and provide them with experience of areas outside their usual job situation.

Third, they can be used as vehicles for the development of a wide range of management skills.

Let us now examine each of these in more detail.

BRIDGING THE 'TWO CULTURE' GAP

Ever since C P Snow gave his famous Reith Lecture (Snow, 1959), the dichotomy that exists between those who have an understanding of science and technology and those who do not has been a matter of general concern. Indeed, the fact that the great majority of Britain's politicians, administrators and managers have little or no knowledge of science and technology is frequently cited as one of the main reasons for our chronic industrial problems.

While it is obviously unrealistic to expect all our managers and administrators to have a degree in science or engineering, we believe they should at least have a basic appreciation of the nature of science and technology, and of the key role that they play in an industrially-based economy such as Britain's. In our opinion, science-based games and simulations, particularly those with a multi-disciplinary background, offer one means of helping to bring such a situation about (Ellington and Percival, 1977; Ellington, Addinall and Percival, 1981).

GIVING MANAGERS AN OVERVIEW OF THEIR INDUSTRY

One of the features of modern industry is the highly specialized nature of most of the jobs, at both management and shopfloor levels. Except in a very few cases, employees are trained to do a specific job in a specific area of operation, and they have virtually no direct experience of other jobs or other areas of operation. Because of this, it is often extremely difficult for such people to gain any real appreciation of the overall nature of the industry or field in which they work and of the relevance of their particular role within that industry or field. We believe that suitably-designed simulation exercises can offer a method of helping to overcome these experiential deficiencies, by placing managers in a situation where they can not only gain a valuable overview of their industry but also have an opportunity to develop their management skills in areas they would not otherwise encounter (Ellington, Addinall and Percival, 1981).

DEVELOPING USEFUL SKILLS AND DESIRABLE ATTITUDES

Games and simulations play an extremely important role in the general training of managers, partly by giving them experience of specific on-the-job situations, and partly by helping to develop the type of skills and attitudes that an efficient manager should possess (Hart, 1978). Technologically-based exercises are no less suitable for achieving the latter set of objectives than 'conventional' management games. In our experience, they can be used to develop a wide range of useful skills (eg, man-management, interpersonal, interpretative, decision-making, communication and presentational skills) and desirable attitudinal traits (eg, appreciation that problems can generally be viewed in different ways) (Ellington, Addinall and Percival, 1981).

Illustration of rationale by examining specific exercises

Let us now illustrate this rationale by taking a look at four specific technologically-based exercises, which have proved useful as management training tools, and showing how they have helped achieve the various aims outlined above.

THE BRUCE OIL MANAGEMENT GAME

The BRUCE OIL MANAGEMENT GAME is a computer-based case study which simulates the development and exploitation of a large offshore oilfield (Ellington, Addinall and Langton, 1978). The game was first developed in RGIT during 1973-74, and, during the following six winters, was used as the basis of an international business management competition which attracted teams from virtually all sectors of industry and commerce, and, in particular, from the various oil companies and service industries that operate in the North Sea.

The game involves six rounds of decision-making in which teams (of up to six people) have to handle virtually all aspects of the management of their field, including the deployment of production platforms, the logistics of getting their oil and gas ashore and the refining and marketing of the various products. Although it is essentially a financial game, the winning team being that which handles its investment and cash flow most efficiently and ends up with the largest overall profits, all financial decisions have to be made on the basis of a thorough understanding of the *technology* of the offshore oil industry. This is the main feature which distinguishes the BRUCE OIL MANAGEMENT GAME from other management games in which in-depth technological understanding seldom assumes such importance.

The original idea for the game came from Roger Nicholson, assistant managing director of Aberdeen Journals Ltd, who wanted to sponsor a competition that would serve as a useful in-service training tool at middle management level for oil companies and offshore service companies, and would also be of interest to banks, local government organizations, and other bodies involved in the North Sea oil industry. During the six years of the competition, over 300 teams, drawn from all the above areas, took part, many organizations entering more than one team at a time (Esso once entered no less than six!). Feedback received from the various participating organizations indicates that the game proved extremely valuable to them as a management training tool, a conclusion that is reinforced by the fact that a number of organizations now use the exercise 'in-house'. Success in the BRUCE OIL GAME also did no harm to the promotion prospects of the people involved; the leader of one of the winning teams, for example, became a director of his company within the year!

THE POWER STATION GAME

THE POWER STATION GAME is an extended role-playing exercise simulating the process by which a large new power station is planned (Ellington, Langton and Smythe, 1977). It is played by three teams of six people over a period of two to two-and-a-half days. Each team has first to carry out a detailed technical and economic feasibility study on one particular type of station (coal-fired, oil-fired and nuclear) and then prepare a case for building a station of this type. This involves deciding on the overall station design and lay-out, choosing the best site (taking account of all relevant geographical, social and environmental factors) and determining the capital cost and the likely operating costs over the life of the station. The teams then present their cases at a plenary session where the most promising scheme is selected by an independent jury, after which a comprehensive public inquiry is held into the chosen scheme.

Although it was originally developed as a 'mind-broadening' exercise for science and engineering students at upper secondary and lower tertiary levels, the game has found a large number of other applications since its publication in 1976 (Ellington, Addinall and Percival, 1981). These include use as a management training exercise by several organizations involved in the supply of electricity, eg, the Central Electricity Generating Board and the United Kingdom Atomic Energy Authority. Both organizations have found that the wide-ranging, multi-disciplinary nature of the exercise makes it an ideal vehicle for achieving virtually all the aims listed above. They have also found that it creates a realistic environment in which technical and non-technical staff can work together effectively on a common project—to the benefit of both groups.

ILE DE PERFORMANCE

In January 1980, we were asked by Phillips Petroleum Company to develop a management game for use at their forthcoming Petroleum Products Group conference. Specifically, Phillips were looking for an exercise which dealt with one or more aspects of 'the energy problem' (one of the main themes of the conference) and would also serve as a management training tool, partly by enabling all delegates to participate in a decision-making exercise, and partly by providing a vehicle for senior staff to develop their man-management skills — both under competitive conditions.

Because of the short time available, it was agreed that we would adapt one of our earlier exercises—POWER FOR ELASKAY—for use at the conference rather than develop a completely new game. POWER FOR ELASKAY is a simulated case study based on alternative energy and involves devising a 50-year rolling programme for meeting the electricity needs of a hypothetical offshore island by exploiting its indigenous energy resources (Ellington and Addinall, 1979). The exercise had already been used highly successfully in management training (eg, as part of an in-service course for bank managers), so we felt that it could easily be adapted to meet Phillips' requirements.

A full description of the resulting exercise, entitled ILE DE PERFORMANCE (after Phillips' in-house newspaper *Performance*) is given elsewhere (Ellington, Addinall, Langton and Percival, 1981). Essentially, it involved four competing teams, each containing one quarter of the conference delegates, preparing detailed proposals on how to meet Performance's future energy demands and presenting them at a plenary session on the final day of the conference. Each team had to assess the technical and economic feasibility of six potential energy resources and then decide which of these should be exploited. The work of each team was co-ordinated by a senior Phillips manager under the guidance of a member of RGIT staff (the three authors and Fred Percival).

The conference organizers and senior Phillips staff to whom we spoke after completion of the competition were of the unanimous opinion that the exercise had been a great success, having been thoroughly enjoyed by the participants as well as having been a highly effective management training tool. This was confirmed by an internal evaluation subsequently carried out by the company. One extremely satisfying fact to emerge from the evaluation was that virtually all the delegates who played the game (104 out of 110) felt that a management exercise of this type should be included in future conferences.

THE NUCLEAR DEBATE

As a result of discussions with colleagues in the British nuclear power industry, it became apparent to us during 1980 that there was an urgent need for a simulation package dealing with the nuclear power issue. Such a package would, it was felt, not only prove useful at school and college level, but would also serve as a valuable training tool within the nuclear power industry, by giving technical and managerial staff an overview of their industry and preparing them to take part in the real-life nuclear debate. It was for these reasons that THE NUCLEAR DEBATE was developed in RGIT over the winter of 1980-81.

THE NUCLEAR DEBATE consists of three separate exercises, each dealing with one specific aspect of the nuclear power controversy (Ellington and Addinall, 1981). The first exercise attempts to put the nuclear power issue in its proper perspective, by analysing Britain's present and likely future energy supply situation and trying to determine whether there is a need for nuclear power. The second examines the various nuclear power options available to Britain. The third deals with what is to most people *the* most important aspect of the nuclear debate, namely, whether nuclear power is socially and environmentally acceptable. The first two exercises take the form of simulated meetings of a government energy policy committee at which 'experts' present evidence and the committee then decides on what its policy should be. The third takes the form of a structured debate at which pro- and anti-nuclear arguments are presented.

As in the case of THE POWER STATION GAME, THE NUCLEAR DEBATE is already proving to be an extremely valuable management training tool within the industry on which it is based.

Assessing the strength of the exercises as management training tools

Figure 1 summarises our assessment of the effectiveness as management tools of the four exercises described above. We have done this by rating the strength of each exercise in each of the areas listed above on a 0-10 scale. These ratings are based partly on feedback received from the organizations that have used the exercises and from people who have taken part. Thus, they should *not* be regarded as the results of a formal quantitative evaluation. Figure 1 shows that all four of the exercises appear to be capable of achieving a wide spectrum of management training objectives.

		BRUCE OIL GAME	POWER STATION GAME	ILE DE PERFORMANCE	NUCLEAR DEBATE
Bridging two-culture gap	Giving appreciation of nature of science and technology	5	8	8	7
	Giving appreciation of role of science and technology in modern industrial society	5	9	8	9
Giving overview of industry or field	Giving appreciation of overall nature of industry or field and relevance of particular roles	10	9	8	10
	Giving experience of other job situations	8	7	7	6
Developing management skills and desirable attitudes	Man-management skills	6	7	10	2
	Interpersonal skills	7	10	10	3
	Interpretative skills	10	10	8	9
	Decision-making skills	10	8	9	8
	Communication skills		9	9	9
	Presentational skills	0	10	10	10
	Desirable attitudinal traits	3	10	8	10

Figure 1. *Assessment of the exercises as management training tools*

Conclusion

We believe that technologically-based simulation exercises of the type described in this paper can play an important part in preparing managers to fulfil the role that modern industrial society demands. They can do this by helping managers to understand the technology on which so much of modern industry and commerce is based while, at the same time, contributing to the development of traditional management skills. Hopefully, this paper will encourage the wider use of such exercises.

Note

Of the five exercises referred to in this paper, THE POWER STATION GAME and POWER FOR ELASKAY are available as commercial packages from the IEE, Station House, Nightingale Road, Hithcin, Herts SG5 1RJ. The former costs £25 (UK) and £30 (overseas); the latter costs £7 (UK) and £10 (overseas) — both inclusive of postage and VAT.

Further information about THE BRUCE OIL GAME and THE NUCLEAR DEBATE can be obtained from the authors. For information about ILE DE PERFORMANCE write to Mr G Dodds, Phillips Petroleum Company Ltd, Portland House, Stag Place, London SW1E 5DA.

References

Ellington, H I and Addinall, E (1979) Building case study simulations into the science curriculum as part of structured lessons. *Simulation/Games for Learning* 9 1: 13-19

Ellington, H I and Addinall, E (1981) THE NUCLEAR DEBATE — a new educational package for teachers. *Simulation/Games for Learning* 11 3: 120-25

Ellington, H I, Addinall, E and Langton, N H (1978) THE BRUCE OIL GAME, a computerised business management game. In Megarry, J (ed) *Perspectives on Academic Gaming and Simulation 1 & 2:* 184-90. Kogan Page: London

Ellington, H I, Addinall, E, Langton, N H and Percival, F (1981) ILE DE PERFORMANCE — a competitive planning exercise built into a company conference. *Simulation/Games for Learning* 11 1: 12-22

Ellington, H I, Addinall, E and Percival, F (1981) *Games and Simulations in Science Education*. Kogan Page: London

Ellington, H I, Langton, N H and Smythe, M E (1977) The use of simulation games in schools — a case study. In Hills, P and Gilbert, J (eds) *Aspects of Educational Technology* XI. Kogan Page: London

Ellington, H I and Percival, F (1977) Science-based simulation games — a means of bridging the 'two-culture' gap. Proc. of 8th ISAGA Conference, University of Birmingham

Hart, R T (1978) Simulations and gaming in management education and training. In McAleese, R (ed) *Perspectives on Academic Gaming and Simulation 3:* 70-75. Kogan Page: London

Snow, C P (1959) *The Two Cultures and The Scientific Revolution*. Cambridge University Press: Cambridge

Biographical notes

Dr Henry Ellington graduated in natural philosophy from Aberdeen University in 1963 and obtained his doctorate from the same university in 1969. He is also a chartered electrical engineer. Since 1973, he has been senior lecturer in charge of the Educational Technology Unit at Robert Gordon's Institute of Technology, Aberdeen. He has published extensively in the field of academic gaming, and has served on the Councils of both SAGSET and AETT, being treasurer of SAGSET 1975-81. He has also carried out a large amount of consultancy work in the field of instructional design.

Dr Eric Addinall graduated in physics from Nottingham University in 1962 and received his doctorate from the same university in 1965. He is also a chartered electrical engineer. He has lectured in physics since 1965, and is currently a senior lecturer in the School of Physics at RGIT. A former member of SAGSET Council and its membership secretary 1977-81, he has been involved in the development of a large number of games and simulations and has also carried out extensive consultancy work in collaboration with Dr Ellington.

Professor Norman Langton was educated at Hull and Nottingham universities. After the Second World War, he held several posts in the Government Scientific Services before moving into the field of education in 1947. He lectured at Loughborough College of Advanced Technology and at the National College of Rubber Technology before being appointed head of the School of Physics at RGIT in 1965 — a post which he still holds. He has been closely involved in the development of games and simulations at RGIT since 1973.

Educational Technology Unit
Robert Gordon's Institute of Technology
St Andrew Street
Aberdeen AB1 1HG
Scotland

17. Some evaluated aspects of the PLANET MANAGEMENT GAME

Barbara Diehl

Abstract: This paper focusses on the *least* researched aspect of simulation games — the objective analysis of differential effects (mental, emotional, communicative) of a game, and evaluation of these effects for providing guidance in the managerial skills training area.

It analyses and evaluates THE PLANET MANAGEMENT GAME, in which participants are required to manage the resources of an imaginary planet similar to Earth. The game's objectives are to develop understanding of the complex interrelated aspects of management and to provide practice in important managerial skills. Data for analysis were obtained from two different evaluation instruments, completed by 155 participants.

The simplest instrument contained open-ended questions, regarding strengths and weaknesses of the game. The responses, subjected to content analysis, provided a general game evaluation. They also indicated potential problem areas for facilitators of this game and this paper makes suggestions for minimizing these weaknesses.

Data from the second instrument, containing 12 simulation gaming attributes contributing to managerial learning, were subjected to multivariate analysis. The interpretation of these results provides a more specific and objective evaluation. This is discussed in terms of the potency of some of the more important mental and emotional processes stimulated by participation in the game process — understanding, strategic thinking, communication, decision-making, etc. The implications for managerial skills training follow.

Overview

Management currently recruits graduates from various fields of study. It then needs to train them in business managerial skills in order that they can operate effectively in different capacities at varying managerial levels. Training these small groups of people from diverse disciplines, for individually different positions, is an enormous challenge for trainers. It is also a potentially very expensive undertaking if the training is to be really effective, so management needs better cost-effective training methods.

Simulation gaming can be a powerful instructional technique for generating learning. There are three sequential ways of viewing a simulation game: description of the game; description of the game's effects on participants; and measurement of these effects. The bulk of simulation gaming literature consists of the first two types of description, there being very little reported research which attempts objectively to measure aspects of simulation games, and evaluate their effects, using appropriate assessment techniques. Most designers state the aims of the game and explain what should happen before and during play, but this information is too general for an educator who wants to use simulation games to achieve specific teaching or training aims. What is needed for each is *objective* information regarding its inherent attributes, their relationships and their effects on different types of participant. Management training, in particular, could be made more effective, and possibly less costly, if trainers had information regarding the similarity and differences between trainees from different disciplines.

This paper is part of a broader research project to investigate and determine relevant specific attributes of selected simulation games, suitable for use in Australian curricula. Previous measurement of the *total* effectiveness of 13 simulation games has resulted in THE PLANET MANAGEMENT GAME being ranked as one of the most effective games (Diehl, 1979), thus meriting further analysis. The research cited in this paper could be regarded as the first approximation of a micro-evaluation of THE PLANET MANAGEMENT GAME. It reports the analysis of participants' responses to two general open-ended questions regarding the strengths and weaknesses of the game, and to 12 questions relating to its specific attributes.

The PLANET MANAGEMENT GAME

THE PLANET MANAGEMENT GAME, developed by Showalter (Horn, 1977), requires participants to manage the resources of an imaginary planet similar to Earth.

They allocate expenditure for selected projects, attempting to improve the standard of living for an exponentially increasing population, without decreasing the quality of the environment. Each 'year', small groups of participants must reach a consensus regarding which projects to propose and how much money to spend on each one. The results of these decisions, as shown by changes in the game's four indices — population, food, income, environment — are obtained from a 'cardboard computer' and this feedback provides additional data for synthesizing a maximizing decision-making strategy. However, successful group management depends not only on these deductive-reasoning abilities, but also upon subtle aspects of communication skills.

Subjects

One hundred and fifty-five tertiary-level students (mostly postgraduate) from five major fields of study—Arts (49 students), Economics (19), English/History (33), Mathematics (28), Science (26)—enrolled in the course Ed BSc 356-1 Gaming and Simulation in Education, at the University of New England.

Instrument

At the completion of each of the simulation gaming workshops in the course, participants filled in an evaluation sheet consisting of two open-ended questions (see below) relating to their general impressions of the strengths and weaknesses of the simulation game. They also answered 12 seven-point Likert-type questions focussing on specific aspects of simulation gaming—motivation, communication, lower cognitive outcomes, higher cognitive outcomes, decision-making, planning, affective outcomes, material complexity, mirrors life, role reality, strategy reality and general learning (see p157). Eleven of the 12 questions are directly from, or slight modifications of, part of Stadsklev's games analysis system for evaluating simulation gaming material (Stadsklev, 1974). Four questions come from the section on rationale and objectives (C1-4) and seven from the content section (D1, 3-8).

Reliability

Coefficient alpha, a measure of internal consistency used for the 12 items, was .83. This reliability level is sufficiently high to allow meaningful interpretation of any existing group differences (see pp156-60).

General evaluation: content analysis

The general evaluation of PLANET MANAGEMENT was obtained through a content analysis of answers to two open-ended questions (Stadsklev, 1974: F4, 5).

What did you *like best* about this SG—what are its strong points?
What did you *like least* about this SG—what are its weak points?

Frequency counts were made of the different ideas expressed in the 155 responses to both these questions. The ideas were then grouped together in appropriate categories and the categories arranged in a frequency hierarchy as shown in Tables 1 and 2. (The frequency of each category could have been expressed as a percentage, but this might have been misleading because answers to open-ended questions can contain a variety of points.)

STRONG POINTS

The consensus of opinion was that PLANET MANAGEMENT's strongest point is 'group involvement', which subsumes involvement, communication, discussion and co-operation. The majority of comments were about the high level of group involvement. Others described the processes for achieving this increased interaction. They felt that the game promotes communication skills by stimulating discussion with other group members to achieve better results, or that it develops co-operation through the need to learn to listen to others and share different people's attitudes, viewpoints and orientations.

Frequency	Category
Highest	1 Group involvement
	2 Decision-making
	3 Interest
	4 Realism
	5 Understanding
	6 Analysis
	7 Subject matter
Lowest	8 Ease

Table 1. *Analysis of PLANET MANAGEMENT's strong points*

'Decision-making' had the second highest frequency count. Comments in this category hinged on increasing decision-making skills, because participants were forced to make decisions which related directly to results. The reinforcement due to immediate feedback of results, and the ability to use this to make better decisions, was widely commented upon, as was the flexibility of decision-making.

The third strongest point concerned player 'interest' which category includes high motivation, enjoyment, excitement, challenge and stimulation of the imagination.

The fourth strongest factor was the game's 'realism', since participants viewed it as having a close relationship to real-life problems which are becoming increasingly important. They thought it encouraged players to think about problems which face their own community, in that it is virtually impossible to achieve maximum production without detriment to the environment.

Although the 'understanding' category rated only fifth, it contained the greatest diversity of responses. Most referred either to the increased awareness of real-life environmental and economic factors and problems, or to understanding the complexity of maintaining a desirable balance of these interrelated factors. Some described the game's strength as aiding understanding of problem-solving from the administrative point of view, and the novelty of assuming management or authority roles.

Closely related to understanding and to decision-making is the next highest factor, 'analysis'. Participants saw this game as stimulating their analytical powers by generating the need to plan ahead. If this planning takes the consequences of actions into account, then players develop the skill to manipulate the relationship between strategies and outcomes.

Several respondents made thoughtful comments relating to the game's subject matter—for example, the interdisciplinary nature of the material; the importance of the game's issues; the complex interrelationships of the four major indices; the well conceived possible outcomes; and the scope of concepts involved (including pollution, conservation, industrialization, trade-offs, wealth, agriculture, productivity, indexation) which could be integrated and elaborated upon, in follow-up work. The graphing aids included in the game material would facilitate visual presentation of follow-up work.

Finally, the game was seen as easy to play. This is rather unexpected since the entire exercise (presentation, play, follow-up discussion) was conducted in one session, not two or three as would be desirable for maximum ease of understanding and effective implementation.

WEAK POINTS

Frequency	Category
Highest	1 None
	2 Limited variables*
	3 Time*
	4 Complexity
	5 Preparation*
	6 Relationships
Lowest	7 Group pressure*

(* Special implication for PLANET MANAGEMENT facilitators)

Table 2. *Analysis of PLANET MANAGMENT's weak points*

The frequency counts on the weak points are perhaps less valid than those on the strong points because many responses could reflect instructional time constraints, facilitator inadequacy or player misunderstanding, rather than game deficiency. These will be noted where pertinent. However, some factors indicate potential problem areas for PLANET MANAGEMENT facilitators (those asterisked above) and these merit special consideration.

The highest frequency category, 'none', covers the responses which were left blank, or contained statements about the game's lack of weak points, or the respondent's inability to find weak points.

The weak point with the second highest frequency was the 'variables' of the game. Most responses here were criticisms, but others were suggestions for improvement. Criticisms ranged from insufficient available strategies (a reflection on player ability, rather than game inadequacy), to a limited range of project alternatives in each colour. (Interestingly, close analysis of the game shows that all alternatives in the one colour give equal results, so additional alternatives would not increase the possible outcomes.) Suggested improvements included the use of chance cards (for example, random insect plagues to simulate the unreliability of agricultural yields) and many pleas for a birth control option to limit an exponentially increasing population. This would be an interesting modification.

The 'time' factor was seen as a weak point by many, who said that 10 rounds was too long and could lead to boredom. Since the participants occupied the dual roles of student and facilitator in a three-hour workshop, they could be registering displaced fatigue. It would be advantageous to know if participants, especially school children, have this same reaction when playing the game over two or more sessions. Since it is a possibility, facilitators of PLANET MANAGEMENT should be sensitive to the participating group's levels of concentration, and choose the number of rounds played to achieve their learning objectives, without inhibiting motivation. To complicate the matter, a few respondents thought the time spent was inadequate.

'Complexity' generated diverse comments. Several participants (half of whom were potential primary teachers) thought it would be too difficult for primary school use. This agrees with the game design specifications which suggest that the minimum playing age is junior high school level. A few, across all teaching areas, thought it would be too complex to explain to school children. (This suggests facilitator inadequacy or late arrival of respondents at the workshop session.) Potential English/History teachers felt it would be difficult to analyse the results mathematically. This problem can be avoided by playing the game in a true interdisciplinary context, after organizing co-operative gaming/debriefing with a teacher or teachers of other subject areas, each of whom is responsible for debriefing and follow-up work related to the objectives of his or her subject area.

Pre-play knowledge relating to game 'preparation' was the next most common problem posited. Respondents felt they had insufficient knowledge of existing conditions at the start of play, or pointed out the length of time required to give players adequate preliminary knowledge so that participants could play with some strategy in mind. This again indicates the need for the game facilitator to organize play over more than one period, so that preliminary information can be digested before actual play. It would, likewise, be beneficial to play the game more than once, as the designer suggests.

The next factor was the 'relationship' between strategy and results. Some participants felt frustrated because they could not see a direct relationship between the amounts spent on specific indices and changes in the four indices. More game experience would help these respondents understand that this is a *strong* point of the game, if it is debriefed perceptively and followed up immediately with relevant subject matter and activities.

Finally, a pertinent concern for facilitators related to 'group pressure', even though this factor rated the lowest. Because simulated games are designed for high involvement, one can erroneously assume that all participants are involved. However, even in small groups, it is possible for one or two powerful members to dominate the group and take over all game tasks. This might be difficult to overcome in some games, but is easily solved in PLANET MANAGEMENT by ensuring that all tasks are shared. Each group member should be responsible for one set of project cards (one colour), and the tasks of reading the four index changes and recording them each round should be shared among the group and rotated each round. Furthermore, an odd number of players (preferably a maximum of five) would avoid a stalemate in decision-making. However, if one has to play with even-numbered groups, then a stalemate breaking device (for example, tossing a coin) should become part of the rules of play.

Specific evaluation: multivariate analysis

Management trainers need cost-effective training techniques for instructing people from diverse backgrounds in managerial skills required for different positions. Training with simulation gaming could be made more effective if trainers had information regarding the similarities and differences between trainees, with respect to a specific game. For example, they need to know if males respond differently from females. They also need to know how people from different major fields of interest react.

DIFFERENCES BETWEEN GROUPS

To find this information for THE PLANET MANAGEMENT GAME, the data from the 12-item simulation evaluation instrument below were subjected to multivariate analysis of variance (MANOVA). This is the appropriate and most

SIMULATION EVALUATION

SIMULATION GAME TITLE: ....

RESPONDENT'S MAJOR FIELD OF STUDY: ....

SEX: M or F *(Circle one)*

Circle the number which best indicates your opinion - 0 represents the poorest (lowest) opinion; 6 represents the best (highest) opinion

1. How well does this SG motivate players to become involved?
    0   1   2   3   4   5   6

2. To what extent does it promote communication skills?
    0   1   2   3   4   5   6

3. How well does it achieve lower cognitive outcomes (knowledge and understanding)?
    0   1   2   3   4   5   6

4. To what extent does it promote process skills (higher cognitive outcomes) such as applying, analysing, synthesizing and evaluating?
    0   1   2   3   4   5   6

5. To what extent does it require the player to make decisions?
    0   1   2   3   4   5   6

6. How much does it influence the player to believe that intelligent, informed planning greatly increases the probabilities of success in an endeavour?
    0   1   2   3   4   5   6

7. How well does it achieve affective outcomes (attitudes and feelings)?
    0   1   2   3   4   5   6

8. How difficult or complex is the material that must be understood to function in the game?
    0   1   2   3   4   5   6

9. How closely does it mirror real life?
    0   1   2   3   4   5   6

10. How closely do the participant roles correspond to real-life roles?
    0   1   2   3   4   5   6

11. How closely do the strategies available to the player in the SG match those available to the participant in real life?
    0   1   2   3   4   5   6

12. How would you rate the simulation in general as a learning experience?
    0   1   2   3   4   5   6

powerful statistical methodology when there is more than one test result for each testee. Since the research questions concerned five subject area groups (Arts, Economics, English/History, Mathematics, Science) and two sexes a two-factor design was required. Finn's (1978) powerful MANOVA computer program was selected because it takes order effects into account, and used (on the University of New England's DEC 2060 computer) for a two-factor design, fitting a model of rank 10, the dependent variables being subject area (five) and sex (two). The main effects and the interaction results are listed in Table 3.

SEX DIFFERENCES

The multivariate F values and their accompanying probabilities showed that there were no differences in the mean vectors across sex, nor was there a significant interaction effect, indicating that males and females have similar opinions regarding the attributes of this simulation game.

SUBJECT AREA DIFFERENCES

The multivariate F for the subject area factor was not statistically significant at the conventionally accepted .05 level, thus prohibiting pure statistical determination of group differences. However, there is a growing consensus that the arbitrary .05 level is unnecessarily restrictive and causes loss of potentially valuable information which might point the direction for more precise research. Since this study was a preliminary investigation, and the low F probability indicated that differences existed between subject groups for one or more variables, further investigation of the variables was warranted, but its results should be interpreted with caution. In order to find which of the 12 variables were affected, univariate F values were calculated. These univariate F values and their probabilities are presented in Table 4. Three of these showed significant differences, and variable 'lower cognitive' having a probability less than .05. However, a significant F value with a low probability of error only indicates that there are significant differences somewhere between two or more groups, but it cannot show exactly where. For this information, pairs of groups must be subjected to a further test. Those variables which contributed to the multivariate significant differences were subjected to a Scheffe multiple comparison test (Glass and Stanley, 1970), which is the most appropriate test because of unequal n's of the five groups. For each variable, Scheffe tests were conducted on each of the 10 possible differences between pairs of subject area means.

Those contrasts which were significantly different from zero by the Scheffe method are listed in Table 5. To make this easier to read, subject areas are cited by their initial letter, and the first member of a contrast has the higher score. For the variable 'communicate', the Arts group (higher) differs from the Mathematics group at the .05 level. For 'lower cognitive', the Science group (lower) differs from English/History at the .05 level, and from Arts (highest) at the .01 level. For 'complexity', the Economics group (lowest) differs from the English/History (highest) and Arts groups at the .05 level.

Summarizing these results, there are significant differences of opinion on only three of the 12 game attributes, the five groups differing most in their opinions about its usefulness for developing lower cognitive skills, such as knowledge and understanding. The second greatest difference concerns its communicative aspect.

Source	Multivariate F	Probability
Subject Area	1.3110	p .0847 —
Sex	1.0007	p .4519
Interaction S.A./Sex	7451	p .8968

Table 3. *Manova results for the 5x2 design*
(Degrees of Freedom = 48,518)

Variable	Univariate F	Probability less than
1 Motivate	.710	.587
2 Communicate	2.586	.040*
3 Lower Cognitive	3.494	.009**
4 Higher Cognitive	0.436	.783
5 Decisions	1.607	.176
6 Planning	0.924	.452
7 Affectivity	1.719	.149
8 Complexity	2.796	.028*
9 Mirror Life	1.465	.216
10 Role Reality	1.081	.368
11 Strategy Reality	1.091	.363
12 General Learning	1.891	.115

Table 4. *Univariate Fs and probabilities for the 12 variables*
over the five subject areas (df — 4,145)

Variable	Between groups (Arts=A, Economics=E, Eng/Hist=EH, Mathematics=M, Science=S)
2 Communicate	A & M*
3 Lower Cognitive	A & S** EH & S*
8 Complexity	EH & E* A & E*

Table 5. *Scheffe multiple comparison test*

Note: ** indicates significance at the .01 level; * at .05 level and — at .1

On the whole Arts respondents register the largest number of differences, but upon studying where these differences occur and between which groups, an interesting pattern emerges. It shows clearly that a person's major area of interest has a distinct effect on his or her responses. Trainers should take this into account when using this game with groups consisting of people who have majored in different subject areas.

Group commonalities

PLANET MANAGEMENT's grand mean for the 12 variables was 4.19, ranking it third highest of the 13 simulation games evaluated (Diehl, 1979). There were *no* significant differences on nine of the 12 variables investigated, which indicates that the game is a strong interdiscplinary simulation. Since the respondents have such a common perspective, it is pertinent to rearrange the variables in a hierarchy of importance, according to their overall group means.

5 Decision-making	5.37
6 Intelligent planning	4.97
4 Higher cognitive outcomes	4.72
1 Motivation	4.65
12 General learning experience	4.55
2 Communication	4.44
9 Mirror Life	4.01
3 Lower cognitive outcomes	3.95
8 Complexity of material	3.60
7 Affective outcomes	3.50
11 Reality strategies	3.25
10 Reality roles	3.25

Table 6. *Variables in decreasing order of overall means*

The highest means indicate the specific strengths of this game. Thus, potential users can expect participants to feel that it trains them in decision-making skills; encourages intelligent strategic planning through the use of higher cognitive processes (analysis, synthesis, evaluation); facilitates the practising of communication skills; and is strongly motivating. The need for participants to combine mental and emotional behaviour in game play apparently generates the impression that they are realistically dealing with management problems.

Most management simulation/games tend to be either complex extended simulations, or highly specific drill tasks. THE PLANET MANAGEMENT GAME is very useful because of its proven *gestalt* approach to management, which can be conveyed, without facilitation difficulty, in approximately two hours.

References

Diehl, B J (1979) Participants' evaluations of 13 simulations in a teacher training course. Paper presented at ADSEGA Conference, Sydney

Finn, J D (1974) *A general model for multivariate analysis.* Holt, Rinehart and Winston: London

(1978) *Multivariance:* user's guide version VI, Release 2

Glass, G V and Stanley, J C (1970) *Statistical methods in education and psychology.* Prentice-Hall: Englewood Cliffs

Horn, R E (ed) (1977) *The guide to simulations/games for education and training* 3rd edition, Vol 1 and 2. Didactic Systems Inc: Cranford

Stadsklev, R (1974) *Handbook of simulation gaming in social education* (Part 1: Textbook). University of Alabama

Biographical note

Barbara J Diehl is a lecturer at the Centre for Behavioural Studies in the Faculty of Education at the University of New England. With research and teaching interests in gaming and simulation, she is currently involved in a major longitudinal measurement project for 13 selected simulation games, part of which is reported here. She has recently completed a year's study leave in the Netherlands and UK.

Barbara J Diehl
University of New England
Armidale
Australia

18. Feedback in the successful application of management games

Chris Brand and Terry Walker

Abstract: Maxim Consultants specialize in developing games to aid management training and development and organizational problem-solving. Several games have been designed to simulate the operation of real-life organizations, in both the public and private sector. It is essential that such games capture the essence of the real-life organization, and individual players should recognize and experience the actual organization in the game. This paper examines the various approaches used to translate an actual organization into a playable game while retaining its central characteristics.

Introduction

Maxim Consultants Ltd is a Brighton-based consultancy which specializes in the design of games to aid management training and development and to aid organizational problem-solving. Games designed by Maxim Consultants range from the simulation of the operation of specific international commercial organizations to situational role-playing games, used in the identification of training needs by a local authority.

This paper examines the role of feedback in the design and use of these games and is based upon both the commercial and academic experience of the authors.

The role of training games

Management games have long been established as an aid to training in both academic and commercial worlds. However, many organizations and individuals are still circumspect about their use. This may be due to the name 'game', or it may be due to inexperience or bad experience in playing or organizing inappropriate or unsuccessful games.

A management game is a very powerful tool for the trainer or teacher but it must be designed properly and applied effectively, otherwise the value of the exercise is lost and games as an educational experience fall into disrepute. This section discusses the successful application of training games, the design of such games and their organization. Feedback is seen to be an essential ingredient in the successful use of management games, and therefore its role must be considered throughout the design process and during the game's application.

Application

The first ingredient in the successful application of management games is appropriateness. A classic mistake made by many teachers and trainers is to choose a game based on an unfamiliar discipline. For instance, using a traditional model-based production-oriented management game to explore methods of improving oral communication would be inappropriate.

Choosing an appropriate game is part of the tutor's skill. Presenting the game appropriately, clarifying the objectives for playing the game and using feedback to apply the game effectively are all opportunities for the trainer to run a successful game.

Games can be designed to be organization-specific. These are easier to apply effectively as participants readily relate to the game material. This does depend on a realistic simulation of the organization. However, the design of such games on a bespoke basis is time consuming, requires a great deal of research and design skill and is therefore expensive. Persuading an organization to allocate budgets to this type of project is difficult. The benefits to the organization, once persuaded, can be great. In these situations Maxim Consultants design and produce a bespoke game which becomes the property of the organization and is eventually run solely by their own training departments. The benefits to the organization accrue from owning a very powerful, pertinent and re-usable training vehicle which can be used in different ways to achieve various objectives. For example, a UK computer manufacturer uses a bespoke management game to induct new employees to their company organization and ethos. The same game with different modules can be used to investigate the organizational implications of new policy.

Games which are not organization specific have to be more carefully applied. It is difficult to design an original game to mean all things to all men. It is important to establish a possible range of objectives for playing the game before launching into the design process. This, at least, establishes the constraints within which the game can be successfully applied. Problems occur when trying to bend a game to fit a need.

Packaged proprietary games also pose a problem. There is a large number of commercial games available in the UK for moderate sums of money. They generally contain notes for organizers as well as notes and materials for participants. What they rarely indicate is what the game should be used for and what sort of feedback to give. It is therefore up to the tutors to become familiar with a range of games, designed by other people, and attempt to apply these successfully. Particularly in academic life, these games are abused and used most inappropriately as 'time fillers' with little thought of objectives and effective feedback. This attitude seeds a poor view of games as an effective learning vehicle. Proprietary games can be used effectively but tutors must understand why the game has been selected, define the objectives and relate all feedback to those objectives.

Design

Appropriateness of a management game will inevitably depend on its effective design. Effective design depends on many factors, from accurate creation of models to designing the logistics of running the game. This section illustrates Maxim Consultants' view of the games design process.

When designing a game Maxim Consultants generally have a target audience and specific purpose in mind. The game will be aimed at a particular training course or client. This could mean that the game is industry-specific, function-specific or situation-specific. Whatever the mode of the final game, a logical approach to the game design is taken as follows:

(a) Identification of game objectives. A range of objectives to meet the client's needs is developed. This will also define the limitations of the game to be developed. This stage will need detailed discussion with the client.

(b) Development of potential game frames. At this stage the games designer will have completed some preliminary research to formulate a broad model. A number of potential game structures are developed to assess their appropriateness to the situation. Here, the place of feedback and the timing of feedback will be considered: all inappropriate game frames are discarded.

(c) Detailed research. A detailed research programme is undertaken in order to distil the essence of the situation into the game. The initial objectives and the selected game frames will determine what information is required from research. Typically, the organization's or situation's major characteristics, patterns of operation and unique features are required to produce the essence, while case, operational or financial material is required for the model.

(d) Production of the model. The model is developed from synthesizing research information. It typically involves producing a list of factors requiring emphasis in the game, an outline statistical picture (if appropriate), a statement of operational or human constraints, future trends, etc.

(e) Formulation of the outline game. This is the stage of challenging original ideas and game frames to accept a suitable game structure. Particular consideration is given to the stated objectives at this stage.

(f) Detailed game design. The outline game concepts are now turned into a full working game including models, environment, operational structure, nature and timing of feedback, overall game logistics, and documentation.

163

(g) Play-testing. In a commercial environment it is not always possible to play-test a game thoroughly, and initial runs often have to be the proving ground. However, every attempt is made to play-test games with sample groups.

(h) Production of final game. The final game will include modification made as a result of play-testing, taking into account any problems in model performance logistics, and feedback. More detailed organizer's notes are generated at this stage, based on the experiences of the play-test and initial runs.

Operation

A management game cannot run effectively, however well designed, unless it is organized properly. The organization depends on many factors including environment, design of material and a well thought-out programme.

It is important in any learning situation to work in an appropriate environment. Some games require separate tutorial rooms for group working and small group feedback. Other games require large rooms for group and individual interaction. Communication links or duplicating facilities may be required to play the game. Poor provision of physical facilities can be detrimental to the success of a game.

Poorly designed material can also have an adverse effect on the game. For instance, a badly designed form that participants have to complete may distract them from the issues of the game. Badly reproduced material will also cause difficulties for participants.

The structure of the programme is also very important. In a highly structured period-by-period game, deadlines for decisions will have to be set. In a more loosely structured game it may be a good idea to introduce checkpoints or regular feedback sessions.

A typical structure of a game programme might be:

(a) Distribution of participants' background game material
   — this often takes place the previous day.
(b) Presentation of the game:
   — stating the reasons for playing the game and the specific objectives
   — giving a background to the game material
   — showing how the game is organized
   — indicating the timetable.
(c) Initial preparation period/first decision period:
   — distribution of intermediate results
   — advice, answering questions, giving indicators
   — other decision periods and feedback sessions as appropriate.
(d) Main feedback and review:
   — discussing game issues, answering questions, posing related issues, etc
   — reinforcing learning experiences via game objectives.

Game programmes will be structured differently depending on the game frame. Feedback will also be structured differently depending on both the game frame and the game objectives, and this is discussed in the next section.

The role of feedback in games

Feedback has been mentioned many times in this paper, without defining it in a games context. The authors' definition, together with the forms it takes, is considered below.

THE NATURE OF FEEDBACK

Standard definitions of feedback relate to control systems which have relevance in all aspects of life from social systems to electronics. In our view, feedback in a game is the major controlling factor but it has two forms. These two forms achieve different sorts of control.

The first is the dissemination of game information by the trainer as a direct result of actions taken or decisions made by the participants. This clearly controls the direction of the game. In a highly formalized game this may take the form of calculating and returning results based on participant decisions. In a less formalized game this could be an oral response from the 'games master' as a result of action taken by a participant.

This form of feedback is essential to most management games where specific learning objectives should be met. This does not in itself achieve learning objectives, but it ensures that the outcome of the game will enable learning objectives to be met.

The second is the tutorial role of the trainer in facilitating and reinforcing the learning experience for the participant. Very often the participant is so involved in 'playing the game' that little learning is realized until it is highlighted by the tutors. The effective presentation of the game, with emphasis on the learning objectives, will help this feedback considerably.

These two forms of feedback can often be used together, using the results of an action to facilitate the learning. In other cases, it is the processes not the results which form the basis of feedback. Again this depends wholly on the learning objectives of the game.

It is our view that the second form of feedback is what gives the game meaning to the participants. Without this, playing a game can have little value in training and education as the learning experience has to be directed.

METHODS OF FEEDBACK

Both game feedback and learning feedback can take many forms. The pertinence of the method depends on the game structure. Some examples are given below.

GAMES FEEDBACK

For games feedback, the traditional method in quantitative model-based training games is a written statement of the state of progress. This may take the form of a revised scenario, a balance sheet, a trading statement or simply a set of performance ratings. It is usually calculated or assessed as the result of formal decisions taken by participants. It is good practice to have pre-printed forms giving the structure of feedback, to facilitate good presentation of material to the participants. Often a master board is kept for all participants to be made aware of overall factors influencing the game, eg, current inflation rates, maximum market sizes, political indicators. This aspect of feedback may also include specially requested reports, pre-prepared market research, simulated consultancy reports, etc.

With this sort of highly structured feedback it is normal to present it at set times during the game, with periods of uninterrupted play by the participants. On completion of the game a comparative analysis is often made if more than one group is playing.

With role-playing games, feedback may be similar to that described above, but usually there is additional oral feedback during play. In role-playing games, the models are often less definite and points of clarification often arise.

It may also be the case that groups have created situations through their role-plays that the designer had not considered. In this case the tutor must feed back definite information during the course of play. The tutor may actually play a role in the game, therefore giving direct and continuous feedback.

One particular game run by Maxim Consultants for a major hotel group in the UK requires continuous feedback by the trainers via telephone and letters. This requires a great deal of pre-planning, attempting to cover all situations that might arise and having reasonable programmed responses to them. This is essential when games of 50 people with five trainers take place, or else consistency in response will be lost and the game models will break down. In this particular game a large set of standard letters has been prepared and rules for answering telephone enquiries have been established to constrain the variation in factual information given when responding. In some situations, participants establish their own results by calculation or inference and the trainer then has an auditing role to perform, to ensure accuracy and consistency.

Learning feedback

Learning feedback is obviously the means by which the trainer reinforces the learning experience of the game, looks at related issues and extends the learning experience. This can be accomplished at many different stages depending on the game frame. In a traditional model-based game the learning feedback will probably be given at the end of play, possibly using a comparative analysis of results. Learning will be reinforced by encouraging participants to explain their strategies, to analyse cause and effect and to explore 'what if' situations.

Often this type of feedback is directed by a questionnaire pointing to relevant issues and using this as the basis for feedback. During feedback sessions, participants will want to discuss many issues, some of which are not central to the learning objectives. It is important for the trainer not to be diverted too far from the central issues but to attempt to steer the feedback back to central ideas. This requires a thorough understanding of the game, the game models and how they relate to the learning objectives.

It may also be pertinent to have learning feedback sessions, on a progressive basis, at each decision period, with a final analysis on completion.

In games based on role-play, learning feedback is generally best left to defined sessions. Interruptions of role-plays, unless absolutely necessary, will disturb the continuity of the game. If behavioural objectives are set, it is useful to have a skilled observer who takes no part in the game. Notes should be made on a structured basis and should be consistent with the objectives stated during the presentation.

On completion of a role-play game, open discussion, tutorial or questionnaire technique can all be applied successfully. Audio or video recording can be used particularly successfully in role-plays, where playback can be used to reinforce observation. However, a certain amount of intimidation can be felt by participants faced with the use of audio-video equipment, which can affect the progress of the game.

All situations will require their own form of learning feedback. Wherever possible, game performance should be directly related to the learning objective, and the most effective games are those whose game feedback and learning feedback are synonymous.

Conclusions

This paper has dealt with the main issues of appropriateness of a game to a learning situation and the need for effective feedback to meet learning objectives. To use games successfully as pertinent training vehicles, it is essential to understand clearly these learning objectives. Without these a game has little or no value in training or education.

To effect the learning situation, feedback is the major control both to keep the game a coherent entity and to direct the learning. It is an enabling device but the tutor must direct the enabling.

If a game is not appropriate to the situation it should not be used other than as an intellectual exercise. Do not bend games to fit needs or bend needs to fit games. Feedback becomes very difficult if the issues raised are mainly outside the learning objectives set.

When designing games, think about feedback as an integral part of the design process. It may influence the choice of game frame used in your final design.

When running games, take care about physical environment, quality of material, physical access to materials and tutors. Consider the methods and frequency of feedback required.

In the experience of Maxim Consultants the success of running a game is a function of the clarity of objectives, the pertinence of the game and thorough, directed learning feedback. Measuring success in running a game is an issue which will never be properly resolved. Consider, however:

(a) the atmosphere created by the game participants during play
(b) the morale of the participants at the end of the game
(c) the extent of unprompted questioning and discussion during feedback.

If these are all favourable, the game has probably been successful. If objectives have been clearly stated, feedback has centred around these objectives and the three points above are all favourable, the game has been successful!

C Brand and T Walker
Maxim Consultants Ltd
19a Queens Road
Brighton
Sussex
England

19. The use of simulation/gaming to facilitate creativity in the development of leadership potential

Linda di Desidero

Abstract: The gaming process fosters the development of creative potential within the individual. Simulations heighten the individual's ability to perceive situations in novel ways and to explore diverse solutions to problems. Simulation/gaming, a heuristic process, usually achieves total participant involvement.

Torrance and other major creativity theorists argue that the development of creative potential is important for many reasons:

(a) It enhances mental health.
(b) It increases an individual's ability to become a fully functioning person.
(c) It adds value to educational achievement in the realms of cognition and memory.
(d) It contributes to vocational success.
(e) It is of immense socio-cultural importance.

Although divergent thinking cannot be taught or learned in conventional ways, an individual's awareness of his or her innovative potential may be heightened as a result of mind-stretching activities. Gaming aids the individual in developing the ability to tap the sources of his or her creative pool.

This paper examines the use of simulation/gaming in the light of its propensity to promote the growth of divergent thought processes. Employment of these techniques ultimately contributes to the development of leadership potential. As confidence in other ways of knowing is strengthened, an individual's sensitivity to group needs is enhanced. Freed from external constraints, the individual becomes a better decision maker.

Introduction

'God has let us down, God seems to have left the receiver off the hook, and time is running out,' wrote Arthur Koestler in a recent work, *Janus: A Summing Up.* In a radically changing world, behind which looms the ever-present threat of atomic destruction, a growing disparity exists between the ability of persons to understand and control the environment, and our ability to understand ourselves enough to solve the increasingly complicated problems of civilization. Humans create things: attempts to do away with poverty, hunger, war and inflation, attempts to improve the human condition through political, social and educational institutions, have at best been only partially successful.

Creativity—whether artistic creation, scientific discovery, technological invention or personal insight—embodies a process that appears to be as essential

168

to life as breathing and eating. At its lowest level, it helps people to understand the world; at its highest level it enables persons to understand their relations to existence and to bring this insight to others. Creative ability and self-actualization are synergistic: more self-actualized people are creative, as more innovative persons reach higher states of self-actualization.

Because creativity is something humans must engage in alone, because it demands that individuals diverge from public consensus reality, and because it details ways of knowing which are not fully conscious nor cognitive, many fail to create. An activity that allays fears surrounding creativity and which increases human potential through the development of innovative abilities is simulation/gaming.

Simulation/games simplify reality while providing a risk-free environment for exercising options. They allow individuals to function originally and spontaneously within the safe parameters of the creative environment. Simulations increase the understanding, power and control an individual can exercise over his or her actions and thoughts, over others, and over the environment. They develop the abilities to cope with and respond to the unknown. This strengthens the development of leadership potential within societies as it increases the likelihood of self-actualization. Games bridge the convergence necessitated by daily living and the divergence demanded by the need to create and the need to improve the human condition. What follows is an examination of creativity and its relation to gaming in terms of the creative process, the creative environment, the creative product, and the creative person.

The creative process and gaming

The creative process has been described by many theorists in many different ways. A synthesis of these conceptualizations shows that innovation demands that the individual engages in thought processes which are not fully conscious or cognitive, and that simulation/games stimulate these mental activities.

One of the first and most widely accepted analyses of the stages of creativity was published by Graham Wallas in a work entitled *The Art of Thought* (1926). After studying artists' and scientists' written accounts of their works (eg, Henri Poincare's classical description of his discovery of Fuchsian functions), Wallas delineated four stages to the creative act: preparation, incubation, illumination and verification.

A problem is posed in the period of preparation for which there appears to be no ready answer. The problem enters a period of incubation within the unconscious during which time the individual is usually engaged in restful or relaxing activity. Poincare has postulated that 'atoms of ideas' are unhooked from the walls of the brain and set into motion. Within the unconscious, disorder, chaos, and liberty reign as ideas collide with one another, producing combinations which would never have been arrived at through logic or conscious analytical thought. Einstein called this a play of the mind's elements. This period of unconscious work is followed by the illumination of a unique idea, whose validity can then be determined in a period of conscious verification.

This description of the creative process may seem simplistic, and it has, in fact, been criticized for its rigidity. It compares to models of the creative process from the more recent work of theorists and has often been used as a base for these paradigms.

E Paul Torrance, advocate of creativity in education, conceptualizes the creative process in a way similar to Wallas. For Torrance, creativity is 'the process of becoming sensitive to problems, deficiencies, gaps in knowledge and disharmonies; identifying the difficulties; searching for solutions, making guesses or formulating hypotheses about deficiencies; testing and retesting these hypotheses and possibly modifying them; retesting them and finally communicating the result' (Vernon, 1970).

The game MASTERMIND illustrates creativity and its synergism with gaming. The initial sensitivity to 'gaps in knowledge' is given in the game's objective: the code-breaker must discover the hidden pattern of colours determined by the code-maker. The code-breaker formulates hypotheses about the pattern, receives non-verbal feedback concerning their viability, then reformulates hypotheses until the code is broken.

This illustration of Torrance's definition of the creative process may, too, seem simplistic and rigid. Where does a sensitivity to problems originate? How do we formulate hypotheses? More in-depth, non-linear descriptions of the process account for these aspects of creativity.

William J J Gordon maintains that perception, learning, and invention are extensions of one another. We perceive through metaphor and make connections between the known and the unknown, the known and the known. Learning is an extension of perceiving, as inventing is an extension of learning.

Learning is a process of making connections between the known and the unknown, a process of making strange things familiar, a process of assimilating what is being learned to what has already been learned. It is a communication with the self. Innovation is a process of seeing the familiar in strange and novel ways, a process of breaking connections, a process of accommodation. It culminates in a communication with the world. Simulation/gaming includes several cycles of both processes.

To play a game, a player must learn objectives, rules, roles, the scope of the game, as well as the sequences of action and interaction. As he or she plays the game, the player may invent new strategies to achieve objectives, new matrices of moves, new dimensions to roles, and new ways in which to communicate with players.

As the game progresses and at its end, the player has a holistic image of the process embodied in the game, as well as immediate feedback concerning the value of what she or he has learned and invented. This *gestalt* is achieved by cycling through periods of preparing for play, incubating rules, roles, and goals, achieving illuminations of how to think and behave in both prescribed and novel ways, and by the opportunity to verify or evaluate actions and understanding on a level commensurate with one's abilities and compatible with individual learning styles.

Figure 1 imposes upon Gordon's learning-innovating cycle Wallas' four stages of the creative act as it illustrates the convergence (learning) and the divergence (innovating) necessitated by gaming.

This picture of the gaming process also fosters the individual's understanding of how his or her psychological processes operate, a condition under which, Gordon maintains, learning efficiency may be increased.

The notion of increasing learning efficiency as well as divergent thinking abilities is one assumed by many theorists. Developing these abilities, or these 'natural' thought processes (as Wallas called them) may be achieved by:

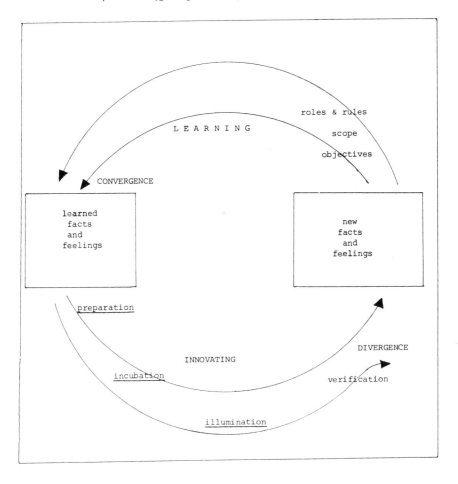

Figure 1. *The cycle of learning, innovating and creativity*

(a) getting persons to understand their own psychological processes better;
(b) according emotional and non-rational components of these processes the
same significance accorded intellectual and rational components; (c) engaging
emotional and non-rational components along with intellectual and rational
components in mind-stretching activities (Gordon, 1966).

Gordon has developed methods and techniques for increasing learning
efficiency in a procedure called *Synectics*. This process expands an individual's
capacity to use metaphor in learning and innovating, through brainstorming
activities and through application of analogy.

To the same end, games—particularly role-play simulations—provide
metaphors of reality as well as the opportunity to connect analogically the
pieces of simplified reality in the learning and invention of play. They accord

importance to emotion as well as to intellect. The motivation to play, the drive to achieve a goal, and the individual's ability to internalize a role as well as the ability to empathize with other players' roles are largely non-rational strengths.

Role-play simulations, although they demand certain intellectual abilities of comprehension, reason and analysis, also demand other ways of knowing and of acting upon this knowledge. In such games, a delicate balance between competition and co-operation among players should be achieved; this is as much affective as it is cognitive. The ability to integrate the emotional and non-rational components of the human psyche with the intellectual and rational components often distinguishes a creative individual from a non-creative individual, and a successful from an unsuccessful game-player.

Other ways of knowing: creative processing and gaming

The mental processes involved in this integration of the rational and the non-rational have long been a perplexing issue for creativity theorists. We may call this integration 'intuitive action', although intuition has too long been used as a catch-all for several thought processes which are not readily explicable. More in-depth conceptualizations of these mental processes, so integral to creative thinking and to successful gaming, are offered by Silvano Arieti (1976), Edward de Bono (1979), Arthur Koestler (1978), and Albert Rothenberg (1971). We may call these forms of thought endoceptual cognition, lateral thinking, bisociating matrices, and Janusian thinking.

In *Creativity: The Magic Synthesis*, Silvano Arieti (1976) posits the concept of tertiary process thinking to describe the articulation between what Sigmund Freud called primary and secondary thought processes. Primary thought processes are primitive forms of cognition prevalent in the unconscious. These are form and process oriented types of knowing; 'paleological' as opposed to logical or illogical. Secondary thought processes comprise logic, reason and analysis; in other words, the mechanisms we use in conscious deliberation. These are content-oriented.

The connection between primary and secondary thinking is essential to creative action. When we can synthesize this in a thought or behaviour, we use what Arieti calls the tertiary process, a function of which is the endocept.

Endoceptual cognition occurs without form. It may be otherwise understood as internal, non-verbal, unconscious, or preconscious thought. The endocept is a 'primitive organization of past experience, perceptions, memory traces and images of things and movements' (Arieti, 1976). Although the endocept works within primary process thinking, it can influence conscious thought indirectly by transformation through verbal or artistic action into a product that retains much of the endocept's quality.

We experience endoceptual phenomena in dreams and in experiences of high emotion, such as an intense simulation. Endocepts are active during what Wallas calls the period of incubation, as they struggle for embodiment in words, actions and ideas. 'Endoceptual processes accrue. They are self-enlarging and self-enriching; they add new dimensions even when higher levels of mentation are present' (Arieti, 1976).

The gaming process, when it demands original and spontaneous thought that is largely unrestricted by precedent, can require and encourage endoceptual cognition and can foster its development within the individual.

Another approach to divergent thinking, not quite so technical psychologically, has been delineated by Edward de Bono. Thinking, according to de Bono, is a skill from which the individual should derive challenge and pleasure, a skill to be exercised in several ways. De Bono draws a dichotomy between vertical and lateral thinking.

Vertical thinking is thinking in patterns that are convergent, sequential, and logical. Although this type of thinking is easy to teach, test and measure, it is not a process that leads to original solutions to problems. De Bono had coined the term 'lateral thinking' to describe a divergent means by which problems are defined and solved. Two important concepts to note with regard to lateral thinking are fragmentation and shift.

When faced with a problem, 'instead of constructing a pathway forward (as in vertical thought), one jumps to different points and then allows the fragments to coalesce' (McBride, 1981). This coalescence of idea fragments is sometimes lucrative, sometimes not. But the divergent thinker can tolerate apparent absurdity or ambiguity because she or he can shift perspectives. This ability to re-orient a frame of reference, or to make 'universe changes', can be enhanced in the gaming situation.

Role-play simulations provide exercise in lateral thinking skills. Not only do players have the opportunity to jump from one conclusion to another, but absurd, unusual or ambiguous solutions to problems can be tolerated within the safety of the environment. In developing empathy for other roles, gamers are encouraged to shift perspectives, a process that fosters understanding of the creative act. Not only do players have the opportunity to try out different solutions to problems and varied strategies in reaching goals, but they receive almost immediate feedback on the viability of these solutions and strategies.

Arthur Koestler (1978) conceives of this as the bisociation of matrices. He maintains that thought and behaviour patterns and abilities are contained in separate matrices. As humans grow older, these accrue. Matrices are governed by codes of rules to operate in accordance with environmentally induced strategies. When two previously separate matrices are related to one another in some way, they are bisociated in terms of the creative act. Their integration is scientific, their collision is humorous, and juxtaposing them is artistic. A given creative act has the potential to enter any of these realms. Gaming relaxes the affiliation between inflexible codes and flexible strategies to promote innovative behaviour. An illustration of this is the societal simulation QUICK CITY.

QUICK CITY (McConatha, 1975) is a societal simulation designed to teach players how to deal with conflicts between various community interest groups, specifically within the context of a capitalist economy and a democratic government. Participants are divided into four interest groups, which represent the powerful factions that exert control over individuals in larger society:

(a) a powerful and highly competitive economic group;
(b) a social welfare group, often in direct opposition to the economic group;
(c) a political group, which ideally should reconcile differences between social welfare and economic groups;
(d) the apathetic public, or the silent majority that often relinquishes its powers and rights to any stronger and more stable group.

Each group has a set of three goals to achieve within the sequence of the play of the game.

Groups first structure their goals on a priority system, then attempt to achieve each of the goals within the ensuing three negotiation sessions of the game; power and money cards are their only tools.

Often the goals of groups conflict with one another. The political group is to distribute power and money as it sees fit, but the economic group must obtain 50 per cent of all the power. Communication problems arise as one group may choose to withhold information from another group or to lie to that group. In the attempt to reconcile the competition induced by this to the co-operation needed to accomplish the game's objective, the formation of a city, players must be innovative in their combination of strategies. Efforts to achieve two seemingly opposed ends at once lead to the consideration of a final type of divergent processing—Janusian thinking.

Psychiatrist Albert Rothenberg (1971) describes a thought process based upon the simultaneous conception of two opposing entities. This Janusian principle—metaphorically represented by the two-faced Roman god who could perceive in contrary directions at once—is prevalent in works of science and art; it is embodied in the concepts of metaphor, paradox, ambiguity and tension. It is also stimulated by the gaming process.

Rothenberg maintains that Janusian thinking occurs early in the conceptualization of a creative act, during what Wallas called the periods of preparation and incubation. Even though Rothenberg insists it is a secondary thought process, neither its presence nor its effects may be obvious until the action is completed.

This is reminiscent of both Gordon and Arieti. Gordon's mind-stretching, through the use of metaphor and analogy, actually demands the integration or relation of opposites or near-opposites. Like Arieti's endoceptual cognition, Janusian thinking is a way of knowing without realizing that you know, until the act is completed.

In the gaming situation we often find the embodiment of contrary goals striving for accommodation. The complexity of a role-playing simulation such as QUICK CITY requires the reconciliation of competition to co-operation, of falsehoods to truth.

Another example of this is found in the cross-cultural simulation CULTURE CONTACT (Abt, 1969). CULTURE CONTACT is designed to teach the concept of cultural relativism, and to have players experience the possibilities of misunderstanding prevalent in situations in which two culturally different groups must communicate with one another. Participants take specific roles of characters in one of two cultures—the Elenians, a horizontally structured, pre-industrial society, or the Grannisters, a competitive and hierarchically structured industrial society.

Cultural differences are at first apparent in physical conduct. The Elenians rub their tummies when they meet people, while the Grannisters scratch their heads and look at the ground. Avoidance of eye contact is proper conduct for the Grannisters but the Elenians feel it is rude. More deeply-seated cultural differences become apparent as the game progresses. Role descriptions are explicit in terms of goals, wealth, power and the place of individuals within the culture.

The Grannisters would like to establish a trading post on the island of the Elenians. They have travelled to Elena by ship to negotiate this. A language barrier exists as only three members of each culture may communicate with the other. Play proceeds by alternating planning sessions with team members of the same culture and negotiating sessions among the six interpreters.

Participants must maintain superficial cultural characteristics, as they internalize both general cultural traits and values and specific role characteristics. The fact that important cultural differences lie beneath role differences and the events of the game offers a unique challenge to players. Not only must these cultural differences be discovered, they must be dealt with in ways that will not negate primary cultural objectives: the Grannisters must trade and the Elenians must protect their sacred groves. Although the simulation may not result in a definitive win or loss for either side, players experience the process of cross-cultural communication and they exercise innovative ways of dealing with it from personal interpretations of role perspectives.

Gaming facilitates the individual's use of her or his innovative thinking powers. The gaming process requires original and spontaneous response, offers opportunity for the more content-oriented forms of cognition called learning, as well as opportunity for the form and process oriented types of thinking conceptualized within the creativity paradigm as innovating, tertiary process thinking, endoceptual cognition, lateral thinking, bisociation, or Janusian thinking. Games and simulations are conducive to creative development not only in the process they embody, but also in the environment they establish.

Game as creative environment

Creative action demands courage. In a world where 'average' and 'normal' are generally synonymous, and where mediocrity is all too often lauded, those who choose to deviate from norms in any way risk social alienation and stigma.

Simulations and games eliminate the fear associated with divergence by offering a safe environment in which the individual may test other ways of knowing, thinking and behaving. The world of the game brings individuals closer to tapping the sources of their creative pools, closer to a state of self-actualization, closer to realising their potential to see life both as it is and as it might be. The gaming environment can foster the growth of creative vision because it can provide both safety and freedom.

Creativity, writes Carl Rogers, must be 'permitted to emerge' under 'nurturing conditions of psychological safety and freedom' (Vernon, 1970). Psychological safety is attained by three related processes:

(a) accepting the individual as of unconditional worth;
(b) providing a climate in which external evaluation is absent;
(c) understanding empathetically.

Psychological freedom, or a 'complete freedom of symbolic expression', is permission to think, feel and express with a primary responsibility only to the self. This helps develop an inner locus of evaluation within the individual, thus promoting the growth of actions which are results of creative, internal processing, as opposed to actions which are prompted by external cues.

These 'nurturing conditions' are often inherent in the gaming environment; when they are not, they may be built in by the nature of the facilitator and the nature of the group. Good game facilitators provide unqualified support for and acceptance of participants. Players are often secure enough in their roles to interpret them freely. The ultimate evaluation of a player's actions is not made by the facilitator nor by other players, but by the gamer. In order for a productive and stimulating game to progress, there must be empathy among players. The higher the degree of total participant involvement a game demands, the more nurturing the gaming environment becomes.

One-person games, games of chance and puzzles are generally predictable, demand minimal involvement, are of low intensity and usually have solutions that are universally accepted. These games least resemble life, and even though they may teach analytical thought and problem-solving skills, they do not teach problem-finding skills. Opportunities to integrate the intellectual and the emotional components of perception are scarce, if they exist at all.

Well-run role-play simulations are more lucrative creatively. Although opposing goals and interests of players as well as rules and basic strategies may be rather well-defined, there are opportunities for divergence in the implementation of strategies and in the combinations of moves. There are no preferable strategies and no single, predictable outcomes. Lack of precedent often requires spontaneity and originality from players, even when they are playing a simulation for the second or third time.

Players are free to interpret roles and devise strategies to meet often more than one objective, within the constraints of the scope of the game. The need to compete must often be reconciled to the need to co-operate.

The gaming environment is one that facilitates creative types of thought processing within the individual. It is also conducive to the production of a creative product that is the embodiment of the synergism between the individual and the environment.

Games as creative product

The result of divergent processing within a nurturing environment may be understood in terms of the development of creative potential within the individual and in terms of the creative product. Carl Rogers writes that creative products are novel and relational, that they 'grow out of the uniqueness of the individual on the one hand, and the materials, events, people or circumstances of his life on the other' (Vernon, 1970).

Games are heuristic, holistic avenues to the creative product. They are languages of the future, according to Richard Duke (1974), a form of *gestalt* communication. Holistic images are products of an individual's creative processes.

Within the safety constraints of the game (ie, role, scenario, sequence), players perceive, create and express perceptions of specific systems and processes. Duke's characteristics of games as the future's languages suggest innovative action: games are mutable, universal, inherently spontaneous, and they are transient in that they permit definition and redefinition during play.

Simulations transmit *gestalts* in varying time frames, Duke maintains, because of three qualities:

(a) specific options 'pulse' in correlation with a holistic image;
(b) details may be understood at several levels of abstraction;
(c) links between major segments of *gestalts* may be made explicit as players perceive the complexity of the process and receive feedback about their actions and perceptions.

These qualities of games as languages of the future reflect the qualities of games as creative products of individual understanding.

There is an implicit synergism between the 'holon' of the game (ie, the process it embodies as well as the context of the process), and the individual creating the play of the game. In *The Courage to Create*, Rollo May writes: 'A continual dialectical process goes on between world and self, and self and world; one implies the other and neither can be understood without the other.'

Following the play of a simulation such as QUICK CITY,, the player has an understanding of the process of negotiation between various socio-cultural groups. This understanding is strengthened by the simultaneous perception of the process from his or her perspective in simulated reality and from consideration of the process in the player's actual life situation. This continual shifting of perspectives refines and enhances the image of the process, the major linkages in the process, and the connections between self/role and process/game.

A more intense simulation such as CULTURE CONTACT reinforces this. Not only do players understand their role commitments to individual agendas, strengths and weaknesses, but they must discover motives, agendas, strengths and shortcomings of others. The complexity of the process is apparent in cultural barriers—communication difficulties, differences in values, reasons for distrust, etc. Although players may create similar understandings of the process of cross-cultural communication and of their own powers of negotiation, for each player it is a unique understanding. It is a product that has grown out of the experience in its totality and the player's individual relation to and within that experience.

The creative gamer and the development of leadership potential

The societal and individual implications of creativity development as a means to reach human potential are many. The work of creativity theorists attests to the fact that innovative potential can be cultivated within individuals. The work of gaming theorists offers evidence that the development of leadership potential and the use of interpersonal power may be maximized through gaming. An examination of the creative gamer shows how these two processes—the development of innovative ability and the development of leadership potential— may, in fact, be synergistic.

Studies of the personalities of creative people indicate that they achieve higher states of self-actualization than non-creative persons, and that they possess many universally desirable characteristics. In *Traits of Creativity* (Vernon, 1970), Guilford delineates several characteristics of the creative person. These compare with traits catalogued by other theorists. They include:

(a) a general sensitivity to problems;
(b) fluency of words, associations, expressions and ideas;
(c) flexibility of thought that is spontaneous and adaptive;
(d) originality;
(e) the ability to redefine or reorganize;
(f) the ability to elaborate, or to construct complexities.

Simulation/gaming contributes to the development of these traits. A successful gamer must be sensitive to problems, must be aware of personal goals, strengths and weaknesses, and must anticipate an awareness of others' objectives. She or he must be fluent and flexible in exploring alternatives, and in conceptualizing new methods to achieve goals. Co-operating with players demands sensitivity and resilience. Often the solution to problematic issues lies in the ability to redefine or reconstruct them. Successful strategies are often original and/or complex.

The nurturing environment of the game fosters the development of these traits. Gaming also makes these traits viable in the development of leadership potential. Miller's (1979) analysis of social interaction games in *Simulations and Games* illustrates this.

Miller analysed interaction games to determine the ways in which playing them contributed to the development of social power within the individual. He conducted the analysis in terms of three components: assets, conversion processes, and interpersonal power.

Assets are stable resources which determine social power potential. They include intelligence, appearance, humour, wit, judgement and social skills. Before these interpersonal assets can be used to exert social influence, they must undergo conversion processes. Conversion processes may be measured by the proportion of assets they convert, the ways in which they convert assets to social power, and the quality of the conversion. Interpersonal power is achieved by integrating assets and conversion processes within a social environment.

Simulation/gaming fosters the development of this integration process. Within the gaming environment, individuals become deeply aware of their personal assets. They learn new ways to use these personal resources in interacting with others, thus learning new ways in which to convert these assets into social power. Miller concludes that gaming facilitates the individual's use of interpersonal power in three ways:

(a) it develops the ability to formulate realistic and fulfilling personal goals and relationships;
(b) it increases sensitivity to how others feel and how they view the individual;
(c) it increases the capacity to adapt to the demands of different social situations.

These traits of socially powerful individuals compare to the characteristics of creative persons delineated by Guilford (Vernon, 1970). They also align themselves with Torrance's assertion that creative thinking, besides enhancing educational achievement and improving mental health, increases an individual's ability to become a fully functioning person, contributes to vocational success, and is of immense socio-cultural importance (Vernon, 1970).

Simulation/gaming, in facilitating the individual's creative development, also aids in the realization of the individual's potential in developing those qualities which make him or her more powerful socially. Persons who can make sound decisions and formulate realistic goals, who are sensitive to others as well as to their surroundings, and who adapt themselves readily to rapidly changing situations are those persons who reach higher states of self-actualization, who are most suited to fulfil leadership roles in societies.

Conclusion

Democracies collapse only when they fail to use intelligent imaginative methods for solving their problems. Greece failed to heed such a warning from Socrates and gradually collapsed. What is called for is a far cry from the model of the quiz program champion of a few years ago... (Torrance, in Vernon, 1970).

Creativity development is necessary for civilized persons to reach their potential. Implicit within the concept of civilization, however, is convergence; divergence is often viewed as antithetical to the maintenance of societies. This perspective must be broadened, as the development of innovative abilities in all facets of human life is required for the survival of the species. The courage to change this perspective, the courage to welcome new ideas and actions and the courage to acquire the sensitivity to people and problems, qualities so integral in strong leaders, may be attained through simulation/gaming.

The nurturing environment of the game allows persons to think safely and behave in original and spontaneous ways; it permits and encourages access to other ways of knowing. As confidence in creative ability grows, individuals attain broadened conceptions of life processes and systems, and of their personal relations to these in terms of understanding and control. This increases human potential within societies as it draws people toward higher, more encompassing levels of not just being, but becoming.

Ultimately creativity development through gaming can maximize leadership potential within individuals: as divergent thinking abilities develop, so, too, do the abilities to implement new ideas in the exertion of interpersonal power and social influence. Our expectations for the development of human potential through creativity cannot be too great. As Arthur Koestler writes (1978):

> To hope for salvation to be synthesized in the laboratory may seem materialistic, crankish, or naive; it reflects the ancient alchemist's dream to concoct the elixir vitae. What we expect from it, however, is not eternal life, but the transformation of homo maniacus into homo sapiens.

References

Abt, C (1969) CULTURE CONTACT. Abt Associates, Inc: Cambridge, Mass
Arieti, S (1976) *Creativity: The Magic Synthesis.* Basic Books, Inc: New York
Davis, M (1973) *Game theory.* Basic Books, Inc: New York
de Bono, E (1979) *Future Positive.* Temple Smith: London
Duke, R (1974) *Gaming: The Future's Language.* Halstead Press: New York
Ghiselin, B (1972) *The Creative Process.* University of California Press: Los Angeles
Gordon, W J J (1966) *The Metaphorical Way of Learning and Knowing.* Porpoise Books: Cambridge, Mass
Koestler, A (1978) *Janus: A Summing Up.* Random House: New York
May, R (1975) *The Courage to Create.* Bantam: New York
McBride, S (1981) Edward de Bono: Teaching the world to think. *Christian Science Monitor,* 6.7.1981: Boston
McConatha, P D (1975) QUICK CITY: A SOCIETAL SIMULATION. Utah State University
Miller, L (1979) (ed) Interaction games for the classroom. *Simulations and Games,* 10 4: 355-358
Rothenberg, A (1971) The Process of Janusian thinking in creativity. *Archives of General Psychiatry,* 24: 195-205
Vernon, P E (1970) *Traits of Creativity,* Penguin Books: New York

Biographical note

Linda di Desidero teaches English at a New Jersey high school. Prior to that, she taught English and German in Sayreville. She has recently completed her Master's degree in Science and Humanities education at Rutgers Graduate School of Education in New Brunswick, where much of her work had been done in the field of creativity and creative development. She has both participated in and conducted workshops in gaming and simulation.

Linda di Desidero
Willingboro High School
Willingboro
New Jersey 08109
USA

20. The philosophy of fallibilism and simulation/gaming

Michael J Rockler

Abstract: This essay provides a rationale for new curricula which is based on the philosophy of fallibilism as well as on viewpoints derived from an aesthetic curriculum perspective, humanistic education, existentialism, and futurism. The paper defines fallibilism — describing its historical development: it indicates how this philosophy of science has been adapted to education. It demonstrates the compatibility of fallibilism with other innovative perspectives. These serve as rationale for new approaches to curriculum. Part of this innovation in education involves the technique of simulation/gaming. In this way, the article offers helpful support to potential users of simulation/gaming.

Introduction

Rousseau's prayer offers a hint of the need for a new approach to curriculum:

> Almighty God! Thou who holdest in thy hand the minds of men, deliver us from the fatal arts and sciences of our forefathers: give us back ignorance, innocence and poverty which alone can make us happy and are precious in thy sight.

The anonymous author of the following also alludes to this need:

> Our past is not our potential. In any hour with all the stubborn teachers and healers of history who called us to our best selves we can liberate the future. One by one, we can rechoose — to awaken. To leave the prison of our conditioning, to love, to turn homeward. To conspire with and for each other. Awakening brings its own assignments, unique to each of us, chosen by each of us. Whatever you may think about yourself, and however long you may have thought it, you are not just you. You are a seed, a silent promise. You are the conspiracy.

These quotations suggest the theme of this paper: a call for a new approach to school curriculum based on a variety of perspectives and particularly including the philosophy of fallibilism. These viewpoints, taken together, provide support for this new approach. An important strategy within it is the technique of simulation/gaming. Before examining this proposed new curriculum perspective, let us reflect upon traditional programmes now present in most schools in the United States.

Current curriculum practice often fails to educate pupils. Designed to serve the needs of another day and age, it does not adequately provide for this day and age. At its inception, the old school curriculum contained two components:

(a) It provided universal education through primary school with emphasis on the basic skills of reading, writing and arithmetic—desired outcomes to train children for simple employment as labourers and clerks and to make them capable of reading the Bible.

(b) It provided education for the elite—college preparatory schools that offered training in academic subjects.

The situation today is different. Universal secondary education now exists in the United States. All children from the age of five to the age of 18 participate in programmes and large numbers go on to some type of post-secondary courses, extending the secondary school population from a privileged few to a diverse many. Curriculum—with perhaps the exception of the limited addition of vocational training—has hardly changed.

Traditional courses of study have failed to be effective, even as preparation for college. Teacher burnout, criticism from parents, and drug abuse help demonstrate this proposition.

TEACHER BURNOUT

Although relatively new in the public's awareness, this phenomenon has existed for a long time. Teacher turnover has accelerated despite larger salaries and improved benefits. People seem unable to endure the stress of teaching for very long.

CRITICISM FROM PARENTS

Esteem for schools has reached an all time low in the United States. Parents demand accountability. Huge numbers of students fail to become fully literate. The movement towards private education has gained momentum and the public demand for tuition tax credit will certainly accelerate this trend.

DRUG ABUSE

This problem grows in significance as the use of drugs in schools increases. Teachers know when a new shipment of marijuana has arrived in the neighbourhood because of the large number of 'stoned' pupils. Students use drugs to make palpable the irrelevance of their studies.

A new approach to the school curriculum

A new approach to the school curriculum can be derived from five significant viewpoints. These include the philosophy of fallibilism, the aesthetic curriculum perspective, humanistic education, existentialism, and futurism.

The philosopher, Karl Popper, developed the philosophy of fallibilism in response to Hume's criticism of induction (see, for example, Popper [1961]). Henry Perkinson, working with other educators at New York University, has translated fallibilism into a philosophy of education. An examination of the formulation of fallibilism will show its usefulness as support for a new approach to curriculum.

The scientific revolution stems from the principle of induction—a way of knowing that helps persons learn from experience. The scientist approaches a series of white swans. After examining one thousand of them, the scientist feels comfortable in making the following generalization: all swans are white. However, suppose swan number 1001 is black. What happens to the generalization? It becomes false.

Hume forced empiricists to understand that the principle was limited. He denied that induction led to truth. At first, he was not taken seriously. Science reigned unchallenged in western thought: Newton's fascinating laws worked. From them predictions were made leading to the discovery of new planets. The universe appeared to be an orderly place. Newton's logical paradigm arose from the inductive principle, giving it renewed credence. Trouble came, however, when Albert Einstein's model essentially replaced Newton's. Einstein proved that Newtonian physics remained true only within certain limited parameters. The logic of induction once again came into question; new analyses of it developed. Two of these can be juxtaposed: the work of Bertrand Russell and that of John Dewey.

Einstein's physics required Russell to examine anew the limitations of induction. He believed that science sought absolute truth. Induction seeks certainty believing that ultimately it can be found. Each hypothesis along the way becomes a refinement of an earlier one; induction is a necessary and useful tool which brings the scientist closer to perfect knowledge.

Dewey too believed that experience can be used to find the truth but he felt that it could not come directly from induction. So he created a way station and labelled it 'pragmatic truth'. Formulations were 'true' (for the time being) so long as they worked (so long as no black swans showed up).

Dewey sought pragmatic truth while Russell searched for absolute truth and refined hypotheses along the way.

Fallibilism and the curriculum

Karl Popper, originator of fallibilism, rejected induction totally: he viewed it as an unnecessary strategy. For him, absolute truth exists but is unattainable. What does this leave for science? Popper argued that its purpose is to demonstrate the *falsity* of theories. Inductive logic can be abandoned and absolute truth can be viewed as a desirable but unattainable goal. The scientist proceeds to demonstrate falsity and does so by employing a critical method, creating a new theory, then proceeding to falsify it. Understanding the fallibility of any notion means that the ultimate task is not certainty but improvement. Each step along the way provides a better, more accurate idea; it leads along a road to understanding but, Popper argues, this path never comes to an end.

Fallibilism can be the underlying philosophy of new approaches to curriculum. Henry Perkinson (1971) applies fallibilism to education. For

Perkinson, the primary purpose of learning is improvement. Schools can perform one of the following tasks: they can be agents of *conservation.* When they conserve, they maintain the past. Centres of learning may *serve.* When they do this, they provide for needs in the present. Schools can also *improve.* When they do, they help orient students to the future. Institutions often attempt all three tasks simultaneously. But this helps to account for their failure since the three tasks are usually at cross purposes. In order to be effective, Perkinson argues, schools should seek improvement of ideas knowing that all persons are fallible and therefore any idea can be wrong. Betterment comes from constantly attempting to rectify error.

'What prevents improvement?' asks Perkinson. Authoritarianism, is his answer:

> Any individual, group or institution that is, or claims to be, immune from criticism is authoritarian. Not being criticizable, they are incapable of improvement.
>
> Authoritarianism encourages people to defend and continually try to prove that they are right. It blinds people to the evils, inadequacies, and falsity of their theories, actions, and institutions. It not only discourages self-criticism, it makes people antagonistic to criticism from others. Authoritarianism represents an attempt to transcend the human condition of fallibility, and thus prevents opportunity to improve. Instead, it turns them into moralizers who fear making mistakes, since mistakes incur condemnation. Moralizing and defending do not secure improvement; they obstruct it.
>
> Authoritarianism sometimes does generate a concern for improvement – the improvement of others. Possessed of the *truth*, authoritarian people or institutions seek to impose it on others: they indoctrinate and manipulate. (*The Possibility of Error,* p19)

Perkinson describes a special kind of authority that prevents improvement in schools – the authority of the expert. Most institutions are plagued by experts; schools suffer most in this regard. In order to be couth and scientific, the profession of teaching has attempted to mimic its sisters in other disciplines, carrying things to ridiculous extremes. There are media experts, bilingual ones, specialists in reading and non-reading, an almost infinite list. Confronted by experts, teachers cringe into conformity. But the fallibilist educator can say: 'Are you sure you are right? Perhaps you are in error – undoubtedly your theory can be improved.'

To attain improvement, Perkinson suggests the use of critical dialogue. This differs from discussion or debate because persons seek not victory but improvement. The participants in a critical dialogue avoid dogmatism and confrontation. They advocate not 'true' ideas, but ones that are potentially wrong and in need of criticism.

In my teaching, I ask students to engage in critical dialogue about issues in American education using group process – a skill for which I have special training. Sadly I report that, even though I am a staunch supporter of Perkinson's position and even though I understand group procedures, critical dialogue is difficult to achieve. Persons experience problems in stepping back from their personal involvement with and commitment to ideas. They quickly become defenders rather than thoughtful critics of their own notions. This serves not as an argument against the pursuit of a new approach to school curriculum but strengthens the case for it. The difficulties that people encounter stem from their failure to be open and accepting. They are defensive largely as a result of having studied the old, traditional school curriculum.

Perkinson, along with Ronald M Swartz and Stephanie Edgerton, has further applied Popper's thought in a volume entitled *Knowledge and Fallibilism* (1980).

The book traces the history and development of fallibilism, first as a philosophy of science and then as a system of ideas for curriculum. In an introductory chapter, Edgerton examines the problem of induction as a teaching strategy and offers criticism of those programmes which have relied on it as the sole or primary strategy. In a second essay, Swartz discusses the importance of mistakes as an aid to learning.

A key chapter in the book is one by Perkinson entitled 'Against Learning'. In it, he offers a new metaphor for conceptualizing the process of teaching. He describes two traditional metaphors. The first he labels the building block method (also called the matching process). In it, students are fitted into studies for which they are thought to be best suited. Perkinson calls his second analogy the carrot and stick process, based on 'motivation'. This approach views children as striving for some end. In order to help them get there, they either obtain carrots or else they receive punishment. Ultimately these devices increase motivation.

In place of these traditional metaphors, Perkinson proposes the clothes closet metaphor:

> And the teacher? No longer the promoter of learning, the teacher will now simply try to help students improve knowledge by helping them to probe, to test, to experiment with — to criticize — the knowledge they already have. Perhaps the best way to convey this construction of the teacher and the function of the school is to case it in a new metaphor.
>
> I suggest we adopt the closet-cleaning metaphor. Every student has a closet full of ideas, skills, and dispositions that he has accumulated in the course of his life. But much of what he has accumulated is false, mistaken, erroneous, mythical, inadequate, and may even be harmful. The educational process is one of closet cleaning. The teacher helps the student clean his own closet by helping him to criticise and test the worth of the ideas, skills, and dispositions he has accumulated. But it is not the teacher's job to replenish the closet. The teacher does not have a pile of official wisdom or guaranteed skills, or approved dispositions to give, sell, install, or foist off on the student. The teacher is not a closet stuffer, not a promoter of learning. The teacher's task is the liquidation of ignorance, the elimination of false, mistaken and inadequate ideas, skills, and dispositions. (*Knowledge and Fallibilism*, p34)

This metaphor, teacher as closet-cleaner, supports a new approach to curriculum because it allows learning to emerge from the needs of the student. When the closet is empty, the person alone must fill it; this requires self-directed learning.

Perkinson and his colleagues pursue these ideas in a number of additional essays. Together these demonstrate how fallibilism becomes a philosophy of education.

Other formulations also lend support for a new approach to curriculum, including the aesthetic perspective, humanistic education, existentialism, and futurism.

Aesthetic, humanistic and existential perspectives

The aesthetic perspective in education, best developed by Elliot Eisner (1979), offers the idea that in an attempt to become respectable, the discipline of education has over-relied on the scientific method to the exclusion of all else. This results in a terrible imbalance; it reduces teaching to topics that lend themselves to objective testing (often resulting in a position that claims that behavioural objectives are the only legitimate ones). Other ways of knowing also exist – deductive logic and jurisprudence, to name two. All of evaluation need not be measurement. People can know with their hearts as well as with their heads. The need for an equilibrium between empiricism and the arts emerges from the aesthetic curriculum perspective.

Humanistic education provides still another innovative viewpoint. The goal of humanism is the development of self-actualized human beings who move from seeking basic needs (food and shelter) to the upper levels of Maslow's hierarchy – esteem and self-definition. It attempts to increase the space of free movement – a concept described by Lewin. It emphasizes an understanding of meaningful work as play – Dewey's basic paradigm. In sum, humanistic education helps persons go beyond normal inhibited limits of development, expanding human capacity, and allows the leading of full, rich lives.

The philosophy of existentialism represents an additional structure supporting a new kind of school curriculum. Existentialism urges persons to create their own selves. Objecting to the idea that all people have an essence by virtue of existing, Jean Paul Sartre and other existentialists insist that persons must define themselves. This requires free choice as well as solitude. Creating one's essence – self-definition – becomes the central task of life; the traditional school curriculum hardly ever focusses on this.

Persons must be prepared for life in the future. Alvin Toffler tells us of 'future shock' – a sense of uneasiness that we all experience, a lingering perception that things are not well. Toffler attributes this sense of malaise, in part, to the fact that we live in a historical time period when the rate of change is itself accelerating. Furthermore, Toffler (1980) argues, the industrial era is ending and is being replaced by a new, yet undefined civilization. How do persons prepare for a time to come of which they have no clear perception? The answer lies in the development of human beings able to adapt and to accommodate. The curriculum of today with its teacher burnout, student drug abuse, and low level of confidence is not the answer.

An emergent approach to the curriculum

This essay does not deny the need for basic skills nor the importance of science. It does reject the authoritarian assertion that basic skills or science (or any topic) is infallibly correct for students. The approach advocated here is *new*, refusing to accept the tired statement: 'I have been doing this all along.' It relies on *emergent* learnings. No one can predict exactly what will occur under such a curriculum plan. It arises from the needs of students led by teachers who are fallibilists, humanists, existentialists, and futurists who employ and emphasize the aesthetic perspective. The training of such instructors may be difficult but not more complex than the preparation of educators in the giant bureaucratic structure existing today. Quite possibly, the education of teachers for this kind of curriculum will be more simple than current procedures.

A new emerging school curriculum, while essentially open as to its construction, can be defined to a certain extent. It focusses on self-definition – asking persons to know themselves as a first step toward knowing how to survive in the future. Because of its existential roots, it requires a good deal of free choice. It denies certainty, avoids assertions, never relies on experts, and continually raises questions about its own validity. It relates to the needs and interests of students and strives to enable them to clean their closets even as they learn to be more effective problem solvers. It teaches students to engage in critical dialogue.

Can such a curriculum ever be achieved? Who knows? Will it be an improvement over the present school curriculum? Probably. The curriculum of today — the old, non-emergent school curriculum — does not work and it grows worse each day. With its over-emphasis on basic skills, science, and objective measurement, it promotes the inhumanities; it contains the danger of producing a society of people who are effective with regard to cognitive skills but who lack heart and the capacity to think divergently. Such a curriculum can be destructive of human endeavour as it leads eventually to a decrease in human dignity.

Simulation games and other instructional strategies

The instructional strategies employed in the new curriculum include techniques for facilitating creative behaviour as well as fantasy and enchantment. Within this programme, people learn to solve problems through psycho-drama and socio-drama. And, of course, this new emerging school curriculum utilizes simulation/gaming as a central strategy.

Instructional games meet all of the requirements of a curriculum based on the philosophic positions described above. In this way the argument developed in this paper represents a reflective justification for the use of simulation/gaming. Games can be used for a wide variety of purposes. Essays in this volume indicate many of them.

The purpose of this article has been to offer instructors a rationale based primarily on Popper's fallibilism, and to a lesser extent, on the other perspectives outlined above. Simulation/gaming can be more clearly understood in relation to these varieties of significant viewpoints.

The kind of curriculum described here — of which simulation/gaming is an integral part — demands much and offers much. It requires teachers who embrace fallibilism and existentialism, humanism, and futurism. It asks instructors to be artists as well as scientists. This programme demands the mastery of difficult techniques so they can be taught to others, including critical dialogue, socio-drama, and simulation/gaming. This programme of studies offers the possibility of effective patterns of learning and helps teach survival in the future.

In still another work, Henry Perkinson (1980, p217) writes the following about Karl Popper:

> Karl Popper was himself a teacher in the Vienna Schools for seven years before migrating to New Zealand when Hitler came to power. In his *Autobiography*, he tells how as a college student he had dreamed of creating the kind of school that those twentieth-century education theorists later prescribed: 'I dreamt of one day founding a school in which young people could learn without boredom, and would be stimulated to pose problems and discuss them; a school in which no unwanted answers to unasked questions would have to be listened to; in which one did not study for the sake of passing examinations.'
>
> Karl Popper never carried out that dream, never founded a school — but he did create the philosophy for the founding of such a school of his dreams.

References

Dewey, J (1938) *Experience and Education.* Collier Books: New York
Duke, R D (1974) *Gaming: The Future's Language.* Halstead Press: New York
Eisner, E W (1979) *The Educational Imagination.* Macmillan: New York
Goble, F C (1970) *The Third Force.* Pocket Books: New York
Kaufman, W (1963) *Existentialism from Dostoevksy to Sartre.* Meridan: New York
Perkinson, H J (1971) *The Possibilities of Error.* McKay: New York
    (1980) *Since Socrates.* Longman: New York
Popper, K (1961) *The Logic of Scientific Discovery.* Science Editions: New York
    (1963) *Conjectures and Reflections.* Routledge and Kegan Paul: London
Swartz, R M *et al* (1980) *Knowledge and Fallibilism.* NYU Press: New York
Toffler, A (1970) *Future Shock.* Random House: New York
    (1980) *The Third Wave.* Morrow: New York
Valett, R E (1977) *Humanistic Education.* C V Mosby Company: St Louis
Vernon, P E (1970) *Creativity.* Penguin Books: New York

Biographical note

Dr Michael J Rockler has been chairperson of the Department of Education at Rutgers University in Camden since September 1977. Before coming to Rutgers, he taught at the University of Nebraska at Omaha, Carleton College in Northfield, Minnesota, and the University of Minnesota where he received his doctorate in 1969. He has participated in the North American Simulation and Gaming Association (NASAGA) for several years and has been on the planning committee of the 1981 conference in Washington, DC. He serves as a social studies editor for Robert Horn's *Guide to Simulation/Games for Education and Training.* Though his experience in curriculum is wide ranging, Dr Rockler's major interests lie in simulation/gaming theory and creativity. His articles on these and other subjects have appeared in numerous professional books and journals.

Michael J Rockler
Department of Education
Rutgers
The State University of New Jersey
Camden
New Jersey 08102
USA

The Society for Academic Gaming and Simulation in Education and Training

Although the power of play in education has long been acknowledged and indeed may be traced back via Bruner, Piaget, Dewey, and Rousseau to Plato, it is only in recent years that serious thought has been given to the practical problems and possibilities inherent in its application. As teachers, lecturers and industrial trainers sought to explore less didactic forms of learning they found that little systematic work had been done to collect and exchange information and ideas.

One of the characteristics of simulation and gaming, however, is that it is experiential. There is a limit, therefore, to the information about it that can be conveyed by the written word. It is necessary for practitioners to meet, discuss and try out games. It was largely to fulfil this need that SAGSET was formed. The Society was founded in 1969; it held its first conference in August 1970 and rapidly established itself as a focal point for activities and publishing in the field.

From the start, the interests of its members have spanned education and training from primary school to university and from trade unions to senior management. Again, right from its beginnings, the Society's approach to gaming and simulation has been from different perspectives. In publications and conferences there are contributions which emphasize the theoretical basis of gaming and simulation, which explore common conceptual frameworks, and which debate the problems of evaluation and assessment. At the same time there are contributions which look at the practical aspects of gaming, the hardware, the difficulties of planning, organizing, debriefing, and the dynamics of the group in action. Equal emphasis is placed on the need for practical help in running simulation exercises and on the need to build from a sound academic framework.

The Society publishes a quarterly journal *Simulation/Games for Learning* (formerly SAGSET *Journal*), which carries articles on use and design, reviews of books, games and simulations, abstracts and references. It is accompanied by SAGSET *News*, an insert which carries members' inquiries, topical references and news, and a calendar of courses and conferences.

Other publications include subject area resource lists, conference proceedings under the series title *Perspectives on Academic Gaming & Simulation* and an anthology of articles under the title *Aspects of Simulating & Gaming*. The

---

*It is the Council's recommendation to the next annual general meeting that the Society's name be changed to: The Society for the Advancement of Games and Simulations in Education and Training

Society also acts as the European distributor for the well-known books by Stadsklev on simulation gaming in social education. Through its contacts with other national and international organizations and by means of its annual conference, local meetings and widespread membership, the Society tries to encourage and develop the responsible use of games and simulations as an approach to teaching and learning. It also endeavours to offer support and encouragement to those who use these methods and provide them with a forum to discuss their ideas and problems.

Officers and Council Members of SAGSET for the Society's year 1981/82

Ian Gibbs	Home Office Unit for Educational Methods	*Vice-President*
David Walker	Loughborough University of Technology	*Chairman*
Alan Coote	Polytechnic of Wales	*Secretary*
Peter Haysman	Royal Military College of Science	*Treasurer*
Jacquetta Megarry	5 Glencairn Gardens, Glasgow	*General Editor*
Roger Brown	Wimpey Waste Management	
John Dudley	Belgrave Comprehensive School, Tamworth	
Geoffrey Fagan	Jordanhill College	
Nancy Glandon	Bradford University	
Lynton Gray	Anglian Regional Management Centre	
Christine Hay	Hounslow Health District	
David Jaques	Hatfield Polytechnic	
Michael Kelly	Manchester Polytechnic	
Fred Percival	Glasgow College of Technology	
Donald Thatcher	Portsmouth Polytechnic	
Bas van der Horst	Free University, Amsterdam	
Morry van Ments	Loughborough University of Technology	

Information about the Society and details of membership may be obtained from:

The Secretary
SAGSET
Centre for Extension Studies
University of Technology
Loughborough
Leicestershire LE11 3TU
England

Index